Blossoming of a Ukrainian Canadian
Savella Stechishin

Natalie Ostryzniuk

\

Order this book online at www.trafford.com/09-0162
or email orders@trafford.com

Most Trafford titles are also available at major online book retailers.

Note for Librarians: A cataloguing record for this book is available from Library
and Archives Canada at www.collectionscanada.ca/amicus/index-e.html

Printed in Victoria, BC, Canada.

ISBN: 978-1-4269-0394-6 (soft)
ISBN: 978-1-4269-0396-0 (ebook)

*We at Trafford believe that it is the responsibility of us all, as both individuals
and corporations, to make choices that are environmentally and socially sound.
You, in turn, are supporting this responsible conduct each time you purchase a
Trafford book, or make use of our publishing services. To find out how you are
helping, please visit www.trafford.com/responsiblepublishing.html*

*Our mission is to efficiently provide the world's finest, most comprehensive
book publishing service, enabling every author to experience success.
To find out how to publish your book, your way, and have it available
worldwide, visit us online at www.trafford.com*

Trafford PUBLISHING® www.trafford.com

North America & international
toll-free: 1 888 232 4444 (USA & Canada)
phone: 250 383 6864 ♦ fax: 250 383 6804 ♦ email: info@trafford.com

The United Kingdom & Europe
phone: +44 (0)1865 487 395 ♦ local rate: 0845 230 9601
facsimile: +44 (0)1865 481 507 ♦ email: info.uk@trafford.com

10 9 8 7 6 5 4 3 2 1

Contents

Dedication

I dedicate this book to my mother, Elizabeth Shewchuk. Her encouragement and devotion to her children was selfless and exemplary. She always emphasized that education was important and higher learning could be attained if desired. I was inspired by her to continue my academic studies and then to write this book.

Acknowledgements

I wish to thank everyone I interviewed for the writing of this book. Many thanks go to Jean Meketiak of Calgary who was a gracious hostess as well as Mary Cherneskey and Mary Harbus, both of Saskatoon. The afternoons spent with these ladies was informative and most enjoyable. I wish to acknowledge the letters I received from Olga Cikalo and Bea Clarke and I thank them for taking the time to write. It was a pleasure to listen to the reminiscences of Jean Matieshan of Toronto. My gratitude is extended to Savella's family in Edmonton and Toronto for the time spent with me. Also, I appreciate the assistance of Zenia Stechishin in arranging interviews with people in Toronto.

The constructive suggestions, encouragement and editing skills of Louisa Kozey of Regina, is greatly appreciate and a bouquet of thanks goes out to her. My very special thank you is to my two sons: Evan for his professionalism in editing and making sense of my rambling manuscript and putting it in a readable form, and to Vincent for his invaluable technical help by getting the manuscript press ready and the lovely design of the cover of this book.

I am indebted to Saskatchewan Heritage Foundation for their generous financial support for my travel in pursuit of the various interviews out of the province and within. I thank Ukrainian Canadian Congress, Saskatchewan Provincial Council and SaskLotteries Inc. for their financial support.

Cover design by Vincent Ostryzniuk
Cover photograph by Wendy Ostryzniuk

Abbreviations

CAS	Canadian Association of Slavists
CUYA	Canadian Ukrainian Youth Association (*Soiuz ukrainskoii molodi Kanady*)
IWC	International Women's Council
UCC	Ukrainian Canadian Congress
UNF	Ukrainian National Federation (*Ukrainske natsionalne obiednannia*)
UNWLA	Ukrainian National Women's League of America (*Soiuz ukrainok Ameriky*)
USRL	Ukrainian Self-Reliance League of Canada (*Soiuz ukrainskii samostiniki*
UWAC	Ukrainian Women's Association of Canada (*Soiuz ukrainok Kanady*)
WFUWO	World Federation of Ukrainian Women's Organizations
WUNR	Western Ukrainian National Republic

GLOSSARY

<u>Common Terms</u>
bursa/bursy - student residence/residences
kylym/kylymy - rug/rugs
narodni domy - Ukrainian National Homes (community halls)
pysanka/pysanky - Easter egg/eggs
ridna shkola - Ukrainian school
rushnyky - embroidered linen towel
sorochka/sorochky - shirt, shirts

<u>Organizations</u>
Soiuz ukrainok - Union of Ukrainian Women
Soiuz Ukrainok Ameriky - Ukrainian National Women's League of America
Soiuz Ukrainok Kanady - Ukrainian Women's Association of Canada
Soiuz Ukrainskoii Molodi Kanady - Canadian Ukrainian Youth Association
Soiuz Ukraintsiv Samostiinykiv u Kanadi - Ukrainian Self-Reliance League of Canada
Svitova federatsiia ukrainskykh zhinochykh orhanizatsii - World Federation of Ukrainian Women's Organization
Svitovyi souiz ukrainok - World Association of Ukrainian Women
Ukrainske Narodne Mystetstvo - Ukrainian Folk Arts Council
Ukrainskyi zhinochyi soiuz - Ukrainian Women's Society

<u>Books</u>
Iuvileina knyzhka Soiuzu ukrainok Kanady z nahody 10-litnoho isnovannia, 1926-1936 - <u>Jubilee Book of the Ukrainian Women's Association of Canada Commemorating 10 Years, 1926-1936</u>

Chvert' stollittia na hromadskii nyvi: Istoriia Soiuzu ukrainok Kanady (1926-1951) - <u>Twenty-Five Years of the Ukrainian Women's Association of Canada</u>

Dorohamy sorokrichchia 1926-1966 - <u>Forty Years in Retrospect 1926-1966</u>

Pivstorichchia 1923-1973 Zhinochoho tovarytsva im. Olhy Kobylianskoi v Saskatune, Saskachevan, pershoho viddilu Soiuzu ukrainok Kanaday - Fifty Years of the Olha Kobylianska Branch, Saskatoon, Saskatchewan, the First Branch of the Ukrainian Women's Association of Canada

Iuvileina knyha 25-littia Ukrainskoho instytutu im. Petra Mohyly v Saskatuni, 1916-1941 - Jubilee Book of Twenty-five Years of the Petro Mohyla Ukrainian Institute in Saskatoon, 1916-1941

Na storzhi kultury - Guardians of Culture

Pivstolittia na hromadskii nyvi: Narys istorii Soiuzu ukrainok Kanady 1926-1976
A Half-Century of Service to the Community. An Outline History of the Ukrainian Women's Association of Canada 1926-1976

Persha Recordova Knyzhka - First Record Book

Newspapers and Magazines
Dilo - Action
Kaliandar-Almankh - calendar almanac
Nashe zhyttia - Our Life
Nova khata - The New Home
Promin - Sunbeam
Ukrainskyi holos - Ukrainian Voice
Ukrainskyi visti - Ukrainian News
Zhinocha dolia - Women's Fate

Introduction

For a master's degree in Canadian history, I decided that my thesis would focus on a woman of Ukrainian descent. I asked myself if there was or is a Ukrainian-Canadian woman who has achieved something outstanding. My subsequent research confirmed that there is a limited recorded history of Ukrainian-Canadian women from the time of their arrival in the late 1890s until the present. Ethnic women are generally invisible in conventional Canadian histories. They have been ignored because of their gender, class and ethnicity, perhaps because these women tended to ghettoize, making them unreachable by the mainstream community. Thus, their works, written in their own language, have remained closed to the outside world. Also, the majority of histories of Ukrainian Canadians written by Ukrainian Canadians have not recognized women's place in history, as these authors preferred to record the stories of men. While women, in general, have been disenfranchised in recorded history, beginning in the 1970s the feminist movement brought a surge of interest in and writings about women. However, stories of the lives of immigrant women remain few.

Fortunately, I discovered that, yes, there was a woman still living in my province, Saskatchewan, who met the simple criteria I had established. In fact, I had been given her cookbook on Ukrainian cuisine, written in English, as a wedding gift many years ago. The book has not only wonderful recipes, but also a wealth of information on Ukrainian traditions and culture, so much so that it can be used as resource material for Ukrainian traditions. The name Savella Stechishin had also crossed my travels in my activism in Ukrainian-Saskatchewan circles.

What was the makeup of this woman that enabled her to have lofty dreams and be so determined to accomplish what she set out to do in spite of many obstacles? After all, she was a member of a minority ethnic group that had not been welcomed by many in the host society. In my first interview with Mrs. Stechishin, I learned that she had certain views and even in her 90s would not be swayed from them. She had a remarkable memory and was precise in what she knew and what she expected others to know. I decided that this unique woman would be the topic of my master's thesis. In order that the facts be correct, she gave me her unpublished autobiography and permission to access her papers at the National Archives in Ottawa, Ontario. She had written the autobiography in the 1980s, beginning with her life in Ukraine as a little girl and continuing through to her arrival in Canada, and ending in 1960. It describes her personal life and her career, including her vision and involvement with the Ukrainian-Canadian women's movement. Those pages which she considered to be of a delicate nature, she removed. The autobiography helped me immensely to put events in perspective and chronological order, as well as to show the strong and determined character of this leading activist.

As my research progressed, it became evident that indeed Savella Stechishin was a Ukrainian-Canadian woman activist who had helped to unite women of her ethnic community and been a motivator for the genesis of a national women's organization. Her vision and mission were to empower women with little or no education, limited worldliness and sophistication, few material possessions, still in a peasant culture of patriarchy and superstition, and a century behind their Anglo-Canadian contemporaries, to take hold of their destiny. While her mandate incorporated 'safe' issues like the retention of Ukrainian culture and visible symbols, the Ukrainian Canadians, among whom women were equal contributors but not leading members, had to be coalesced into a vibrant cohesive force to take their rightful place on an equal basis alongside other nation builders in Canada. Savella wrote exclusively in the Ukrainian language and in this manner precluded non-Ukrainian women from reading her works or to be aware of her activism.

When Ukrainian immigrants arrived in Canada at the turn of the 20th century, there were many challenges for them to overcome. With few exceptions, they were poor and illiterate and were unable to speak with non-Ukrainians. There were no facilities for their customary religious observance and no traditions to support a Ukrainian national identity. To meet these challenges, male Ukrainian immigrants of a nationalistic persuasion formed an 'intelligentsia' and took steps to resolve them in most expedient ways possible within their limited means. The formation of an intelligentsia began in the 1910s with the founding of educational institutions in the prairie provinces to house and educate young adults with the hope of making them into leaders of the fledgling Ukrainian flock. They, in turn, would elevate the immigrants and Canadian born to Canadian standards. The issues of illiteracy, backwardness, insecurity, and lack of pride in their culture were identified and were to be resolved.

Women, meanwhile, were expected to participate in helping to solve these problems. Savella, living in the hub of the activists milieu and married to a man who was a leading activist and very supportive of his wife, was aware of the many obstacles and was determined to be instrumental in finding a solution to overcome them. Education was of prime importance, Savella realized, as did all the activists. There was a urgent need for leaders and Savella had the ambition to take her place alongside the male leaders as an equal partner. A nationwide organization for Ukrainian women was another solution. The first national Ukrainian women's organization in Canada, the Ukrainian Women's Association of Canada (UWAC), was established in 1926 with membership open to all women of Ukrainian descent regardless of political or religious affiliation; Savella Stechishin was one of the group at the helm. Their goal was to gather women – to create a commonality – to share their culture, gender and class. It was desirable for not only Ukrainian-Canadian women, but the entire Ukrainian-Canadian community, to improve the position of women in their own communities, as well as in the mainstream. Branches of the UWAC, scattered across the prairies, were sent directives from the National Office. As president for the first decade, Savella was responsible for the majority of the directives.

Although the times were rife with the suffragette movement and progressivism, Savella and her fellow activists were more concerned with ethnicity and class rather than with 'women's rights' and 'female issues,' as defined by the Anglo-Canadian elite. In order to be good Canadian citizens, they believed it was imperative that each man and woman of Ukrainian descent thoroughly know about his/her heritage and be proud of it. Women were assigned the task to be knowledgeable in everything Ukrainian and be in charge of the upbringing of their children. Children were to be immersed in a Ukrainian home which included being literate in the Ukrainian language and knowledgeable about Ukrainian history and literature, and to cultivate Ukrainian arts.

For a variety of reasons, not all Ukrainian-Canadian women joined the UWAC. Some simply chose not to be members of their ethno-cultural community, while others chose alternative organizations. However, Savella Stechishin and the UWAC did play a fundamental role in the consolidation and elevation of women to an important place within the Ukrainian ethnic group in Canada. In the initial years of the UWAC, young middle-class educated women in their twenties and early thirties guided the women's movement. While older women joined the Association, the leaders were usually young married women with children. This youthful leadership was unlike that of most Anglo-Celtic women's organizations in which the vast majority of members were middle-aged, middle-class women in their forties and fifties.

Several themes are evident in chronicling the life of Savella Stechishin and her activism with the women's movement. Her determination to enact her vision to transform these women, barely out of a peasant culture, into modern women is unmistakable. National (Ukrainian) consciousness was foremost and superseded women's consciousness. Women were to subordinate female issues to all things Ukrainian, and individual issues to that of the group. Three components were inextricably intertwined: gender, class and ethnicity.

Her husband, Julian, a nationalist leader in his own right, was her greatest supporter and admirer. They shared common goals and ambitions; their marriage was a love story of fictional proportions, according to contemporaries. Even though Julian was a lawyer, they were not money-rich, but were rich in the satisfaction of living together and achieving their goals.

In interviews with her, when she felt I had interpreted her activism and views accurately, her verbal confirmation would always be, "Exactly!" And she had an 'exacting' and assertive personality, yet could be thoughtful of others and was loved and respected by her close friends and family. Savella Stechishin was a bright light in the Ukrainian-Canadian milieu and a mistress of her own fate.

Over months of research, I learned about my subject and 'her people.' I received my master's degree, then continued my research after deciding to write a book about this remarkable woman, so that others could appreciate the work of a woman on the fringe of Canadian history. It is my hope that this book will give someone the inspiration and determination to dare to achieve her goals.

1

A New Beginning

Church bells rang out on August 19, 1903 in the village of Tudorkowychi as they did in every village in the province of Galicia (*Halychyna*), Austria. After all, it was one of the most important feast days for Ukrainians – the Transfiguration. Trofim and Eva Wawryniuk had another reason to celebrate; their fifth child, a third daughter was born. Eva wanted this child to have a distinctive name unlike anyone in the village. In accordance with the practice of the Ukrainian Greek Catholic Church, the child was to be baptized shortly after her birth and the selected godparents were instructed to have her named Izabella. As the survival rate amongst infants was not high, it was imperative that the child be baptized as soon as possible, otherwise the child's soul would not be cleansed on its way to heaven. When the godparents arrived at the village church with the intention of having the Wawryniuk baby baptized Izabella, the priest refused, since the name was not that of a saint. Custom dictated that a Christian's first name be one of a saint, with the intention that that titular saint would becomes the child's guardian and intercessor before God and that child should imitate the life of the saint whose name he/she bears. The priest instructed the godparents to return to the parents to tell them that they should look at the list of saints in their calendar and chose a more appropriate name. Both Trofim and Eva, unlike many Ukrainians, were literate. Meanwhile, he suggested the feminized version of Savel (Saul - St. Paul).[1] The parents agreed to Savella.

The village Tudorkowychi was in the county Sokal, twenty miles north of the city of L'viv in what was then known as the crown province of Galicia, in the Austro-Hungarian Empire. Today, the eastern portion of Galicia (*Halychyna*) is part of Ukraine, consisting of the three western regions of L'viv, Ivano-Frankivsk and Ternopil, but in 1903 Ukraine as a sovereign state existed only in the minds of national activists. The Austrian emperor had annexed this region from Poland in 1772 via dubious hereditary claims, and it would remain a part of Austria until the end of the First World War when, after a bout of civil war between Polish and Ukrainian nationalists, it would be refashioned as part of a resurrected independent Polish state. Like the rest of the empire, Galicia was ethnically mixed, with a Polish nobility dominating politics, a German minority running the provincial bureaucracy from the capital L'viv, a range of urban classes that consisted of Poles, Jews and Armenians, and a large, isolated peasantry numerically dominated by Ukrainians, or *Ruthenians* as the Austrian government liked to register them. Due to numerous invasions, suppression and serfdom, the majority of Ukrainians were poor illiterate peasants. Although freed from serfdom in 1848, lack of education, heavy taxation by the government and an acute shortage of land kept them poor and oppressed. In 1900, forty-nine percent of the land-holdings were less than two hectares and the illiteracy rate of the Galician population was fifty-seven percent.[2] At this time almost ninety percent of the peasant women were illiterate.[3]

This was Savella's heritage. Her father, Trofim Wawryniuk, tall, blue eyed, with brown hair, was a typical man of his generation and a man of influence and ambition. He was the village mayor, an elected position that required the approval of the local *pan*, or landlord. He would be considered middle class by our standards today, as he owned more land than the average peasant, enough to feed his family and to hire labourers. He also held a large share in a flour mill in the village. As with most Ukrainians, religion played a large role in his life. He was a church elder and cantor in the local Ukrainian Greek Catholic church. These important positions made him a prominent member of the community. After his first wife died of tuberculosis, leaving behind three children, the most natural option then was to marry again. He needed someone to look after the children and be in charge of the household.

Eva Kostiuk was born in the neighbouring village of Konotopy. After her parents died while she was still in her teens, she found work as a housemaid to a childless widow, an educated woman of a middling background. In this employment she, a peasant girl, received very useful training in the domestic arts in a middle-class home: housekeeping, fancy cooking and baking, and preserving, skills with which few peasant women were acquainted. Within a few short years she married, but early in her marriage she became a childless widow, thus eligible for marriage again.

In the Galician countryside during the late 1800s, news came by word of mouth and over short distances. It is likely that Trofim learned of Eva's recent widowhood and proposed marriage after a few solicitous inquiries. Eva agreed and took upon herself the task of looking after three stepchildren and a busy household. Fortunately for Eva, Trofim had hired help in the home and on the farm, making the physical burden of running a household relatively light. In time the couple had six children of their own: Helen, Eugene, Apolonius, Maria, Savella and Stephania, with Eva managing the vibrant household and raising nine children in all.

The Wawryniuk home was larger and more lavish than the typical peasant cottage. As was common in the region, the cottage was divided in half by a fairly wide hallway (*siny*) with a front and a back porch. While many cottages in the village and area had earthen floors, the Wawryniuk home was distinguished enough to have a wooden floor. The living area consisted of two rooms. The larger room served as the parlour where guests were entertained. It was furnished with two single beds, a large oak table, wicker chairs, benches along one wall, a cabinet for fancy dishes and in one corner a type of built-in heater (*pikolok*). The smaller room was the kitchen. It was equipped with a big clay oven (*peech*) consisting of a stove and a hot water reservoir. The chimney was also housed in the kitchen where it gave off needed warmth. Alongside and on top of the oven were small platforms suitable for sleeping. This is where the children slept. Also, a wide bench with a drawer for bedding called a *bambatel* was used as a bed. With two adults and nine children, the Wawryniuk household was indeed a crowded one.

During the winter months, the wide hallway dividing the cottage was used as a cold pantry where large wooden barrels of sauerkraut and other non-perishable preserves were stored. During the summer months, it became a dining room for the hired men. This hall did not have a wood floor but a hard packed earthen floor. The other half of the cottage consisted of unheated storage rooms: two large and one small, which doubled as bedrooms when the need arose. These rooms also had wooden floors. A trap door led to a small cellar where root vegetables were stored. The attic was available for storage as well. A thick, thatched roof protected the cottage.

As was common in the village, flower beds beautified the cottage on either side, while at the back in an orchard grew apple and pear trees as well as bushes laden with an abundance of red currants and gooseberries. A large vegetable garden beside the orchard produced a cornucopia of fresh produce to sustain the large family. The family had access to a water well located just behind the orchard. This well was conveniently located next to a manmade pond for the family's ducks and geese, which along with the chickens, were an essential source of meat. Meadows and fields of wheat and other crops stretched away from the orchard in long strips.

Children began school at the age of seven, learning the Polish language and the history of Poland while speaking their native tongue, Ukrainian, at home and at school. Every morning during school days, facing the portrait of Emperor Franz Joseph, the Ukrainian children sang the Austrian national anthem in Ukrainian because the children did not know German. Although few Polish families resided in the village, Polish was imposed in schools and government offices because it was the dominant official language of

Galicia, even though Ukrainians had the right to education and administration in their own tongue. Nevertheless, Savella had a happy childhood amidst a large family with caring parents.

The school, a one storey two-room building, and the church were situated in the middle of the village. Every morning and afternoon the school bell rang out loudly throughout the village calling the children to school; the senior grades five to eight were taught in the morning and the junior grades were taught in the afternoon. There were two teachers, one for each half day, and they did not hesitate to use a ruler/stick for corporal punishment when they saw fit to do so. In this setting little Savella completed the first three years of her schooling.

All was not work at home and in school for the young children. In their traditional everyday folk dress, children played games on the dirt streets or in the open meadows where red poppies, white daisies and blue cornflowers nodded their heads in the warm summer winds amid the tall green grass. The daywear of Ukrainian peasant children and adults alike was made of a white fabric home spun and woven from their home grown flax. The *sorochky* (shirts/blouses) were stitched with fine brightly coloured embroidery around the neckline and on the end edging of the sleeves. Embroidery on the clothing tended to be simple patterns, designed and stitched usually by the mother or older daughters. Over the *sorochka*, commonly the girls wore skirts and the women wore a woven *plakhta* (wrap around skirt) and apron.

The most popular entertainment was ritual spring songs and games celebrating the rebirth of life. *Hahilky-vesnianky (Hayivky)* was performed by young girls on Easter Sunday in front of the church in observation of the resurrection of Christ. In pagan times, group dances, songs, games and dramatic scenes (*hayivky*) were believed to serve the magical function of enticing spring to return and chase winter away. These celebrations personified a funeral for frost and winter. Through the magic of music, words and body motion, children and young adults enacted the planting and growing of crops, and in this way ensured a bountiful harvest.

Spring started in March with a gradual unfolding of buds. Ukrainian families would tap birch trees and collect their juice, a practice similar to the collection of maple syrup in Canada. With its richness in Vitamin C and other nutrients, birch juice was a healthy drink after a cold winter when staples were in short supply and fresh fruit and vegetables were depleted. The flavour of the drink was pleasant and especially fresh particularly after the long winter of consuming sauerkraut, potatoes, onions and black radish, and preserves, along with the cereal grains buckwheat, millet, barley, and wheat, not to mention the legumes (beans, peas and lentils). Families gathered and dried these food stuffs in the fall for use in winter meals.

The important task of tending the geese was given to Savella when she reached the age of six. This work was usually given to young girls of this age, since each member had to contribute to the maintenance of the household and young girls could handle easily this chore and at the same time have fun playing together. Every family had a flock of geese and ducks, as they were a source of not only meat but also down and feathers. Pillows and duvets (*peryna*) made from each family's flock were necessary for the warmth they provided during the winter months, particularly since the houses were not well heated at night. The wood in the oven/stove would only last a few hours into the night. Pillows and duvets also formed an important part of the trousseau for girls of marriageable age. The Wawryniuk flock consisted of about sixteen geese with a very aggressive hostile gander overseer.

To tend the geese, Savella, along with other girls in the village, had to herd the gaggle of geese into the nearby meadows or summer fallow fields to feed. Although the task was an easy one, the girls had to be vigilant so that the geese would not rush into neighbouring fields and damage crops but remain within the narrow grassed area set aside for them. One day Savella got so involved playing games, singing and telling stories with her friends that she forgot to mind the geese. Her flock, led by the gander, waddled off to a neighbour's field and started nibbling at his crop within sight of the neighbour who happened to be walking in his field. He scolded Savella and reported the incident to her mother, who in turn scolded her for her neglect. The incident taught Savella a well deserved lesson that inspired her to come up with a solution. She reckoned that if she could control the gander, then the flock would stay where she wanted. However, in order to contain the gander in the appointed meadow, she would have to hobble him. The next day, Savella ripped the inside of the hem on her skirt to make strips, and with the help of her friends she captured the gander and tied his legs together. This incapacity rendered him helpless and in Savella's control, with the result that the geese remained in the meadow grazing the grass, while their leader sat quietly nearby unable to move. With her new found freedom, Savella resumed playing with the other girls. When the time came to return home, she simply released the gander's legs and off they all went.

In her autobiography, she writes of a time when she was so afraid that she rushed to bed as soon as it turned dark. The reason was the appearance of Haley's comet in 1910. Ukrainian peasants, living very close to nature, were greatly affected by unexpected changes in their environment, and so many considered the comet a bad omen leading to some tragedy in the village. Children were told that if they misbehaved the comet would sweep them off with its tail and take them away.

Impending doom was indeed looming over Europe. Austrian military was performing their manoeuvres and there was talk that the soldiers were training for war. Rumours of war were rampant. People were beginning to consider alternatives to remaining in a country where poverty was prevalent and political, economic and social conditions unstable. Many families who had emigrated to Canada wrote to their relatives and friends of their successes in the new land. The Wawryniuks considered these factors and in 1912 made the decision to emigrate. They were also concerned that their two teenaged sons would be conscripted into the Austrian army when they came of age. The future did not look bright for their children should they remain in the land of their ancestors.

With the decision to emigrate firmly in place, Eva ordered western style clothes for the entire family so that they would be appropriately dressed for their arrival in Western Europe and Canada. The folk dress would be left behind – given to friends. Savella's outfit consisted of two dresses, knee high socks and shoes. She was excited and very proud of her navy blue sailor dress and the lovely red dress with long sleeves. Instead of the usual boots, she was able to take delight in her very own pair of patent leather shoes. The time came to sell off or give away the furniture, implements and clothing that they were not taking with them. What was left fit into two wagon loads of boxes and trunks. The family left in the middle of May, so they could arrive in Canada before the weather turned very cold.

The Wawryniuks drove the two miles to the town where they boarded a train. Eva had prepared food for the family of two adults and six children; the three stepchildren were adults and could be left behind. The food lasted for several days, after which Eva bought food staples at various station stops on the cross-continental trip to Antwerp in Belgium. At Antwerp, the Wawryniuks had to wait two weeks for the arrival of the ship that would take them to Canada.

The hotel where the Wawryniuks stayed was teeming with emigrants from different countries and speaking many languages. The close knit village and the comfort it exuded was now a memory. From Antwerp, the emigrants were sent to Hamburg, where the trans-Atlantic ship that would take them to Canada had finally docked bound for Quebec, Canada. The *S.S. Barcelona* sailed on June 14, 1913 with three ports of embarkation: Hamburg - 377 people, Bremen - 436 and Rotterdam - 402. The ship, a converted cattle ship, sailed from Hamburg, the last port, to Canada with a total of "1,215 passengers in steerage only; cabin no passengers."[4] All the emigrants were herded on board in an orderly fashion. Families were kept close together and each person was recorded on the ship's manifest. The manifest read: Trofim - 53 years old, country of birth - Austria, race - Ruthenian, destination - Rosthern, Saskatchewan, occupation - farm labourer, religious denomination - Greek Catholic. His wife Eva was listed as 40 years old, while the children were inscribed as: Helena - 18 years, Eugen - 15, Apolinary - 15; Maria - 13, Sawela - 9, and Stefania - 4. The manifest also recorded that the Wawryniuk family had brought two thousand dollars cash with them. This was a substantial amount of money for a Ukrainian immigrant family. Historian Orest Martynowych states, "A survey of Ukrainian rural settlers in western Canada in 1916 revealed that 50 per cent had arrived without cash and 42 per cent had amounts up to five hundred dollars with one hundred dollars the norm."[5]

The Wawryniuks, along with all the emigrants, walked along the deck, descended a narrow, steep and slippery stairway to steerage, located below water level. There they came upon row upon row of bunk beds. In the centre of what initially once had been a storage room, sat several long tables where food was served. To accommodate the vast number of passengers in this steerage and only class, meals were served continuously, with people taking turns at the tables. The dish most often served was a kind of stew made with tough meat and potatoes and turnips cut into big chunks. Beet jam with bread passed as dessert. The motion of the ship took its toll on some of the passengers. Some became sea sick and vomited from the upper bunks as they attempted to rest and stop the dizziness and nausea. Hot water did not exist and cold water was rationed for personal hygiene; drinking water was grudgingly doled out. The pungent smell of garlic, onions and whiskey that the immigrants had brought along with them, added to the foulness below deck.

Two weeks of crowded, noisy, ill-smelling and dirty quarters finally came to an end when the *Barcelona* steamed into Quebec harbour on July 1, 1913. It is not surprising that the immigrants were overjoyed at the sight of the shores of Canada. Most of the passengers had never seen the ocean must less experienced the rolling and heaving of a ship at sea. All the children were lined up on the upper deck and their hands and faces were washed with warm water. How wonderful the warmth of the water felt coupled with fresh air! Upon disembarking, the immigrants were told to produce their passports and prove that they had twenty-five dollars. The families were then given a routine medical examination. Ten people were held in quarantine. Within a short time, those who were going to western Canada were taken to the train station and together with all their baggage put on a train bound for Winnipeg – Canada's West. The Wawryniuks gathered all the children, boxes and trunks and followed the rest of the hopefuls looking forward with apprehension and anticipation towards a new beginning. Spacious colonist cars were fitted with comfortable wooden seats that could be converted into sleepers, washrooms with cold running water, heaters and cooking stoves. All this luxury was afforded the immigrants free of charge by the Canadian Pacific Railway. It was a great improvement to being holed up in the depths of a ship.

The Wawryniuk family was part of the first wave (1897-1914) of 171,500 Ukrainian immigrants arriving in Canada with the majority settling the Canadian west. By 1911, Saskatchewan alone was home to 22,276 Ukrainians, giving first place only to Manitoba with its 32,053 Ukrainians. Large numbers of Ukrainian immigrants crossed the ocean to the shores of Canada in three waves. World War I ended the first wave and initiated the second wave (1920-1939) when approximately 67,700 Ukrainians arrived. Like the first wave, this second group consisted mostly of peasant farmers, who also gravitated to the prairie west, settling into the bloc settlements established by the first wave.[6] A third wave occurred after World War II between 1947 and 1953, when 34,000 displaced persons chose to make Canada their home rather than be repatriated to the Soviet Union.[7] After the independence of Ukraine in 1991, Ukrainians again began to emigrated, beginning a fourth wave that continues into the 21st century. However, times had changed, and unlike the Wawryniuk family and other early immigrants, the immigrants of the third and fourth waves were considerably more educated and tended to gravitate toward large urban centres.

Over the three day journey to Saskatchewan, the passengers saw woods, towns and villages as the train clacked mile after mile. The scenery changed gradually, as the undulating hills and woods of central Canada gave way to the unpopulated and rocky wilderness of northern Ontario and then the bush and fertile prairie farmlands of Manitoba. As the big city of Winnipeg loomed ahead, the immigrants were told that this was to be their last stop. Tired and disoriented, they were ushered into the Immigration Hall near the CPR station and the ostentatious Royal Alexandra Hotel. The Wawryniuk stayed for several days at the hall with other newcomers to receive instructions about their final destination.

When all documentation was completed and seats made available, the Wawryniuks boarded a train bound for Saskatoon, and then another train that took them 45 miles north to Rosthern. Trofim had requested a homestead in the Rosthern area because their former neighbours had settled in that vicinity. Mrs. Pshebyla, a woman from their village who was now working as a maid in Rosthern met them at the train station. She was able to secure them a suite above the general store owned by a Jewish family, the Ostrowskys, to rent for a few days before they could move to their homestead. A day after they settled into the suite, a young man, Andrew Worobetz, a storekeeper from Wakaw, came for a visit. He, too, was originally from the neighbouring village in Ukraine and had even worked as a hired hand on the Wawryniuk farm. He had been sweet on Savella's sister Helen in Ukraine and was very much still romantically interested in her. In a couple of days, he proposed and hastily married her, taking her back to his home in Wakaw, a hamlet 30 miles east of Rosthern.

Minus one member of the family, Eva and her children were driven 53 miles west of Rosthern to the hamlet of Krydor, where they moved in with the Krawchuk family, yet another family from their village. Trofim, in the meantime, found a farm with buildings in the Wakaw area, NE quarter section of Section 21, Township 43, Range 27, Meridian W2, owned by Mike Syroishka. Trofim paid cash for what he believed was this land with buildings, cattle and machinery. Unfortunately he was unaware that the purchase was for the house, cattle and machinery and not the land. To add insult to injury, Trofim found that the farm had several alkaline sloughs and was very stony. He then made an Application for Entry in the Prince Albert District for a Homestead No. 20862 on August 4, 1913 for "SW quarter section of Section number 20 in Township 44, Range 8 west of the 3rd Meridian in Krydor" and paid the $10.00 registration fee.[8] In the late summer of 1913, the family moved into their new house on the Syroishka farm.

When fall arrived, four of the children, Eugene, Apolonius, Mary and Savella went to the closest school, Sokal, about two miles from their home. It was a typical prairie one-room school with about 45 children from grades one to six. Jacob Stratychuk, a Ukrainian immigrant, was the teacher. The language used during recess, noon hour and after school was almost exclusively Ukrainian since most, if not all, the children came from Ukrainian homes. This was a typical situation in the Ukrainian bloc settlements. Understandably, a Ukrainian teacher, though as yet uncommon, was favoured because he could explain school problems in the language of the immigrants while they were learning a new language. Often non-Ukrainian teachers were not interested in teaching these new immigrants who did not understand the English language and whose culture and traditions were alien to them. Since the four Wawryniuk children had been going to school in the 'old country', they were able to progress well in the new educational system. Eugene, the eldest son, remained on the farm to help his father. The value of education was instilled into the children by the parents. Apolonius, the second son, was free to pursue a higher education and was given individual instruction in the evenings to learn the English language giving him an advantage in attaining his goal of a higher education.

The Wawryniuks spent only one winter in the purchased house. On June 11, 1914 Trofim filed a Statuary Declaration stating he had taken up residence on the homestead on April 15, 1914 in a cabin, had three oxen and was now in the process of building a proper house on an adjoining quarter which he had purchased. This property was near Krydor. Meanwhile, in the spring Eva and the children were able to live in Justin Worobetz's vacant old pioneer house while theirs was being built on the homestead. Since the settlers in Krydor were from neighbouring villages in Ukraine, they found great comfort in being with their own people. Many of these settlers were already well established and were able to give the Wawryniuk family advice and a helping hand in the ways of their new country. In 1917 Trofim applied for title to his land. A homesteader had to reside on his homestead for at least six months each year for three consecutive years, cultivate thirty acres within that time and construct a habitable dwelling in order to receive title to his homestead. By November 1917, Trofim had broken 32 acres, cropped 30 acres, had a 16 feet by 36 feet log and lumber dwelling valued at $300.00, 30 acres of fenced land valued at $25.00, a stable valued at $400, a granary valued at $200.00, and 12 cattle and 5 horses.[9] On January 28, 1918 Trofim Wawryniuk received title to his land.

Having finished grade six, Apolonius was sent to North Battleford to complete grades seven and eight. After completing grade eight, he was allowed by the provincial government to teach at Dominion School in Whitkow, a hamlet in the Ukrainian bloc settlement, 50 miles west of Krydor. With the serious shortage of teachers caused by enlistment in the Canadian army for service in World War I, men and women fortunate enough to have obtained a grade eight education were sought out to replace teachers. During this time, Savella lived with her sister Helen in Krydor, where she and her husband owned a general store. Savella helped to take care of their baby boy, Walter, and attended school in Krydor to take grade seven, since Sokal school only offered grades one to six.

Life for Savella blossomed as she finished grade seven in the spring of 1918 with good grades. She proudly remembered that her teacher was Orest Zerebko, the first Ukrainian Canadian to graduate from the University of Manitoba, in 1913. Her most memorable elementary school year was in Saskatoon, where her parents decided to send her to take grade eight. Because most one-room schools on the prairies taught only grades one to six or seven, students had to either drop out or go to a city to continue their education. The year 1918 was memorable for Savella for another reason. During her last evening in Krydor before leaving for Saskatoon, she met Julian Stechishin, a young man who was teaching school in the neighbourhood. That particular evening a group of teachers from the Hafford district put on a play in the Krydor Hall. Julian had a leading role. After the play there was a dance. Fifteen year old Savella immediately took special notice of Julian and was "dying" to meet him and was delighted when a friend, Anna Perch, introduced her to Julian. She learned that Julian, like she, would be staying at the Petro Mohyla Ukrainian Institute, a residence that catered to the sons and daughters of Ukrainian pioneers.[10] He would be taking his second year of Arts and Science.

Education was the vehicle for a bright future and it was offered in cities like Saskatoon which in 1916 boasted a population of 21,054 souls. Local politics were on the conservative side, as at this time Saskatchewanians voted for prohibition of alcohol and on December 31, 1916 Saskatchewan officially became 'dry.' In this year women won the right to vote in municipal and provincial elections, but suffrage was extended only to those women who were over the age of twenty-one years and who were British subjects. Statistics on the ethnic population in Saskatoon for this year are not available, but there were enough Ukrainians residing in the city so that in March 1916 the Ukrainian Students' Club formed a committee to establish a student residence and school in Saskatoon for rural students pursuing secondary and post-secondary education.[11] The committee eventually purchased an old hotel on 401 Main Street and converted it into a student residence. This kind of residence/school was called a *bursa* in Ukraine and was modeled on those in Galicia. The new *bursa* was named Petro Mohyla Ukrainian Institute after the distinguished 17th century scholar and Orthodox metropolitan in Kyiv. The activists who established the institute became known as nationalists or *narodovtsi*. These immigrants established an economic, spiritual and social framework in their new society and vigorously opposed assimilation of Ukrainian immigrants into Canadian society.

In 1918 the Wawryniuks took the opportunity to send both Savella and Apolonius to Mohyla to further their education. In Candace Savage's *Foremothers*, Savella explained that she was "anxious to get on" in life and Mohyla would help.[12] At Mohyla, a school called "The New Canadian School" had been established for children and even young adults from the rural area to obtain their elementary school standing. The school had two classrooms with the highest grade being grade 8.[13]

In her first year at Mohyla, two events were instrumental in crystallizing Savella's beliefs and goals: a visit to the school by a woman medical doctor and the attendance at an annual convention at Mohyla by Dr. W. Simenowych, a medical doctor and Ukrainian activist and writer who had immigrated to the United States.[14] Regarding the woman's visit, she later reflected, "[I was] amazed that a woman was a doctor. It awakened a spark of feminism in me that kept growing ever brighter all my life and served as a stimulus for organizing Ukrainian women later on."[15] Dr. Simenowych urged women of Ukrainian descent in Canada to take control and direction of their own lives by uniting and organizing a Ukrainian women's organization. He also told them that the Ukrainian-American women were publishing their own magazine, *Rannya zorya* (Morning Star). These ideas so deeply affected Savella that years later she remembered, "They remained with me and later served as an impetus in organizing Ukrainian women."

Life at Mohyla Institute was centred on inculcating pride in one's heritage and culture coupled with practising the social graces of Canadian society. The boys were to be addressed by 'Mr.' and the girls by 'Miss' and each had to be dressed appropriately. The girls wore dresses and the boys always wore jackets or sweaters with dress pants. Learning etiquette and good manners went hand in hand with the study of Ukrainian language, history, literature, and the arts.[16] Traditional female classes in cooking, embroidery, sewing, interior decorating, and hygiene were offered to the girls. Days at Mohyla were strictly regimented. The wake-up bell rang at 6:45, and after breakfast at 7:45 the students attended university, Normal School, business college, or high schools, returning to have their lunch (if possible). After supper they were instructed in Ukrainian language, literature and history. Also at this time there was singing, dancing and music practice (the archives are silent on sports). The hours between 8:00 and 10:00 p.m. were devoted to homework.[17] Students were obliged to attend the church of their choice every Sunday. Dances were held for the students on Saturday evenings. The girls were given dance card programs which they filled out when the boys asked them for a dance. "May I have number 4 dance?" would be the proper form of request by the young men.[18] Protocol and etiquette were new experiences for the children of the poor, unsophisticated immigrants of a peasant culture. The directors of Mohyla (members of the Ukrainian Canadian intelligentsia) actively exposed their students to the social values of British-Canadian youth while maintaining a dignified respect for Ukrainian culture. The students were groomed to be intelligent, well-mannered young men and women projecting a favourable image to society at large.

The directors at Mohyla were impassioned believers in elevating all Ukrainians in Canada. Women were very important players in the whole picture of this progression. Their role was to be self-enlightened guardians of Ukrainian culture and most importantly to be responsible for the upbringing of future generations to be educated Canadian citizens, yet be knowledgeable and proud of their heritage. Mohyla did not discriminate on the basis of gender; the importance of higher education for girls was stressed.[19] At its inception and to this day, Mohyla was open to boys and girls. In its first year (1916), the residence housed 35 students, 31 boys and 4 (13 percent) girls, but within ten years the ratio of girls to boys dramatically increased to 35 percent. In 1926 there were 37 girls in a student body of 107.[20]

The Institute was fertile ground for prospective leaders who could promote the enlightenment of women. Mohyla's policies promoted equality amongst its students. At a time when many girls with Ukrainian immigrant parents were not encouraged to strive for a higher education but to marry at a young age,[21] the Institute established the following objectives:

> To promote, establish, maintain and manage institutions for students of Ukrainian descent, both male and female, of any religious denomination in those Saskatchewan centres inhabited by Ukrainian people, for the purpose of furnishing board and lodgings to said students at a moderate charge, or entirely free of charge, as may be deemed advisable by the Board of Directors of said Company, whereby said students may be able by means of such assistance to pursue courses of study in public schools, high schools, collegiate institutes, normal schools and universities in the said province.[22]

Although Mohyla was designed to accommodate students from the large rural Ukrainian bloc settlements in the parkland area of Saskatchewan, it attracted not only rural Saskatchewan boys and girls but also those from other provinces and even outside the country. The teachers were fervent believers in upholding Ukrainian culture, yet at the same time acculturating into the Canadian society. It was important, the students were told, that Ukrainians should participate politically, economically and socially within the Canadian milieu while avoiding assimilation. Speakers from Ukraine touring North America were always welcome at the Institute and were asked to speak to the students. The mandate of the teachers of Mohyla

Institute was to instil pride in the students concerning their ethnic heritage, promote self-worth and encourage active participation within their community. In essence this was the formulation of a positive identity for Ukrainian Canadians. The Institute profoundly affected and influenced Savella and the many other female and male students who resided there, who in a few short years became the educated leaders with middle-class values, of the unsophisticated Ukrainian-Canadian flock.

There were many empty lots on Clarence Avenue near Mohyla Institute and several of these lots were bought by the directors of Mohyla with the intention of building a new institute there. The empty lots were then used for planting potatoes that, in turn, would provide food for the students. One particular Saturday at the end of September, Wasyl Swystun, the rector, sent the students to dig up the potatoes that were ready for harvest. The students were paired up: male students dug up the potatoes while the girls collected them and dumped them into gunny sacks. With this team work, the chore was soon completed. As a reward for work well done, the students were allowed to go to the movies after supper. Plans for building Mohyla on the empty lots were never realized; instead the directors bought an old hotel on the corner of Main Street and Victoria Avenue.

Savella began Grade 8 at Mohyla Institute along with 17 other students. In total there were 4 girls and 14 boys, the majority in their mid-teens with the boys a little older. Their teacher, Miss Ellen Ward, was sent by the Saskatoon Public School Board to teach them. Savella many years later remembered Miss Ward fondly, "Our teacher, besides teaching academic subjects, instilled in us values of human relationships and Canadian citizenship."[23] Savella was both an enthusiastic and good student and that year ranked first in the class. She won first prize for the essay "Canada's Part in the First World War" in a competition for all Saskatoon grade eight students and received a book award from the Imperial Order of the Daughters of the Empire (I.O.D.E).[24] Her talent for writing was evident and this essay served as the beginning of a successful and prolific writing career.

In 1918, the First World War ended and Saskatchewan soldiers returned home, bringing back with them the highly contagious and deadly Spanish Influenza that was ravaging Europe. Tragically, the flu claimed over 4,000 lives in the province. The epidemic reached Saskatoon and in November Mohyla closed its doors, sending the students home for a month. Savella returned to Krydor and in short order the entire family fell ill with the disease. A popular home remedy for cooling fevers among Ukrainians at that time was the consumption of garlic, and this remedy was applied to cure the strange new illness. A concoction of crushed fresh garlic cloves was mixed with hot milk, and Savella along with her family drank this 'medicine.' Thankfully every member of the family pulled through the ordeal. Perhaps the garlic elixir was indeed the 'cure'! Upon returning to Mohyla at the end of November, Savella learned that one of the girl students had died from influenza.

Savella participated in all student activities at the Institute: Ukrainian language classes, Ukrainian grammar, Ukrainian history, Ukrainian literature, choir, drama and concerts. Julian Stechishin was the drama director and he chose Savella as his leading lady to his role as the lover in the historical play "*Stepovey Hist*" (A Guest from the Steppes). Savella was thrilled, as being one of the younger girls she never expected to play such an important part. The rehearsals for the plays held at the community hall on Avenue I were in the fall leading up to the performance in December at the national convention for all Ukrainians held in Saskatoon.

In the spring of 1919, Savella completed grade 8 with good marks. The Department of Education set the departmental exams that every grade 8 student in Saskatchewan had to write. The exam papers were sent to Regina for grading and the results were then published in the newspaper: The *Saskatoon Star Phoenix*. At the end of June Savella returned home to the farm and had to take up the chores her older sister, Maria, used to do. Maria had married Harry

Charko, a neighbouring farmer, in the fall of 1918 after Savella had gone to Saskatoon. Now that Savella was home for the summer vacation, it was her duty to do the daily chores that consisted of milking cows and separating the cream from the milk through the cream separator, driving the cattle to the pasture owned by the Hudson's Bay Company that they had the use of and tending the cattle there and then feeding the pigs.

Farming on the prairies in the early 20th century was labourious. Horses and manpower were the means of haying, and seeding and harvesting of crops. Savella was expected to help in many of these chores. When her brother Eugene and father brought the hay home in a hayrack, she was responsible for laying out the stack evenly and trampling it down. When her mother witnessed her attempts to make a haystack, she realized that Savella was not strong enough for the heavy work and assigned her to preparing the meals and baking. Savella remembers, "I thoroughly enjoyed it. We had plenty of eggs, cream and butter for the baking. I learned to cook early in life."

With the summer of 1919 coming to an end, Savella was excited about going back to Mohyla to begin her Grade 9. But before she could escape to Saskatoon, the month of September was a busy one on the farm and she was needed for harvesting. The ripened crop was cut with a binder pulled by horses, tied into sheaves and then stood up to make stooks to dry, and then finally threshed with a threshing machine. Threshing required a gang of 18 to 20 men, consisting of team men, field pitchers, an engineer and grain haulers. All had to be fed and some had to be housed. Neighbouring women came to help prepare food for the regular meals as well as four o'clock lunches every day. With no refrigeration, the food had to be prepared each day. Though labour intensive, days of threshing were social occasions. The women took the opportunity to chat and gossip and to exchange news. At times the reputation of the hosting family was at stake. The family with the exceptionally good meals was looked upon with favour!

A month into the school year, the harvest was nearly completed and off Savella went to Saskatoon where she enrolled at Nutana Collegiate. Nutana Collegiate accommodated the rural children arriving in the city to continue their education. Her brother, Eugene, followed a few weeks later after helping to finish off the harvest. Many Ukrainian students from the bloc settlements in the surrounding Saskatoon area missed a month of school in the autumn to help with the harvest. At Nutana, Savella and the other Grade 9 latecomers, 24 students all of Ukrainian descent, were placed in a separate class, 1G Form. Meanwhile, the Grade 10 Ukrainian late comers occupied 2F Form separate from the other classes. Savella's high school experience was one of joy.

Activities at Mohyla commenced again in the fall. A students' club, *Komeniari* (Stone Cutters), had been organized at Mohyla Institute the year of its establishment.[25] The name was derived from a poem written by the eminent Ukrainian writer, Ivan Franko (d. 1916), who had advocated an independent Ukrainian nation in the late nineteenth century (see Appendix A for information on Ivan Franko). The students participated in debates in the Ukrainian language on current topics and also discussed Ukrainian culture and history and news of Ukraine. There was exciting news to discuss. In January of 1918 the fledgling government in Ukraine proclaimed an independent Ukrainian National Republic. But alas, it was short lived as Soviet troops regained control of Ukraine in 1922 making it one of the republics of the Union of Soviet Socialist Republics (USSR). This event, of course, was of great interest and certainly was published in the student newspaper *Komeniari* to which students contributed stories, articles, poems and jokes.

Studies and culture work were not the only activities at Mohyla. Students enjoyed social times and entertainment at the Saturday evening dances. From where they stood clustered together against the wall, boys would cross the dance floor to where the girls sat together to ask them to dance. This ritual was performed every dance night in an orderly fashion.

Once a week, while Savella was at Nutana Collegiate, the girls in her class went to Victoria School on Broadway to take Household Science (today known as Home Arts). The boys in the class took Manual Training. The class was divided into two semesters: the first semester the students studied foods, their composition, digestion and proper methods of cooking and serving; the second semester they focused on studying textiles and clothing. As a practical project, the girls sewed blouses. This was a unique experience for a country daughter of immigrant parents. "I couldn't get over the idea that such seemingly unimportant or rather menial tasks of women as cooking, housekeeping, and sewing were included in a school curriculum as respectable academic subjects. . . . These ideas remained with me throughout my life."[26] Coming from a background where a woman's traditional role of household chores was considered menial, Savella was pleasantly surprised with the school subject of household science. Through the study of the nutritional value of various foods and the most effective method of their preparation, along with the study of textiles and sewing, she understood women's work in the home to be respected. Women could be looked upon as contributing equally to society as men.

Because of the shortage of teachers in the rural communities, while Savella was at Mohyla and still going to school, she was asked by the Krydor school trustees in April 1920 to come back home to teach at the one-room school, Zaparoze, near her parents' farm. Despite not having completed Grade 9, she agreed. During this era, some individuals were allowed, if they had some education, if not high school, to teach with only a permit, rather than a teacher's diploma. Savella taught the five grades at Zaparoze school from April to September. "I felt I managed very well. Frankly, I was proud that I was a teacher."[27]

That fall Savella was able to get into Grade 10 at Nutana Collegiate, apparently having completed Grade 9. The year 1920-1921 was an exciting one at Mohyla for Savella. Wasyl Swystun, the rector, asked her to teach the beginners to read and write in

Ukrainian. The students in the beginner class spoke Ukrainian but had not had the opportunity to learn the Ukrainian written language. What a thrill to be considered qualified by the rector to teach! She was given another task, as well, to be monitor of the girls, a role that included keeping order and ringing the bell at 10:30 p.m. for lights to be out. She was also to take charge of the new girls and introduce them to the other girls, and to show them how to set the table in the dinning room and participate in serving the students when their turn arose. This duty was performed by each girl in turn.

Mohyla was growing and so was Saskatoon. In 1921 the population of Saskatoon rose to 26,700 with Ukrainians at one per cent of that figure at 332. Both Apolonius and Julian graduated that year: Apolonius with a law degree and Julian with a Bachelor of Arts. Wasyl Swystun resigned as rector and together with his wife left Saskatoon to take up teaching positions in Kamsack. This left a vacancy at Mohyla – no rector. The Board of Directors then asked Julian to accept the position of rector and Apolonius to be the manager. Julian in 1921 was registered in the Henderson Directory as "principal, Ukrainian Institute, 401 Main". As he was a young man, only 26, and unmarried, the Board insisted quite rightly that the rector must be married since there were girl residents. This decision brought Savella into the heart of Mohyla Institute. To Savella's delight, Julian proposed marriage and she accepted with love and enthusiasm. "I was crazy to be married to the man I loved . . . " she said in an interview.[28] Having just completed Grade 10 and only 17, Savella married Julian on July 23, 1921.

The wedding took place in Saskatoon in the newly established Ukrainian Greek Orthodox Church of Canada on Avenue P with Julian's friend, Rev. S.W. Sawchuk, officiating. Savella's bridesmaids were Marion Lazorko (Apolonius' girlfriend whom he later married), her sister Stephania and a friend, Mary Niles. The bestmen were Apolonius, Michael Chorneyko and Onufry Derbowka. Savella wore a white wedding dress and Julian a business suit.

Though Julian could not afford to buy an engagement ring, they each had a gold wedding band.

The wedding was not a traditional Ukrainian wedding. In the countryside a Ukrainian wedding lasted two to three days with many guests coming from the surrounding area, thereby making it an important festive celebration and social event with tables laden with food and drink. Music with a live band was an essential part of the wedding; traditional wedding marches were played and wedding songs were sung by the mother of the bride and the bridesmaids. Days in advance of the wedding, a wooden platform would be built outside for the purpose of the dance. After a sit-down dinner, guests would present gifts of money or whatever they could afford to the bridal couple – sometimes even a live chicken. The night before the wedding, the women of the wedding party sang the appropriate songs while braiding a wreath (*vinok*) of periwinkle (*barvinok*) or myrtle (*mirt*) and silver coins. This wreath was worn by the bride around her head under her veil on the day of the wedding to bring her good luck. The groom would wear a smaller version around his boutonniere. Each set of parents met their respective children with bread and salt and gave them their blessings. Weeks prior to the wedding, banns announcing the engagement were read in the church three times at three different church services before the wedding arrangements were ready to proceed.

In contrast with traditional Ukrainian weddings, the Stechishin-Wawryniuk wedding was a quiet simple affair: a church service followed by a dinner and dance at the Mohyla Institute. With her brother Eugene making all the wedding arrangements, the wedding guests consisted of Mr. and Mrs. Wawryniuk, sister Helen and her husband Andrew Worobetz, sister Mary and her husband Harry Charko, Julian's brother Michael and his wife Anastasia from Yorkton, and brother Myroslav and his wife Ann from Winnipeg. Michael was a lawyer. Myroslav was the editor of the Ukrainian language weekly in Winnipeg, *Ukrainksyi holos* (*Ukrainian Voice*). Both men were members of the intelligentsia. And so Savella, at a tender age, found herself enmeshed in an ambitious family as well as within the 'movers and shakers' in the Mohyla milieu.

2

With Her Husband's Encouragement

The young Stechishins began married life together in the suite reserved for the rector in Mohyla Institute. It consisted of a bedroom, living room and a bathroom; meals were provided by Mohyla staff in the main dinning room along with all the students in residence. This was a new beginning for Savella. She had now moved from the girls' residence up the ladder to the wife of the man in the top position, albeit a position with a great deal of responsibility. Tradition dictated that a respectable married woman assumed the role of a typical housewife, that is, stay at home keeping house, look after her husband and children and perhaps in her spare time volunteer for some worthy cause. However, Savella had different ideas and decided to break with tradition. "I wanted to be an educated person, to stand on my own feet, to reach for the stars."[1] And so she did. With the encouragement of her husband, she enrolled again at Nutana Collegiate to take Grade 11, and thereby complete junior matriculation. In the 1920s it was unusual for a married woman to return to high school. The Stechishins lived rent-free at the Institute and had their meals with the students in the dining room. Savella had virtually no household chores since all chores were performed by the Institute staff giving her freedom to pursue her dream.

However, a bump appeared in the road to her dream. Savella became pregnant shortly after marriage. At school Savella wore a bulky jacket to hide her impending motherhood until her condition became obvious even to the most sympathetic. At about 4 or 5 months pregnant in early spring, she was forced because of her size to quit attending high school. Upset and unhappy about having to quit going to school, Julian cheered her up and encouraged her to continue her studies at home with his help. She recalled, "My husband encouraged me. Frankly, he wanted an educated wife." Determined to achieve Grade 11 standing, she studied all the requisite subjects, finding math and chemistry difficult without the help of a school setting and a regular teacher. She persevered and wrote the departmental exams in June at Nutana Collegiate. At that time Grades 11 and 12 exams were set by the Department of Education in Regina and exams were taken in schools across the province. Approximately a month later, Savella was overjoyed to receive the results of her exams – she had passed all her Grade 11 subjects.

September rolled around and Savella was unsure when her baby was due. She was naive about motherhood and did not prepare for the coming of a newborn with a layette or the equipment necessary to welcome a new baby. Julian was off traveling the countryside soliciting and collecting funds from Ukrainians in the bloc settlements to help pay off the mortgage held on Mohyla Institute. Savella decided that rather than be alone in Saskatoon, she would visit her parents in Krydor. However, the expected-unexpected happened one evening when, while her mother had gone to help Savella's sister Mary with some harvesting chores and her sister Stephania and brother Eugene were away at school in Saskatoon, Savella began to experience labour pains. Mr. Wawryniuk did not have a car to take Savella to her mother so he tried to phone his daughter Mary's place to ask his wife to return home. Savella's mother was an experienced midwife, having delivered many babies in Ukraine and in Canada and had, in fact, even delivered many of her grandchildren. But telephone central closed at 10 o'clock and by the time they even attempted to call central it was well after 10 o'clock. Fortunately, near midnight, as the pain began increasing, Julian arrived by car. He had been in the Whitkow area on business concerning Mohyla and felt the need to see how Savella was holding up in her impending state of motherhood. Julian bundled Savella into the car and as quickly as the poor roads would allow, they drove to Mary's home.

A baby boy arrived at 5 o'clock in the morning on September 18, 1922. The delivery went well and both mother and child were healthy. Eva, mindful of old country superstitions, poured holy water on the child and baptized him without giving him a name, a practice enacted to ward off evil and spiritually protect him. They decided to name him Anatole. Savella had been very fond of the name ever since she had read the novel *Luboratsky* by Anatole Swydnytsky, a Ukrainian writer. Most often a baby was baptized within three months of birth, following the tradition in both the Ukrainian Orthodox and Catholic denominations.

After the birth of Anatole, who was affectionately called 'Tolio' throughout his life by his family, Julian returned to Saskatoon and Savella remained with her parents so that her mother could help look after the baby. In November, feeling confident to be on her own with her newborn, she returned to Saskatoon with her baby. In the spring, leaving Julian in Saskatoon, she and Tolio returned to her parents' home and stayed into the summer, helping a little with various chores. As rector, Julian was kept busy running Mohyla Institute and trying to solicit donations for the upkeep and payment of the mortgage on the Institute. There was little money available from the Ukrainian immigrants who were themselves trying to keep their heads above water as they coped with poverty, discrimination and unaccustomed ways of living in a new land. However, Julian was able to collect sufficient funds to cover mortgage payments for a few months and Mohyla was able to continue in operation.

Savella had set a goal from which she was not to be diverted. At the farm, she formulated a plan: she would leave her baby with her mother and she would resume her path to obtaining a teaching certificate and thus acquire a profession. She considered teaching a good profession and a quick way to become a 'professional' – her ultimate goal. A teacher in the Ukrainian milieu was looked upon with high regard. To be educated and to be able to educate others was indeed a prestigious position. Many young men and a few women used teaching as a stepping stone to obtain higher education and in a few years went into professions such as law, dentistry and pharmacy. They were able to save from their salaries as teachers to pay for university tuition and gain valued and valuable teaching experience. Savella was surrounded by friends who were obtaining a higher education and who wanted to be middle class and have the better things life could offer them.

In September of 1923, Savella returned to Julian and Mohyla Institute and enrolled at the Saskatoon Normal School for teacher training. Although he had graduated with a Bachelor of Arts, Julian decided to obtain a teacher's certificate himself should Fate dictate that it become necessary. Julian and Savella attended Normal School together. After a couple of months, Savella visited her one year old son at her parents' farm and "was overjoyed to see my little boy Tolio."[2] In the spring, she was granted a Second Class Certificate while her husband had received his First Class Certificate at Christmas. Savella obtained a Second Class Certificate because of having only Grade 11 (junior matriculation) standing. "I was a liberated woman in those days long before it was fashionable to be liberated," she told reporter Nancy Russell in 1976 on the occasion of her receiving an honorary doctor of canon law degree from the University of Manitoba.[3] She was "liberated" in the sense that she did what she felt necessary to achieve her goals and she was not hampered by a demanding husband or the social norms of the day, i.e., to be a stay-at-home mom.

The 1920s were a time to abandon old conservatism and embrace great social change. From the world of fashion to the world of politics, forces clashed to produce the most explosive decade of the century. Youth ruled everything, from the young styles of dress to the latest celebrities. If it was young, it was the thing to wear or do. It was the age of prohibition, it was the age of prosperity, and it was the age of downfall. Saskatoon was not immune to change and advancing technology. For instance, on July 18, 1923 CFQC-Radio made its first broadcast in Saskatoon and from then onward news was quickly transmitted, bringing the world much closer to home. The plebiscite in Saskatchewan ended prohibition in 1924 and a system of government liquor stores was adopted to purchase alcohol. Margaret Newton, a young graduate student of plant pathology and the first Canadian woman with a doctorate in agriculture science, was a pioneering cereal rust researcher between 1920 and 1925 at the University of Saskatchewan in Saskatoon. This research, in response to the disastrous stem rust epidemic of 1916 in Western Canada, enabled Saskatoon to bcome the main centre for cereal root disease studies. Saskatoon's Ethel Catherwood won the ladies running high jump at the Olympics with a jump of 5' 3" in 1928. The first ever air mail delivery from Winnipeg arrived in Saskatoon that same year. It was the 1920s and when Savella was in her early 20s, she formulated definite ambitions and goals.

Making the most of her free time with no household chores at Mohyla and her baby living with her parents on the farm, Savella threw herself into what she saw as her role as the wife of the rector. While she was expected to fulfil the role of dean of women (*nastoyatelka*), which she did in earnest, she believed that it was her duty to institute a program of activities for the girls in residence. Most of the girls came from farms and small towns and so were often very shy and had difficulty in expressing themselves in public. To remedy this situation, Savella developed a program in which each girl would speak in front of the other girls on a particular topic and in this way gain self-confidence. Additionally, "In order not to be outdistanced by the more daring boys, the girls formed their own oratorical circle, where every female student had the opportunity to acquire some experience in public speaking."[4] Savella was in fact promoting equality and a social feminism amongst the female students. In addition, she often introduced topics about their own heritage so that the girls would obtain more knowledge about Ukrainian culture and affairs.[5] These social gatherings gave birth to the formation of the Mohylianky Society in 1923. The name 'Mohylianky' was in honour of Raina Mohylianka, a noblewoman living in Ukraine who supported the Ukrainian Orthodox Church.[6] All female students were members of the society and an executive was elected with Savella as its first president.

Ukrainian embroidery piqued Savella's interest in 1923 when an immigrant family, Bohuslav Shashkewich, his wife and young son, arrived from Ukraine and came to Mohyla hoping to find work. Shashkewich was the grandson of the popular Ukrainian poet Markian Shashkewich who was involved in the birth of Ukrainian nationalism in Ukraine (Galicia). Julian embraced most of the newly arrived educated Ukrainians to Saskatoon, presuming that they would be a good influence on the students, by helping them to become patriotic towards Ukraine and become more knowledgeable about their ancestral home. Mr. Shashkewich was engaged to teach Ukrainian history and Mrs. Shashkewich was employed in the kitchen. Savella was amazed at the beautiful Ukrainian embroidery Mrs. Shashkewich had brought from Ukraine. She had never seen such intricate and beautiful patterns on teacloths, centerpieces and various runners. That same year, another Ukrainian family arrived, a woman and her daughter from the province of Bukovyna. This woman had a blouse exquisitely embroidered in a Bukovynian pattern on a thin marquisette type material.

Contemporary fashions were changing; girls bobbed their hair and hem lines went up. Girls at Mohyla were no different than others in Saskatoon and Canada. They were concerned with the latest fashions. But these young women had an additional element to consider: learning and even 'living' Ukrainian culture. In the fall of 1923 Savella introduced a Ukrainian embroidery program to the Mohylianky. The first project was for each girl to embroider a blouse for herself. Savella took it upon herself to select the embroidery patterns, setting an example by embroidering her own blouse and a small teacloth that could serve as a centerpiece on a large table. The embroidery program continued until 1925, when a change in focus was brought about by Mohyla's subscription to *Nova khata* (The New Home), a monthly journal on Ukrainian arts first published in 1923 by *Ukrainske Narodne Mystetstvo* (Ukrainian Folk Arts Council) in L'viv. The Institute also subscribed to the bi-monthly women's magazine from Kolomeyia (Galicia), *Zhinocha dolia* (Women's Destiny) first published in 1924.[7] Savella discovered that *Nova khata* carried informative articles about Ukrainian arts and crafts, which included embroidery patterns, *pysanky* (Ukrainian Easter Eggs) patterns and woodcraft. She studied the articles on embroidery and *pysanky* and shared them with the Mohylianky by reading them aloud at the meetings. Savella then expanded her program with the help of this information.

Articles embroidered by the Mohylianky were often used to help raise funds for Mohyla Institute. In 1925 the Mohylianky held a bazaar where they sold some of their embroidery to financially aid the cash-strapped Mohyla Institute.[8] Donations were solicited from across Canada. The bazaar was also useful for bridging the cultural gap between the immigrant Ukrainian community and the established Anglo-Canadian one. As Savella wrote, "This bazaar was opened specifically to the English public and was similar in style to a typical English bazaar."[9] The bazaar accomplished its two aims: it was a successful fundraiser for the Institute and it increased the visibility of the Ukrainian Canadians in the Anglo-Canadian community in Saskatoon.

In 1936, Daria Yanda, a student at Mohyla at the time of Savella's deanship (1921-24), in *Iuvileina knyzhka* (Jubilee Book, 10th Anniversary) credited her own active participation in women's activities to her stay at Mohyla and her involvement with the women's organization in Saskatoon. She further stated that Savella was responsible for implanting Ukrainian nationalistic ideals in her charges:

> Mrs. Stechishin taught . . . that each of us had to become activists in the Ukrainian community, and be a leader of women in those communities where we would eventually take up

residence, and further that we were obliged to do this and
practise what we learned at the Institute, and at school, and also
the etiquette learned at the Institute. Mrs. Stechishin reminded
us to carefully prepare ourselves for important future obligations
to our Ukrainian community and to our family, all that we will
encounter in our lives. She also reminded us that we were to be
not only good and sensible wives to our future husbands, but also
we were to be equal partners working for our community in the
uplifting and enlightening of our Ukrainian people.[10]

Savella's drive to form a women's organization was always
foremost. She envisaged the organization as infusing self-esteem and
self-worth in Ukrainian-Canadian women. Once they achieved
confidence and pride in themselves, they would be better mothers
who could then take control of the upbringing of their children to be
good Canadians as well as be proud of their Ukrainian heritage. Daria
Yanda further wrote of Savella's resolve and her maternal feminist
concepts: "At these meetings of the girls [Mohylianky], Mrs.
Stechishin pointed out to us that another obligation– as future
mothers– . . . was the upbringing of our children to be [Ukrainian]
nationally conscious and progressive [Canadian] citizens."

Various books and publications from Western Ukraine, which
were regularly subscribed to by Mohyla Institute, piqued the interest
of the Mohylianky regarding women's activism in Ukraine. It was
the close links forged between Ukraine and the Ukrainians in
Saskatoon that helped to plant the germ of uniting Ukrainian women
in Canada. They became aware of a women's movement in Ukraine
and soon the idea of organizing women of Ukrainian descent in
Canada was enthusiastically adopted. Interestingly, they were not
aware that the first recorded secular women's organization in Canada
was the Ukrainian Women's Educational Society formed in
Winnipeg in 1916, the other major centre of Ukrainian cultural
activity in Canada. Its members were from the non-denominational
organization Ukrainian National Home.[11] At this time, however,
communications were poor and the Mohylianky were not aware of
this organization.[12] The Mohylianky appear to have had better

knowledge of the activities in Ukraine via publications than of those in Winnipeg a few hundred miles away. In Saskatchewan, the first recorded Ukrainian women's organization, *Trud* (Toil), was organized in 1917 in the rural area of Dana.[13] In other localities, women of Ukrainian descent who were beginning to organize themselves were almost exclusively on the prairies where the Ukrainian population predominated. Melville (1924), Sheho (1925), Redfield-Richard (1926), Mazeppa (1926), Ituna (1923), and Canora (1926)[14] were communities within the bloc settlement in Saskatchewan which had spawned organized women's societies.[15]

In the spring of 1923, Savella along with several other women called a preliminary meeting to solicit opinions on the idea of a women's organization.[16] Though response was favourable, a decision to formalize an organization was postponed to September when most community activities began. Historian Frances Swyripa agrees that "the Mohylianky launched the first concerted campaign among Ukrainian women in Canada. . ."[17]

Ukrainian Canadians in Saskatoon, regardless of their religious affiliation, congregated at the Ukrainian Community Hall that was built in the late 1910s as a venue for social activities. As there were only 332 Ukrainians living in Saskatoon in 1921 according to official statistics, many of these people had to be committed to their cause to make things happen. Savella's kindred spirit was Tetiana Kroitor from Canora, a married woman, a year younger, also with a baby whom she left with her mother to pursue higher education in Saskatoon with her husband. On September 23, 1923 Savella, together with Tetiana Kroitor, her now close friend and fellow Mohylianka, formally organized the non-denominational Olha Kobylianska Association with 30 women.[18] Some of the enthusiastic members were young single girls: Anatasia Greschuk, Anna Popowych, and Vera Fediuk, and included Mohylianky members Ann Raychyba, Doris Kanasewich, Doris Werezak, Sophia Kalenchuk, Mary Eliuk, Anne Chonko, Stephania Wawryniuk, Mary Chycoski, Anne Makowski, and Thelma Radyk. Since it was customary to name organizations after an outstanding Ukrainian personality, two names were proposed: Lesia Ukrainka and Olha Kobylianska. Savella and Tetiana favoured Olha Kobylianska, a Ukrainian popular contemporary novelist, whose name was selected (see Appendix A for more information on Kobylianska). Her novels featuring strong independent women were read in Canada by enlightened women and students. Thus, the first Ukrainian women's organization in Saskatoon was named Olha Kobylianska Women's Association. The executive consisted of: President - Savella Stechishin, Vice-President - Anna Bachynska, Secretary - Tetiana Kroitor, Assistant Secretary - Anastasia Greschuk, Treasurer - Palahia Wedmedyk.

Primarily, the new rganization was to, as Savella wrote in 1937, "manifest a break with the long established tradition that a woman's place is exclusively in the home, around the *peech* (stove) and not in the community."[19] The Olha Kobylianska Association in Saskatoon was the culmination of the hopes and dreams of Savella and like-minded women in the Mohylianky Society for a women's organization in Saskatoon. While its first members were mostly Ukrainian Orthodox women, some Ukrainian Catholic and a small number of Ukrainian Baptist women were members.[20]

A non-denominational Ukrainian-Canadian women's organization was indeed a liberal idea in 1923. Ethnicity was more important than religion to Savella and her young cohorts. The Ukrainians in Canada, and more specifically on the prairies where the majority had settled were divided into primarily two religious groups: Ukrainian Greek Orthodox and Ukrainian Greek Catholic. The majority of Ukrainians came from Galicia and were of the Greek Catholic denomination with the Bukovynians adhering to Orthodoxy; approximately 85 percent were Greek Catholic and 15 percent belonged to the Orthodox denomination.[21]

Ukrainian pioneers in the early twentieth century found themselves deprived of any spiritual guidance since Ukrainian clergy did not accompany the emigrants. The main obstacle to Greek

Catholic clerical immigration was the Vatican's demand that only celibate priests could minister in North America while in Ukraine the majority of Greek Catholic priests like the Orthodox were married. In Canada, since the Ukrainians did not have their own clergy to minister to their religious needs, three religious groups vied to 'save' the Ukrainian souls: the Protestant (Presbyterian and Methodist), French Roman Catholic, and Russian Orthodox clergy. Only sporadic visits by priests from the United States (both Greek Catholic and Russian Orthodox) alleviated the vacuum created by the lack of priests of the traditional Ukrainian churches. These three religious groups added to the factionalization within the Ukrainian communities who already had their own denominational differences (i.e., Greek Catholic and Orthodox). The majority of Ukrainians rejected all three religious groups as alien to their original churches that were steeped in Ukrainian tradition and ritual.

The establishment in 1912 of a Greek Catholic bishop in Canada, Nykyta Budka, directly responsible to the pope, helped the immigrants of that denomination to achieve consolidation, stability and expansion.[22] However, due to the bishop's compromise with the Roman Catholics to have only celibate priests and the demand for all community buildings to be under the ownership of the Catholic church, a rift developed amongst Ukrainians. The intelligentsia through the *Ukrainskyi holos* (*Ukrainian Voice*) that began publication in 1910 in Winnipeg, Manitoba strongly questioned the wisdom of this demand. In 1916, students at the University of Saskatchewan, teachers on the prairies and the intelligentsia who were the inner circle of the *Ukrainian Voice* established the Petro Mohyla Ukrainian Institute in Saskatoon.

It was Mohyla Institute that became the focus of the bitter feud between Bishop Budka and dissatisfied secular critics. In spite of secular opposition, Budka demanded that the Institute allow only Ukrainian Catholic students and that the Institute be registered under and accountable to the Catholic church. Under the leadership of Wasyl Swystun and Michael Stechishin, leading members of the intelligentsia, a confrontation in June 1918 by the discontented Catholic laity culminated in the establishment of the Ukrainian Greek Orthodox Church of Canada (UGOC) in Saskatoon.[23] The emphasis of this new church was a married priesthood and a democratic structure governed by laity. It was distinct in its differences from both the Canadian Ukrainian Greek Catholic church and the other Orthodox churches whose real power was hierarchical. The UGOC created by the laity would be directed by the laity. Saskatoon was the site for the first *sobor* (general council) in December 1918 whereby the establishment of the church was approved. The new church absorbed Mohyla Institute establishing it as the centre of Ukrainian activism within Saskatchewan and to a significant extent in Canada.

The dynamics of the new women's organization were focussed on promoting self-confidence and self-education amongst Ukrainian women, to elevate them in Canada. Heeding the words printed in the *Ukrainian Voice* a decade earlier (1914) in which an appeal was made to the Ukrainians in Canada: "To uplift us from our lower position, we need leaders, educated leaders, who would be aware of their duties . . . ,"[24] these young female activists encouraged women to actively participate within both their immediate and the host communities and most critically maintain Ukrainian culture. Since 56 percent of Ukrainian-Canadian women in 1921 were illiterate and the majority lived in rural areas, it was the somewhat educated women that the organization at first was looking toward, those who were literate and higher up the socio-economic ladder (the Ukrainian middle class).[25]

Ukrainian-Canadian males' illiteracy rate was 32 per cent while only 5 per cent of Canadian women of all origins were illiterate. By 1931, illiteracy for Ukrainian-Canadian women had decreased by almost half to 30 percent and women in the rural areas began to participate more vigorously within their own communities. During that year, there were 29,092 women of Ukrainian descent living in Saskatchewan, 4,712 in cities and 24,380 in rural areas. In 1921, 54 per cent of Ukrainian-Canadian women in the labour force were engaged in service occupations, compared to 51 per cent of the total Canadian female work force. Agriculture engaged 31 per cent while only 4 per cent of all Canadian women were so engaged. The greatest number of both urban and rural females in 1931 were in the age bracket 20 to 29 (1,072 and 3813 respectively). The rural females dominated in all age brackets (ages 30 to 39 at 563 and 2,248); (ages 40 to 49 at 291 and 1,767); (ages 50 to 59 at 95 and 1057); (ages 60 to 69 at 72 and 659); (ages 70 to 79 at 45 and 325) and (ages 80 to 89 at 8 and 61).[26]

In summary, women activists in the countryside were between the ages of 20 and 40 who had some education. Therefore, Savella and the other activists were reaching out to women who were in the 20 to 50 age bracket, had some elementary education at the least, and who were perhaps more prosperous than those who were below the poverty line. Older women who were uneducated and still entrenched in the old country ways did not have the drive or the wherewithal to develop the vision that younger educated women did, nor were they modern and accepting of Canadian values.

The executive of the Olha Kobylianska Association with Savella as president organized a study group with emphasis on self-education through reading. Their reading material primarily consisted of Ukrainian books and newspapers. The women were also encouraged to read English language newspapers so that they would be familiar with Canadian current affairs. Libraries containing Ukrainian books were set up; no mention is made of recommended English materials. In order to become further enlightened, it was essential for the women to initiate and/or participate in the observances of outstanding Ukrainian historical events, raise funds to provide financial aid to Ukraine and teach their children the Ukrainian language, culture and arts.

Through the years 1921 to 1924, Savella juggled the roles of wife and mother, dean of women, and student at Normal School. In the spring of 1924, upon graduation from Normal School, Savella was hired as the sole teacher of forty-eight children at a one-room school, Zaporoze, located one mile from her parents' home. This arrangement was convenient for her; she lived with her parents at no cost and her mother provided free babysitting. She received a monthly salary of one hundred dollars up to the end of December, when the school term terminated because of inclement weather. Her salary resumed with the onset of spring, as the next school term began in March when improved weather allowed children to walk to school. At the end of term, she kept her promise to donate one hundred dollars to Mohyla Institute to help pay off its mortgage. It was customary for Mohyla teacher-trainees to promise "to donate $100.00 of their first year salary to the Institute. . ."[27] She commuted to Saskatoon by train on weekends and during the long school breaks to be with her husband who remained at Mohyla Institute. At the age of twenty-one, leaving a husband to his own devices while working miles from the home and seeing him on weekends and holidays only was indeed unusual for a woman during the 1920s.

In the 1920s, educated and community active emigres were fleeing Ukraine and settling in the diaspora. One such emigre was Kharytia Kononenko, an active participant in the women's movement in Eastern Europe and a family member of Ukrainian nationalists in Ukraine. Before coming to Saskatoon in 1924, she had graduated from the university in Prague. In Saskatoon, she hoped to study English and complete her graduate work. During her stay in Saskatoon, she lived at Mohyla Institute and participated in the Mohylianky's evening gatherings. Aware of her background and knowledge of the women's movement in Ukraine, Savella invited her to explain the movement and its aims to the young women at Mohyla with the hope that the women's organization in Saskatoon, Olha Kobylianska, would follow a similar path. Rather than turning to the example of the women's movement in Canada, Savella decided to look primarily towards the homeland of her ancestors. Although she sought help and advice from the women's movement in Ukraine, she wanted to incorporate aspects from the Canadian women organizations. This way the new Ukrainian-Canadian women's organization would have the best from both worlds, as she saw it. It would be an organization observing, preserving and promoting all things Ukrainian, yet be in a Canadian setting and valuing Canadian living standards and Canadian institutions. The organization would be in harmony with the old and the new.

Soiuz Ukrainok (Union of Ukrainian Women) in Western Ukraine and *Ukrainskyi Zhinochyi Soiuz* (Ukrainian Women's Society) in Czechoslovakia exerted a great deal of energy in helping Ukrainian women in Western Ukraine. Kononenko had been associated directly and indirectly with both these organizations. She became the first link between the Ukrainian women and the women in Canada of Ukrainian descent. It was she to whom Sofia Rusova, the leading Ukrainian woman activist/feminist in Western Ukraine, appealed for financial aid. In 1925 Rusova wrote to Kononenko in Saskatoon asking for help to cover the financial expenses of the Ukrainian delegates who hoped to attend the Congress of the International Women's Council in Washington in May 1925.[28]

In her article *"Do Ukrainiskukh Zhinok v Kanady i Ameritsi"* (To Ukrainian Women in Canada and America), Kononenko, as President of the Olha Kobylianska Women's Association in Saskatoon, requested the subscribers of *Ukrainian Voice* to aid the Ukrainian women financially.[29] Appealing for donations, she and Savella, who was then secretary, wrote:

> K. Kononenko, as President of the Olha Kobylianska Association, has received a plea from Mrs. S. Rusova which we are putting before you. We think that this plea will find sympathy with Ukrainian women, and that you all understand that our sisters in the Old Country need help in their patriotic work. We think that it would be shameful not to help them at least materially because a great deal of their energies are expended for the good of our native land. It will not be difficult for us to give a dollar for we do not even mind wasting it, but there this dollar will greatly help these patriotic women in their honourable work, and . . . in the name of Sofia Rusova, who all her life has worked for her

countrymen, who was not afraid of Russian prisons nor
Bolshevik arrests but always works for the national cause.
Ukrainian women in Saskatoon have taken upon themselves
the leadership role in this task in Canada and are turning to
everyone regarding this urgent request to help those in their
patriotic cause.

Kononenko and Savella's expectation of individuals to donate
one dollar to the Ukrainian cause was an onerous burden on the
women in Canada. As a result, a modest amount of two thousand
crowns (in Czechoslovak currency) was collected and sent to Rusova.
At this time, poverty on the farms in the bloc settlements was not
uncommon. In the early 1920s, Ukrainian farm labourers seeking
employment during the harvest in southwestern Manitoba, North
Dakota, southern Saskatchewan or south central Alberta earned $240
for two or three months of backbreaking work.[30] In Winnipeg
(Saskatoon would be comparable) the weekly salary for a female
domestic was $9.00, charwomen earned $9-$10.00 weekly, while
waitresses earned about $10.00.

There were few professional Ukrainians in Canada, and very
few of them were women. For example, the first Ukrainian female,
Mary Sawchuk-Dyma (b. 1899), to graduate from a university in
Canada was in 1923. Up to the 1930s, Winnipeg was the home to the
only two fully qualified Ukrainian urban public school teachers in
Canada, both women.[31] These statistics show that the majority of
Ukrainian families in Canada, and more particularly in
Saskatchewan, did not have a dollar to donate since their annual
income would not allow it. The foregoing plea did not recognize the
financial hardship that a large portion of the Ukrainian Canadian
population was enduring. Kononenko was unable to adjust to
Canadian life and returned to Prague, Czechoslovakia in October
1925.

Savella's first call to unite women under one women's
organization in Canada appeared in an article titled "*Do
Orkhanizatsui Ukrainskoho Zhinotstva*" (To Organize Ukrainian

Women) printed in *Ukrainian Voice* on April 1, 1925. In this article she focused on the promotion of (Ukrainian) national consciousness amongst women and not women's consciousness; she gave no evidence of concern for the emotional welfare or rights of women. Savella earnestly urged women to focus their activities and subsume their lives to Ukrainian matters almost exclusively:

> What kind of contribution do the English women make to their country? Their organizations, whatever they may be, always strive to improve everyday life for all. Would it not be worthwhile for us to follow in their footsteps? In our lifetime, we have learned that no one will form our nation [Ukraine] if we do not do it ourselves. Women should care and organize women's clubs to discuss women's issues. Without question, work for such a club is to be directed to national consciousness, for without this there will be no path to follow to fight for a free Ukraine. For those whose interest is freedom for Ukraine, they should form an association and should help women to organize themselves . . .
> We, Ukrainians in Canada, should form a branch of the Women's Association here, which would be affiliated with the Women's Council in Ukraine. This [Canadian] national organization should take the initiative in all national concerns and give direction to all branches how to enlighten the membership.[32]

Savella believed she could advance the concept that Ukrainian Canadian women from all walks of life should unite for the welfare of Ukraine. At this time in her life, she felt this to be the most important issue.

> Members of this organization may be from any women's club in Canada regardless of their religious or political affiliation. Because Ukraine is most important, we should not divide ourselves along religious or political lines. Let's work together! I believe that this kind of organization will be of great benefit. First, it will give us the possibility to strengthen and maintain our nationality while living in Canada. When Ukrainian women will

take more interest in maintaining their nationality, Ukraine will be able to slowly attain independence. . . . because of national consciousness we become good Canadian citizens. We know from our own experience that nationally conscious Ukrainians are better Canadian citizens than those who know nothing about themselves as Ukrainians.

The last two sentences of the foregoing quote demonstrate that Savella believed one must first respect oneself in order to respect others; if one has a strong sense of identity, then one can give with confidence to others and become a better contributing citizen. Could any person who forsakes their own heritage and completely adopts another be trusted to be a proud contributing citizen? Savella believed, as did the intelligentsia, that those Ukrainian Canadians with a national consciousness would become not only leaders in Ukrainian organizations, but also leaders in the building of mainstream communities in Canada. Furthermore, the skills learned within their own organizations would benefit them outside their immediate communities.

Savella's was the first published appeal of its kind in any press in Canada. This first appeal produced no results at all.[33] A second call to women to organize was printed on July 29, 1925 in *Ukrainian Voice*, titled "*Soiuz Ukrainskiv Ameryky i Kanady*" (Ukrainian Women's Association in America and Canada). Growing up and teaching in the bloc settlements, Savella had first hand knowledge of the lower station of Ukrainian women, their lack of activism in their communities and their lack of sophistication and education. To remedy these deficiencies, in her personal published appeal she put more emphasis on 'women's consciousness' along with 'national consciousness.' She believed a woman should sacrifice herself for her family as well as for the Ukrainian nation.

I believe that this kind of an association can greatly help the Ukrainian cause. Until now our women have had little interest in community affairs and this has resulted in no gain for the Ukrainian community. When a woman does

> not understand the value of nationalistic work, she not
> only is a hindrance in this work but also because of her
> ignorance prevents her husband and children from
> actively participating. Should we be surprised at her?
> No. Where would she have been able to receive this
> knowledge?

Savella, at the age of 22, chastised the more enlightened women for not performing their duty to take an active role within their immediate community in the bloc settlements.

> Why don't informed women in the community take upon
> themselves the job to organize a women's club where a
> woman could receive practical household advice, as well
> as more knowledge about our Ukrainian matters? ... Our
> past shows us a clear path which we must strive to follow
> in order to become good Ukrainians. This pathway is a
> women's organization. A woman who cares for her
> children as well as supports her country should be more
> informed than her husband about many important
> Ukrainian affairs. A women's organization will give a
> new direction to women. Positive influence by mothers
> in the home leads the children on the proper path, because
> a nationality is measured not by the present generation but
> by the upcoming one.

The men of the Ukrainian communities do not go unscathed. Savella argued that "[a]mongst us, unfortunately, there are many men who know very little about their country [Ukraine]." She believed that it was specifically the women who must shoulder the responsibility of the preservation of Ukrainian identity in Canada and fight for the freedom of Ukraine. At that time it was the men who were the leaders guiding the fledgling Ukrainian flock and uplifting them as a whole community entity to the levels of the general Canadian population. To attract the attention of women, she mentioned a topic customarily of interest to women – domesticity.

> I think that the easiest way to encourage women to organize
> would be through discussions of the many useful household
> practices which would lighten the load of women's work in the
> home.

Her idea was to attract women with household topics and at the same
time stimulate their interest in more intellectual issues.

> Additionally, at every meeting each informed individual could
> give a short reading and open a discussion – here a woman will
> have the opportunity to express her thoughts and feelings. Later,
> each woman could read a book and give a report. This spreads
> knowledge. It would be beneficial from time to time to read
> aloud important articles from newspapers.

Although Savella appeared to recognize that women needed
to improve the efficiency of their domestic responsibilities, the
ultimate goal was to uplift women to begin practising Canadian social
values so that they could project a good image to the host society.

> If all women's clubs, regardless of their religious or political
> persuasion would become members of the Association, the
> English both in America and Canada would look upon us in a
> different light because all cultured peoples belong to some
> organization. We will improve our fate in Canada and America
> and simultaneously become supporters of the Old Country. I am
> sure that we all wish this. If so, we must take this to task,
> organize women and where possible join the Ukrainian Women's
> Associations of America or Canada. Benefits will be great, so go
> to work. Patriots, you must work for Ukraine.[34]

In the first half of the twentieth century the Ukrainian
Canadians were factional: Greek Catholic, Orthodox, Protestant and
socialists. Each faction vied to increase women's membership in
their respective communities since women's contributions were
greatly valued, particularly as fund raisers. Most often it was women

who were the backbone in the building of social meeting places, be they churches and/or halls by holding bazaars, dinners and other food-related activities. Although Savella was a member of the Orthodox community, she attempted to gather all Ukrainian women together to further the cause of Ukraine. To Savella, nationalism far outweighed religious and political biases.

The Congress of the International Women's Council in Washington in May 1925, where a delegate from Ukraine was to attend and for whom Savella earlier had appealed to Ukrainian Canadian women to donate money to the delegate gave Savella an idea. She decided to invite the Ukrainian delegate to Canada after the Congress to help organize Ukrainian women in Canada on a national level. Savella then proceeded to invite the delegate by letter. Hanna Chykalenko Keller, a prominent activist in Western Ukraine, attended the Congress as the Ukrainian delegate. Hanna acknowledged the invitation but unfortunately was unable to come to Canada because of her limited time abroad. Keller's presence in the United States was the impetus needed for the Ukrainian American women to organize in 1925 to form the *Soiuz Ukrainok Ameryky*, the Ukrainian National Women's League of America.

Savella set aside her work for her goals during weekdays and continued to teach. Although her school was outside Saskatoon, she often returned to the city. On holidays and during the months of January and February when rural schools were closed she remained in Saskatoon. She continued her intense interest in the Olha Kobylianska organization and was elected secretary for the year 1925 with Kononenko as president. In March 1925, in order to be closer to her husband and the organization, she accepted a teaching job at Sandy Lake School in the district of Petrofka (in the bloc settlement) which was closer to Saskatoon. As a small two-room teacherage was available, she and two year old Tolio moved in along with Mary Procenty from Krydor as nanny to look after Tolio while she taught. Because the teacherage was very cold and drafty in winter, plenty of coal and firewood were needed for fuel. Water was pumped from a nearby well and carried in pails to the teacherage. On one occasion, after spending a weekend in Saskatoon, Savella returned to find that she had been robbed, but only her mandolin was stolen. She had a suspect in mind but could not prove it so did nothing about it. It was not common at that time for a woman to live in a teacherage with only a baby and a young nanny.

Ukrainian-speaking teachers frequently taught the Ukrainian language in schools located in the bloc settlements as did Savella. As at the previous school, she taught the Ukrainian language and history for approximately 45 minutes to one hour after school hours. During this period, she taught the beginners reading and writing, and for those who could read and write she moved on to the history of Ukraine. Sometimes lunch break would be shortened to one hour from one and one-half hours so that these lessons could be accommodated during the day. Often during the lunch hour she taught the girls Ukrainian embroidery and crocheting. Most children responded favourably to the additional lessons and were anxious to learn. She often would teach her nanny to read and write in Ukrainian in the evenings. At this time she began to contribute articles to the *Ukrainian Voice* and wrote a short story, "*Zov Krovy.*" In her autobiography, Savella gives only the title of the story and does not explain what the story was about nor does she give the English translation of the title.

In 1926 Savella took a position to teach at Riel Dana school in the Vonda area, later called Smuts. She, her son Tolio and nanny Maria Melnyk arrived in Vonda by train at the end of February. Savella was surrounded by neighbours of Ukrainian descent and, in fact, her sister Stephania was teaching at Rak School nearby. Several other teachers in the vicinity also had been residents at Mohyla Institute and were acquainted with Savella. On weekends, Julian would sometimes visit by car and at other times she took the train with Tolio to Saskatoon.

Although pleased with her school and the community, her passionate desire for higher learning superseded all other obligations and conventional female traditions. To this end, she resigned her teaching position in August 1926 and in the fall enrolled at the University of Saskatchewan. "My heart was set on getting a university education. My husband encouraged me to go to university."[35] Since her husband was the rector at Mohyla, he was able to look after their four year old son when Savella went to university classes. Nevertheless, Savella selected classes that gave her free time in the afternoon to share in child-rearing. While at university, her vision for a women's organization drove her to accept the presidency of the local Olha Kobylianska Association at the same time as being president of the Mohylianky. While these time-absorbing activities resulted in her receiving low marks in her university classes, it did not undermine her determination to achieve her objectives, and so she pressed on with the unwavering encouragement of her husband. "It is true I was really obsessed with the idea and it gave me the driving force," she writes in her autobiography. The women in her social group looked to her for leadership because she lived at the Institute, which was the apex of Ukrainian cultural life in Saskatchewan, and also because her husband was one of the leaders of the intelligentsia that was setting the framework to guide Ukrainians into the mainstream of Canadian society.

Savella felt that Ukrainian women needed to unite in their struggle against the "snobbish dominant society that felt that if you weren't Anglo-Saxon you just weren't that good."[36] Prejudice and discrimination were rampant against the Ukrainian 'foreigners' and derogatory terms like 'bohunk' were often used by non-Ukrainians. In 1926 the Ku Klux Klan arrived in Saskatchewan and found the province fertile for discriminating practices. At its peak, some 25,000 people were attracted to the Klan meetings. However, not one to be deterred by discrimination and perhaps because of it to a certain extent, Savella believed her mission was to unite the Ukrainian women in Canada. She purposefully targeted all Ukrainian women, those who were cloistered in the bloc settlements as well as women in cities. She chose the Ukrainian language newspaper, *Ukrainian Voice,* as her first vehicle, as this was the newspaper read by most of the educated and 'movers and shakers' in the Ukrainian Canadian communities. Also, her brother-in-law was the editor and in tune with her goals.

At the beginning of 1926, Savella's article, *"Zhinka, a Buduchnist Ukraina"* (The Woman and the Future of Ukraine), attempted to provoke women in what she believed was their obligation to Ukraine and the preservation of Ukrainian identity in Canada. At the age of twenty-three, her perception of the role of women in Ukraine was expressed as follows:

> Up to now, Ukraine has not achieved her significance in the world as a cultured state. Why? There are many reasons for this but one of them is that the state was being built by one sex - almost exclusively men, and the women were left to the side. If the state demands only one or the other, men or women, then consequently our state cannot be complete and fully developed. Rather it will become more crippled.[37]

Perhaps due to the prevailing discrimination against Ukrainians in Canada during the first half of the twentieth century, she displayed the paranoia her circle of acquaintances were experiencing. In the same article she wrote,

> The English here in Canada are convinced that the assimilation of foreigners with the help of school and church has not been successful. So now there is great movement among the English to encourage intermarriages. They propose to marry with foreigners and by this method through the influence of the wife on the husband, or the husband on the wife, in family life, will draw them into their camp.

As the *Ukrainian Voice* was the most popular newspaper amongst Ukrainian Canadians at this time, the article was read by a large percentage of Ukrainians in Canada. Savella's article may have made a strong impression. However, it is most unlikely that 'the

English' would have had any such designs on foreigners. Nativism was embraced by a significant number of Anglo-Canadians, and the widespread attitude of the majority of Anglo-Canadians was that Ukrainians were undesirable immigrants and therefore undesirable marriage partners. Rather it is likely that the article was to discourage Ukrainian Canadians from intermarrying with persons of other nationalities in order to preserve the integrity of the Ukrainian heritage.

Ukrainian Voice on November 27, 1926 published Savella's final attempt to inspire women to attend, as delegates or observers, a women's convention. In the article, *"V Spravi Zhinochoho Zizdu"* (The Purpose of a Women's Convention), she again lamented that women have no pride in their own culture and are not interested in uplifting themselves and their community. Hence, such passivity reflects on the family and ultimately on the preservation of Ukrainianness and on Ukraine. She wrote:

> Our past teaches us that no one but we ourselves will be responsible for our fate. Consequently, it is necessary for us to appropriately prepare all members in our communities to this task. A great deal of attention must be placed on the (national) consciousness of our women . . . The best way to do this is with a women's organization.[38]

She went on to explain that the Mohylianky Society had taken the lead in organizing an agenda for this convention with the preparation of a "constitution, resolutions and other plans." Her dogma and assertiveness were evident:

> Since I have before me a definite plan and a definite purpose, there should be no difficulties in working in the direction of promoting awareness amongst women, who will then be useful and functional members in the Ukrainian community.

"I always turned to my husband for advice whenever I was in doubt,"[39] Savella credits her husband, Julian, for encouragement and offering sound advice on the method of procedures in the formation of a women's organization. Additionally, it was fortuitous that Julian's brother, Myroslaw, was the editor of *Ukrainian Voice* (1921-1946) so that access to this newspaper would have been relatively easy for Savella. Another family connection was another brother-in-law, Michael, who was a practising lawyer in Yorkton, Saskatchewan. The three Stechishin brothers were prominent members of the intelligentsia and had been part of the driving force in the establishment of the new Ukrainian Greek Orthodox Church of Canada. Michael's wife was also a believer and supporter of a Ukrainian women's organization. Savella was at the heart of the embryonic Ukrainian elite and middle class who were directing this ethnic minority on the fabric of the Canadian mosaic.

On the advice of Julian, in the fall of 1926 the young women activists in Saskatoon, Daria Yanda, Mary Hryniuk, Maria Maduke and Savella Stechishin, established a Founding Committee to organize a women's session at the Ukrainian National Convention to be held in Saskatoon in December 1926.[40] Then they sent out invitations to all the progressively-minded women they knew, particularly the female teachers in the rural areas who had boarded at Mohyla, inviting them to attend the conference.[41] By now there would have been approximately 10 to 15 female teachers in the bloc settlements. The invitation was signed by Savella while Maria Maduke's name was signed by her husband, John (then residing at Mohyla and going to university) since Maria was teaching at Vonda and unable to come to Saskatoon. Also, it was important to communicate with the wives of the men who were the activists in the intelligentsia and get their support. There were no women acting as leaders in the Ukrainian elite and it was entirely men who guided the growing Ukrainian community. To get support from Winnipeg, which was home to a large number of Ukrainians, Savella wrote to her friends Olha Swystun, Olha Sawchuk and Olha Arsenych, all of Winnipeg, whose husbands were nationalists and prominent members of the Ukrainian community.[42] They, too, embraced the idea and gave it their enthusiastic support.

The chief promoters to establish a women's organization along with Savella were activists Tetiana Kroitor, Daria Yanda, Mary Hryniuk and Maria Maduke. They all had been residents of Mohyla and after completing their Normal School had gone into the bloc settlements in Saskatchewan to teach school and promote the idea of a national Ukrainian women's organization in Canada. Much younger and more highly educated and higher on the socio-economic ladder than most Ukrainian-Canadian women in Saskatchewan, these young social feminists with urban middle-class values were determined to guide the Ukrainian female population that was barely out of a poor peasant culture. Savella and the others did not stress equality for women or women's consciousness (e.g., concerns with physical abuse, birth control, and poverty) as the organizations of mainstream women did, such as the Women's Christian Temperance Union, Young Women's Christian Association, Canadian Federation of University Women and the National Council of Women, to name a few. The Ukrainian women's interest was education for women and Ukrainian national consciousness. Whereas some male Ukrainian activists had immigrated to Canada, Ukrainian women activists/ feminists had not. The number of female activists/feminists in Ukraine had always been small and had preferred to remain there.[43] Thus, in Canada it was up to the young Mohyla educated activists/feminists with energy and vision to lead the women of Ukrainian descent and Savella Stechishin was a major player in this pursuit.

3

Daring to Achieve

Ukrainian-Canadian farm women living in the bloc settlements on the prairies, were not formally organized in any manner. An active social life is an important component of most women's lives and so it was for Ukrainian-Canadian women in the first half of the twentieth century. The many Ukrainian churches with their *banyas* (domes) dotting the prairie landscape became the lightning rod of women's needs to converge to work for a cause and at the same time to interact socially with like-minded women. Here, women formed sisterhoods within the church as they met to decorate and maintain the church all within a religious context. These activities led to much needed social interchange that alleviated the isolation of those living on the prairies during the pioneering era.

The organizing of the Ukrainian National Convention in December 1926 took its toll on Savella. As the rector's wife, she was in charge of the women's session of the convention and the preparation took much of her time. Her midterm university marks were low since she had little time to study for the exams. Fortunately she did not have any household chores because the family ate with the residents. However, she had other community activities, including singing in the choir and preparing items for a concert to be held in conjunction with the convention. Tolio was a quiet contented boy who played in the office while his father did his office work. Her low marks were an incentive to Savella to study diligently after the new year. Her efforts paid off and in the spring her marks greatly improved.

Savella was aware that Olha Swystun, who had married Wasyl Swystun in 1918 and for whom Savella had been a bridesmaid, had addressed the 1918 convention at Mohyla Institute, speaking on the "Role of Women in the Community."[1] Concern for the socio-economic and ethno-cultural conditions of Ukrainian-Canadian women was articulated publicly for the first time in 1918 by Olha Swystun and Anna Bychinska at the third Ukrainian National Convention in Saskatoon. Anna Bychinska, wife of a Ukrainian Protestant minister, chided the men for ignoring women's contributions and concerns. It was imperative that men "place the matter of elevation of our women in the first place."[2] Olha Swystun emphasized that women had an important participatory role to play in building their community. Supporting feminist principles, she asserted that women were to be equal members with men in guiding Ukrainian Canadians to strive for prosperous and progressive communities.[3] The *Ukrainian Voice* published her address, informing all its subscribers scattered across Canada that women and men had to "pull" together to take their place alongside Anglo-Canadians in the building of their country, Canada.

Not until 1925 was the subject broached again. Savella was at the convention when Leonida Slusar, a Ukraine-educated wife of an Orthodox priest (both had emigrated from Ukraine), addressed the Ukrainian National Convention. In her address titled "Women's Obligations," she promoted feminist thought with the opinion that women had equality with men in the sense that they could be educated like men and be leaders within the Ukrainian-Canadian community.[4] Further she believed that women must be educated and have self-respect to enable them to educate their children to take their rightful place in Canada. She was the first in the Ukrainian community to adopt the phrase: *an educated woman makes a better mother*. Ukrainian-Canadian women, she contended, should not only uplift themselves to equal non-Ukrainian women's organizations in Canada, but also keep in close contact with women's organizations in Ukraine. She strongly expressed the desire that all Ukrainian-

Canadian women's organizations should be brought together under the umbrella of a national organization. They could then work hand-in-hand with the Ukrainian women's organizations in the United States and in Ukraine. Leonida's address strengthened Savella's and the Mohylianky's resolve to proceed with their idea of uniting all women as they had discussed previously at their meetings.

An important event in Saskatchewan women's history occurred in 1925. Violet McNaughton, a suffragist and the first president of the Inter-provincial Council of Farm Women, was named women's editor of the *Western Producer*, a Saskatoon-based newspaper. Violet used this position to quietly exert a great deal of influence on farm women in particular and even in the political arena. She and women discussed many issues, such as birth control and safe water, not found in other newspapers.[5] Undoubtedly, these discussions and the atmosphere created permeated through to many women and women's groups.

These issues were not on the agenda for most Ukrainian Canadian women. Their mandate differed in that their concern was adjustment to the Canadian way of life and raising their social standing to Canadian economic standards along with the retention of Ukrainian culture. With these concerns in mind, Savella and the women activists in Saskatoon realized that they lacked the organizational skills necessary to proceed with their idea of founding a formal organization on a national scale; they needed outside help. Contact was made with "English women who were at the head of national societies, so that the methods of organization could be understood and knowledge acquired to carry out work among women's groups."[6] Upon being asked in 1997 whether she remembered which organizations these "English" women represented, Savella replied by letter:

> It was so long ago that I do not recall. It must have been me inquiring personally from my own initiative. Probably I spoke to someone I knew either at the Saskatoon Women's Council or probably someone from the Imperial Order of the Daughters of

the Empire. This group was active in those days. I did not speak
for any group, just inquired personally.[7]

Mohyla Institute was not the only subscriber to the *Zhinocha
dolia*, published in Kolomaiya, Western Ukraine (Galicia). A small
number of immigrant women in Canada also subscribed to it.
Through this magazine, Ukrainian women in Canada became familiar
with the work of the *Soiuz Ukrainok* (Union of Ukrainian Women) in
Ukraine. The *Soiuz Ukrainok* was the most significant women's
organization to emerge after the First World War in Western Ukraine.
Promoting self-reliance and self-help, it encompassed various
women's clubs, including philanthropic societies, nationalist women
and young socialist women.[8] *Soiuz*, a women's movement, not
political or class oriented, was established at the Ukrainian Women's
Congress in 1921 in L'viv. For economic and cultural reasons, *Souiz*
initiated the production of embroidery articles using traditional
Ukrainian patterns as well as 'writing' *pysanky* (Ukrainian Easter
Eggs) as a cottage industry. The word 'writing' is used because in
Ukrainian the root word of *pysanky* is *pysaty* which means to write.
These products provided the village women with not only badly
needed cash and encouraged preservation of their culture, but also
instilled in them a national pride. Female activists made frequent
trips to the villages to organize courses and lectures. These women
were in fact, to use the modern term, feminist, since they were
organizing activities for the sole purpose of improving the lives of
women. Their work reported in the *Zhinocha dolia* served as an
incentive for the women activists in Saskatoon to hasten their own
work towards creating a national women's organization in Canada.

The new organization that the Mohylianky and Savella were
planning was to be unique in that it had to combine the ideals of
'Ukrainianness' within an 'English' Canadian setting. The idea of a
national women's organization was based on a model similar to the
one in Ukraine and also incorporated advice from the English
women's societies.[9] The span between the Ukrainian and Canadian

psyche and the respective conditions and modes of life was obviously vast. Since older women did not participate (most were illiterate), the planning and implementing of the aims and goals were left entirely to the young, determined trailblazers within the Mohyla Institute milieu.

With Julian as one of the organizers of the Ukrainian National Convention at Mohyla and a strong supporter of women's enlightenment, it was not difficult for Savella to persuade the exclusively male organizers to set aside a room and a specific time for women to meet for the sole purpose of proposing the formation of a women's organization.[10] Savella admits in her autobiography, "There was a kind of fear hanging over our heads that it may not be successful." However, the persistence of Savella and her friends came to fruition at a session for women at this convention.

The two-day convention convened on December 26, 1926 at Mohyla Institute in Saskatoon. Saskatoon was now a thriving city with a population of 31,234, and Ukrainians were a large part of this growth, so it was an ideal centre to host the convention. It also provided a good opportunity for women from the rural area to browse and shop in a larger centre. At the women's session, Savella was elected chairwoman of the session where approximately one hundred women, mostly from the prairies, were present. This first Ukrainian women's session at the convention was well planned with four "prominent women"[11] outlining the organization's program of activities as follows: Anna Stasiv: *The Need for a Women's Press*; Maria Maduke: *The Role of Women in World Progress*; Olha Swystun: *Women's Contribution and the Tasks Confronting Them*; and, Savella Stechishin: *The Women's Movement in Ukraine*.[12]

The first national Ukrainian-Canadian women's organization was established. The name *Soiuz Ukrainok Kanady*, translated into English as the Ukrainian Women's Association of Canada (UWAC), was unanimously adopted. This name reaffirmed the organization's unity with its counterparts in Western Ukraine and in the United States. In Western Ukraine, the women's organization was *Soiuz*

Ukrainok (the Union of Ukrainian Women) and in the United States it was *Soiuz Ukrainok Ameriky* (Ukrainian National Women's League of America). Savella presented an outline of the constitution for the UWAC which she had drafted beforehand with the help of her husband and Reverend Vasyl Kudryk.[13] Rev. Kudryk was a patriot, a prominent member of the intelligentsia and importantly a supporter of education for Ukrainian women in Canada.[14] The Ukrainian Orthodox clergy were nearly all members of the intelligentsia and supporters of the enlightenment of women and hence, of a national Ukrainian women's organization. The final version of the constitution was to be formulated by the newly elected executive and then presented at the next convention.

It was proposed that two independent sections of the national executive be formed: the Western (Saskatoon) responsible for the territory west of Manitoba, and the Eastern (Winnipeg) as head office responsible for Manitoba and Eastern Canada. Each section could carry out its mission more efficiently within a designated smaller area. The elected executive was:

> **Winnipeg**
> President: Olha Swystun
> Secretary: Hanka Romanchych
> Treasurer: Olha Sawchuk
> **Saskatoon**
> Vice-President: Savella Stechishin
> Vice-Secretary: Maria Maduke
> Vice-Treasurer: Daria Yanda
> Editorial Committee: Savella Stechishin, Leonida Slusar
> Auditing Board: Maria Eliuk, Anna Chepesiuk, Anna Bunka[15]

Not everyone was supportive of the women's organization at the convention. Savella wrote in the *Iuvileina knyha 25-littia Ukrainskoho instytutu im. Petra Mohyly v Saskatuni (*Jubilee Book of Twenty-five Years of the Petro Mohyla Institute of Saskatoon) that the chairman of the presidium at the convention announced the formation of a "women's section" in a mocking tone and it was viewed by some as a joke, as if these women were not to be taken seriously.[16] Even a few women at the convention were skeptical and had to be convinced that a women's organization was essential. It is most likely these doubting women were not delegates to the Women's Section of the convention and had only accompanied their husbands.

A strong link with Ukraine was evident by the inclusion in the program at the National Convention of a requiem service and the presentation of the life and work of Simon Petliura, who had been assassinated in Paris by a Bolshevik agent in May of 1926.[17] Simon Petliura had been the Supreme Commander of the Ukrainian Armed Forces and President of the Ukrainian National Republic in Exile. He was considered Ukraine's finest son, a great statesman and a champion of Ukraine's rights and liberties.

The Ukrainian-Canadian women made the first charitable donation as a national body for Petliura's widow, who was living in Paris. A total sum of $65.45 was collected and sent to her. Natalia Kohuska,[18] the editor and compiler of a number of books on the UWAC, wrote "It was presented not simply as financial assistance, but also as an expression of respect, love and sympathy for a woman who had been widowed in a foreign country after the tragic death of her husband."[19]

In her speech at the organizational session, Savella explained what was expected of the Ukrainian-Canadian women and what their role was to be:

> Our women's movement in Canada and in Ukraine should have one objective: to help Ukrainian women develop intellectually, to prepare them for civic, domestic and public life. The preparation of our women to be good mothers is a matter of far greater importance than politics, electoral rights or office-holding. Today, when our homeland, church and schools are in the hands of foreign conquerors, the women of Halychyna (Western Ukraine) and central Ukraine must pay particular attention to the upbringing of children. Only the home remains in our hands and the home must provide a national upbringing.[20]

She wanted to improve women's lot, but not in the 'equal rights' feminist sense of political and economic equality of the sexes, rather in improvement of a social and maternal nature. These sentiments were in line with that of the intelligentsia. The prevailing thought for the role of the Canadian woman was that they should be educated, modern homemakers and responsible for the upbringing of their children to be contributing Canadian citizens. However, Ukrainian-Canadian women's duty was threefold: first, to become educated and a modern homemakers; second, to ensure that their children be educated activists within the Ukrainian Canadian and host societies while projecting a good image; and third, to teach their children to be 'Ukrainian patriots.' Savella was a very serious, focussed and sincere young woman with strong leadership abilities. She admits, "It so happened that the women looked to me for leadership, partly because I lived in the Institute, the centre of Ukrainian life in Canada at that time, and my husband was the leader of this life; partly because I was more assertive . . ."[21]

Unwavering persistence by Savella and her colleagues resulted in bringing their dreams to fruition. At the convention they achieved their ultimate desire: the first non-denominational national Ukrainian women's organization in Canada open to all women of Ukrainian descent. However, the majority of the women who became members were actually of the Orthodox faith. Seven branches signed up, constituting the base: the Olha Kobylianska Women's Association, Saskatoon; the Olha Kobylianska Women's Association, Meacham; the Daughters of Ukraine Women's Association, Regina; the Lesia Ukrainka Women's Association, Goodeve; the Hanna Barvinok Women's Association, Vonda; and the Olha Kobylianska, Whitkow all in Saskatchewan; and the Lesia Ukrainka Women's Association, Capon, Alberta.[22]

Savella Stechishin, along with Leonida Slusar, was elected to initiate a women's page in the *Ukrainian Voice*. They were to provide appropriate material and to request other women to contribute to the page. Sympathetic to the women's movement, P. H. Woycenko, publisher of the *Ukrainian Voice*, offered one entire page, the *Zhinochyi kutok* (Women's Corner), to the newly established UWAC.[23] Since the weekly *Ukrainian Voice* was subscribed to by socially and economically enterprising Ukrainians across Canada, this publication could reach the majority of women, especially those in rural areas. The *Ukrainian Voice* attracted prairie farmers (many were leading activists in their communities) and the urban middle class (businessmen, lawyers, university students, school teachers and other professionals). Women of the urban middle class were regarded as the leaders in their communities and promoters of the women's movement.

A year later, the page became known as the *Viddil Soiuzu Ukrainok Kanady* (Section of the Ukrainian Women's Association of Canada) and was edited by Savella Stechishin. For reasons unknown, Leonida Sluzar did not contribute to the page. Other leading members such as Maria Maduke, Olha Swystun, Tetiana Kroitor, and Daria Yanda assisted by providing relevant and well-written articles. Topics included Ukrainian history, short biographies of Ukrainian authors, and household hints and 'awareness' articles of concern to women, for example, the *Idealnay Muzhyna* (The Ideal Man) written by Tetiana Kroitor.[24]

A strong representation of the branches from Saskatchewan was evident, most likely due to the influence of the administration and staff at Mohyla Institute and the rippling effect it had on the surrounding bloc settlements. Many of the former Institute residents returned to the bloc settlements as teachers or petty entrepreneurs and became leaders in their communities. Another factor was the siting of the convention at Saskatoon, resulting in cheaper transportation costs and distance for those from Saskatchewan than for those from other provinces. The central location of Saskatoon in relation to the three prairie provinces, where the Ukrainian population was most dense made it an ideal setting for Ukrainian national conventions.

Approximately sixty years after the first convention, Savella wrote in her autobiography:

> Its objectives were primarily: to encourage women to better themselves through reading and adult education so that they could take their rightful place as Canadian citizens; to promote a deeper understanding of the value of preserving Ukrainian cultural traditions and Ukrainian language in their families and in the Ukrainian community; to encourage young people to higher education; to support the efforts of Ukrainian people in their native land to attain freedom and independence; and to support worthy causes.

Ten years after the establishment of the UWAC, Savella in the *Iuvileina knyzhka* asserts that the most important aim is "the enlightenment of Ukrainian [Canadian] women and the Ukrainian education of children [in Canada]." In investigating the preliminary writings and discussions, research shows that the church did not play a major role in the mandate of the UWAC. Support for the church was encouraged with emphasis on teaching Sunday School, but it was only individual branches that took upon themselves the onerous task of financially contributing to, and affiliating closely with their church. At present, this is true of the majority of the branches, but they are truly independent of the church, as the early activists envisioned it.

At this first women's convention, Canada was looked upon as a free and democratic country from which Ukraine could be helped to ultimately gain its independence. Independence would give Ukrainians (in Ukraine) a place on the world stage as a secure and proud people, and this would also positively reflect on the Ukrainians in the diaspora. Having appealed to the Ukrainians living in Canada to help their countrymen, neither the leaders of the UWAC nor the intelligentsia made any suggestions that anyone should return to Ukraine to live, for any reason. Canada had truly become their country and the advantages of living in Canada with its institutions based on British laws and values were embraced and appreciated.

The National Executive began preparing its first concrete program of activities for the local branches to follow. To fulfill the UWAC objectives, emphasis was placed on the promotion of the following projects: Ukrainian schools, Sunday schools, libraries (members were encouraged to acquire Ukrainian books and to promote knowledge about Ukrainian literature by organizing special readings), and lectures on the education and health of children, as well as on domestic skills such as sewing and cooking.

Through the local branches and through the Association's organ, the *Ukrainian Voice*, the executive hoped to reach even into the most remote regions inhabited by Ukrainian families. Since Ukrainian women in the other provinces were fewer in number and not concentrated in blocs, the UWAC focused primarily on the prairie bloc settlements in the parklands of Alberta, Manitoba and Saskatchewan. However, their ardent hope was to educate Ukrainian women throughout Canada. The Association's motto was *Our Strength is in Education*.[25] Showing the importance of education to the Ukrainian-Canadian women in rural Western Canada, many of whom were poor and illiterate or semi-illiterate or indifferent to self-education or education of their children, was a complex task for the Association. Because prairie farm women, isolated on their homesteads, worked arduously from early morning to late at night, it was difficult for the executive to effectively reach women across the entire country. It was up to the comfortably established and ambitious women to lead their sisters in their communities.

In early 1927, the Association encouraged the branches to celebrate the fortieth anniversary of Olha Kobylianska's literary activity and to donate funds to her in Ukraine. Several branches marked the occasion and sent a modest amount of cash. This was the first formal celebration of a Ukrainian notable figure earmarked by the Association. A second plea for monies was to aid the victims of a major flood in Ukraine. Though a fund-raising campaign was initiated, donations for this campaign were also nominal. The building of new communities on the newly opened prairies, that is, churches and *narodni domy* (community halls called Ukrainian National Homes), occupied the community activists' energies and finances; the cost to educate their children also was a financial drain. Historian Orest Martynowych argues that "most Ukrainian farmers in Saskatchewan" were "fairly comfortable"[26], but, on the other hand, the author of the history of the Redfield-Richard branch of the UWAC writes that in 1929, "Money was scarce, but to the women, their obligations to the church came first."[27]   Land in the Saskatchewan bloc settlements was mostly more fertile than in Manitoba and Alberta and, therefore, the farmers were in comparison more prosperous. It is understandable that donations to Ukraine, a distant land, by the mostly cash strapped Ukrainian-Canadian women were modest.

At the 1927 Ukrainian National Convention, women were expected to participate within their own session. Culture and education were the main themes. About one hundred women delegates attended the second annual national UWAC convention, held in conjunction with the eleventh Ukrainian National Convention in Saskatoon. Leading speakers at the early conventions were young women in the twenties, most often married to activists in the intelligentsia circle. The number of branches represented dramatically increased, almost fourfold over the initiating year to 26 branches. Saskatchewan led the numbers with 22, Manitoba had 1, Alberta had 2 and there was 1 in Fort William, Ontario. The UWAC executive had been successful in spreading their message through *Ukrainian Voice*, word of mouth and through the female students who had attended Mohyla Institute and were now residing throughout Canada, particularly in the prairies and northwestern Ontario. Orthodox priests, many of whom were members of the intelligentsia and the enlightenment movement in Canada, also promoted the active participation and education of women and encouraged them to organize and/or join the UWAC.

Tetiana Kroitor, Savella's friend, married to a school teacher and a school teacher herself, was the keynote speaker at the 1927 convention. She spoke on "The Work of theWomen's Associations in Rural and Urban Districts." She, of course, was on the same wave length as Savella and she spoke of the necessity of women to unite and share their resources (books and experiences) to improve their lives, their children's lives and their community. The speech was an affirmation of what the young female activists were promoting. Other speakers were Anna Chepesiuk, Maria Maduke, Katherine Pukish, A. Pyliuk, Olha Swystun and Savella Stechishin.[28] Kohuska contends that "[w]ith respect to content, the outstanding speech, *Prohrama nasha na sliduchyi rik* (Our Programme for the Next Year), was delivered by Savella Stechishin." This speech became part of the Association's statement of purpose:

> All of our people's efforts are directed toward national liberation; they are directed toward transforming our people into free and able masters in their own home and worthy human beings in general. In Canada our work should be concerned with making the masses conscious of who they are and where they come from, as well as with familiarizing them with our tasks and obligations in this country. Our work should focus on this objective. As women we must assume our share of the burden. It follows that our first task will be to awaken national consciousness among women in general. Nationally conscious women will establish relations with the old country, and this contact may have a beneficial influence on both groups. We in Canada stand to benefit from suggestions and encouragement received from the old country; while women in the old country will receive material assistance and benefit from the experience we have gained by living in different circumstances, in foreign countries with people of various origins . . .
>
> We are contained within a foreign culture and we are unconsciously abandoning our way of life. This is especially true of our young people for whom Ukraine exists only in the realm of imagination. They were born here, and if their parents fail to pay special attention at the appropriate time, they will

certainly never be as proud of their origins as are the Scots and
the Irish. . .[29]

Savella urged that in order to take their rightful place in Canada
women must inspire pride of their heritage in their fellow Ukrainian
Canadians at the community level – that is their primary obligation
and task. Both those living in Canada and in Ukraine will benefit if
the lines of communication are kept open between the two countries.
The parameters she places for the role of women are confined to the
retention and promotion of Ukrainian culture. She, together with the
intelligentsia, felt that it was inevitable that Ukrainian Canadians
would automatically embrace Canadian norms and would value
Canadian institutions because of the constant exposure in schools,
businesses and everyday life.

Mohyla Institute was the core of operations of the Western
section of the UWAC. Since Julian was the rector of the Institute and
the Stechishins lived there, it was convenient to use its office
equipment for all written material. Even male students helped in
typing and mimeographing articles.[30] This was an enormous
financial help to the Association. Julian also helped in the
encouragement of the organization of women in the outlying areas,
mostly in Saskatchewan. He arranged for Savella to address women
at the meetings, which he organized for the purpose of soliciting
donations for the operation of Mohyla Institute.[31] At the meetings,
she explained to the women the aims and goals of the UWAC and the
method of organizing; this approach proved to be successful in terms
of the number of women she recruited and branches she initiated.[32]
As a result of this activity, the Western section was more successful
in its work than the Winnipeg one. With the substantial increase in
the number of branches in Saskatchewan in the first year, as
previously noted, it is apparent that the UWAC was Saskatchewan
driven.

The division of the executive proved impractical with such a
distance between the two cities, Saskatoon and Winnipeg. It was

decided at the 1927 convention that the National Executive be moved to Saskatoon. Mohyla Institute and its staff could then give assistance. The new national executive for 1928 was comprised of:

> President: Savella Stechishin (Saskatoon)
> Vice-President: Olha Swystun (Winnipeg)
> Corresponding/Recording Secretary: Maria Maduke (Saskatoon)
> Financial Secretary: Anastasia Stechishin (Yorkton)
> Treasurer: Rose Dragon (Saskatoon)
> Editorial Committee: Tetiana Kroitor (Saskatoon) and Olha Swystun
> Auditing Board: Olha Sawchuk (Winnipeg), A. Michasiw (Saskatoon) and Katherine Pukish (Regina)

Seeking camaraderie in a familiar social milieu, the mostly prominent and upwardly mobile Ukrainians in Canada, both female and male, eagerly attended the annual Ukrainian conventions held at Mohyla Institute. It was most often the active community participants with enquiring minds who could be found at the conventions. Because most Ukrainians were divided along religious lines, it was the Orthodox Ukrainians who congregated at these conventions. Here, they shared their thoughts and opinions, established friendships and discussed issues relating to the community. Officially, there were lectures and reports discussing the political circumstances of the Ukrainian people in their homeland, what political stance the Ukrainians in Canada should adopt (i.e. primarily anti-Communist) regarding Ukraine and Canada, and the economic and civic issues in Canada. The intelligentsia, exclusively male, provided the guidelines for the Ukrainian flock to follow. Ukrainians adhering to the Greek Catholic church held their own conventions.

At the 1927 convention, the UWAC, although still open to all women of Ukrainian descent regardless of religious or political biases, affiliated itself with the Ukrainian Self-Reliance League of Canada (USRL) (*Soiuz Ukraintsiv Samostiinykiv u Kanadi*)[33], "the avant-garde among Ukrainian organizations."[34] The USRL was formally organized in Saskatoon in 1927, though a self-reliance movement had originated in 1910 with the first Ukrainian teachers' organization and the *Ukrainian Voice*, encompassing the largest and most influential faction of the intelligentsia.[35] The UWAC was totally independent of the USRL, although they held their conventions together for convenience since many husbands of the UWAC members were involved with the USRL, which was exclusively male-driven. The Ukrainian Self-Reliance Association, the men's club parallel to the UWAC, was not formally organized until December 28, 1938.[36]   By the late 1930s, the USRL included all the lay organizations of the Orthodox Church, i.e., the men, women and youth groups.[37]

First and foremost the USRL's mandate was the preservation of the Ukrainian culture and second, to become good Canadian citizens adopting Canadian societal values. **Self-reliance** was their credo. Members of the self-reliance movement became influential members on the national scene – part of the blossoming Ukrainian intelligentsia in Canada.

Other Ukrainian-Canadian women began organizing their own clubs. In 1934 female members of the Ukrainian National Federation (UNF) (*Ukrainske natsionalne obiednannia*) organized themselves in Saskatoon under the name Ukrainian Women's Organization of Canada   (*Orhanizatsiia ukrainok Kanady*) with Anastasia (Greschuk) Pavlychenko, a former member of the Olha Kobylianska Association, as president. The UNF was formed in 1932 by Ukrainian immigrants who had arrived in Canada after the First World War, many of whom were veterans of the Ukrainian armies for the independence of Ukraine from 1917 to 1921. They were nationally conscious in a political sense and found the existing Ukrainian organizations in Canada too Canadianized. The Ukrainian Catholic Women's League of Canada (*Liga ukrainskykh katolytskykh zhinok Kanady*) was established in Winnipeg in 1944 uniting various regional and local women's organizations connected with their church.

An Editorial Committee of the UWAC was responsible for the publishing of timely and informative articles in the Women's Page of the *Ukrainian Voice*. Of the two women elected, only Tetiana Kroitor contributed articles and oversaw the page. Savella's opinion was: "Tetiana Kroitor had inborn talent for writing . . . wrote good articles." Savella, as national president, believed it her responsibility to see that the page was respectable with appropriate material. She enjoyed writing and occasionally contributed articles, recipes, household hints and so on as official organization directives for the branches. Receiving two women's publications from Ukraine, *Zhinocha dolia* and *Nova khata,* helped the newly organized UWAC by carrying articles that UWAC reprinted in the page. Savella, in order to enrich her own Ukrainian language with proper vocabulary and proper expressions, studied these publications carefully. "I listed new words or whole expressions for myself – a kind of dictionary. I also needed expressions for my speeches for in those days I had to address gatherings of women or students."[38] She could refer to her "dictionary" when necessary. There were no Ukrainian-English dictionaries available, or printed for that matter. Since Savella was often in the limelight, giving speeches to students and women's groups in the province, she felt it necessary to master proper usage of the Ukrainian language.

The UWAC took up a lot of Savella's time. Monthly circular directives had to be written and sent to the branches, the majority of which were researched and written by Savella. Besides the work with the UWAC, Savella was taking a full set of courses at university, caring for Tolio and teaching Ukrainian Literature I, at the Institute five days a week. She managed to do all this and pass all her university exams.

The years 1928 to 1930 were critical formative years for the UWAC. While the Mohylianky were composed of young women pursuing their education, the UWAC now attracted older pioneer women along with middle-aged women in the urban and rural areas. Preservation and development of the Ukrainian language, tradition and culture together with respect and retention of religious practices appealed to the older pioneer women. As for the younger women, Ukrainian literature and the arts, i.e., music and theatre, piqued their interest. The executive made a concerted effort to accommodate women of all ages in their efforts towards unity. Literature and notable Ukrainian authors became an effective vehicle for expanding cultural-educational work within the community. The branches were encouraged to hold concerts where children could perform the works of authors such as Taras Shevchenko, Ivan Franko, Lesia Ukrainka, and Olha Kobylianska (see Appendix A) and to mark historical events like Ukrainian Independence Day (January 22, 1918). In this way, the children as well as adults would become acquainted with important authors and the history of Ukraine.

Often a lecture on the life and creative activity of an author was presented at monthly meetings of the branches. For example, according to the *Persha Recordova Knyzhka, 1927-28*, (The First Record Book, 1927-28) of the Daughters of Ukraine Branch, Regina, it was agreed at the first executive meeting to have weekly *shittia vecherok* (embroidery evenings).[39] During the embroidery evenings, one member would read aloud Ukrainian literary works (by Lesia Ukrainka, Natalia Kobrynska, Olha Basarab or Olha Kobylianska or Taras Shevchenko) while the other women embroidered and/or taught various Ukrainian stitches or patterns.

By 1930, the National Executive had incorporated into its cultural-educational programme for the branches to follow an activity commemorating national anniversaries for almost each month of the school year. They were as follows: January 22 - Ukrainian National Independence Day; February - anniversary of Lesia Ukrainka's birth; March - anniversary of Taras Shevchenko's birth; May - Mother's Day/Ivan Franko's death; October - *Sviato Knyzhky* (Book Month) and Thanksgiving Day; November - Olha Kobylianska's birth.[40] As these observances were celebrated by an ever widening circle of women, children, and spouses, uninformed women were drawn to the specific epochs in Ukraine's history and were encouraged to read books, journals and newspapers in the Ukrainian language as prescribed by the UWAC Executive.

One of the most important celebrations was Mother's Day. The UWAC, on Savella's initiative, was the first Ukrainian women's organization in the world to honour mother on an annual basis. Prior to the early waves of emigration to Canada, Ukrainians did not have the tradition of observing mothers on a special day. The Ukrainians in Western Ukraine (Galicia) were introduced to the new holiday by an announcement in the newspaper *Dilo*, on May 5, 1929, a year later than in Canada.[41] Initiated in the United States, celebration of Mother's Day began both in United States and Canada in 1914.

In a letter to the branches on May 4, 1928, Savella wrote that all cultures will be celebrating Mother's Day on the 13th of May. She explained how Canadian schools have celebrated Mother's Day, and suggested ways fathers and children could honour the mother. She also suggested that each branch celebrate Mother's Day each May, that they ask their parish priest to honour mothers in a church service and after celebrating this important day that they write to the *Ukrainian Voice* as to how they celebrated Mother's Day.[42] Writing another letter on May 6, she appealed to Orthodox priests across Canada to have a service honouring mothers: "This holiday is international and all cultures observe it. The purpose for this holiday is so that every person can undertake to show appreciation to their mothers. . . To emphasize this holiday more and in a more positive light, it would be good to discuss this subject in the churches. This is why we are discussing this with you, Father, and we believe you will do everything you can to make it into an important celebration."[43]   After taking the initiative and boldness to write letters promoting Mother's Day to the branches and priests, on May 14, 1928, Savella wrote to the leading women in the UWAC extolling the virtues of celebrating Mother's Day, "The celebration of Mother's Day should be one of the most important events. The UWAC should teach women to be good mothers."[44] She then dedicated the UWAC page to articles on Mother's Day writing an article on the history of

Mother's Day, publishing an article written by Taras Shevchenko in the 1800s and poems dedicated to mothers by various authors.[45]

Aggressively promoting Mother's Day would bring Ukrainians closer to Anglo-Canadian social values. But of equal importance, the Day would be celebrated in the Ukrainian language in a Ukrainian-Canadian setting. A concert arranged within a Ukrainian context (songs, poems, etc. by Ukrainian authors in the Ukrainian language) was an ideal way of celebration. The children would be proud of their heritage within the Canadian environment – acculturation but not assimilation. Ukrainian Canadians would be like other Canadians yet not lose their own identity. Mother's Day was to be a character-builder for both the mother and her children

The executive of the UWAC shouldered the difficult task of disseminating cultural and educational information to a far-flung, isolated and unsophisticated audience. They had high expectations for each member to preserve and promote Ukrainian culture, religion, language, tradition and maintain the Ukrainian spirit within the family home. The dearth of funds in the Ukrainian community prevented the executive from totally fulfilling its mandate so that the work proceeded more slowly than hoped.[46] It was believed that direct personal visits by the executive would be most effective in uniting the women, and so Savella, as President, visited the branches in Saskatchewan "many times" as well as in Ontario and Manitoba.[47]

The UWAC was not philanthropic nor was its direction focussed primarily on economic or emotional aspects of the lives of Ukrainian-Canadian women. Forced early marriages of girls, domestic violence, alcoholism and birth control were of great concern to Anglo-Canadian organizations, but were taboo subjects to Ukrainians in Canada. The Ukrainian cultural moral norms of the day did not allow discussion of these topics. However, at the convention held on December 28-30, 1927, Savella, outlining directives to the women's assembly for the branches of the UWAC to follow, touched upon some of these issues.[48] One of the subjects dealt with forming of a benevolent society to help the Ukrainian poor and orphans, as it appeared that other nationalities were looking after this problem, whereas Ukrainians were not. Another topic she spoke of was the harmfulness of alcoholism. She encouraged women not to have any alcohol at home, to demand that their husbands not drink and to be a good role model by not drinking themselves. She spoke of the working mothers in cities who needed assistance with day care and she felt that day cares should be established by Ukrainians for Ukrainians rather than by the host society. On reflection seventy years later, Savella recalled that the attitude of Ukrainians was to ignore the subjects of birth control, abuse and alcoholism – it just was not talked about.[49]

Savella urged equality for the woman in her role as a community member, but within social maternal parameters. She felt that the woman had no place in the political arena; her sphere was circumscribed by educational and maternal concerns. Neither Savella nor the other women leaders were politically active; they were satisfied to concern themselves with women's issues. Men were expected to lead the Ukrainians in their immediate community as well as nationally by way of effectively organizing them, giving sound advice, setting a good example and support and encourage them to improve their social and economic standards – all this and also promote and preserve their Ukrainian heritage. Women's interests were restricted to the following: having knowledge of Ukrainian culture and history so as to educate their children in all things Ukrainian; keeping 'Ukrainian homes' via the observance of Ukrainian holidays and display of Ukrainian symbols, i.e., Ukrainian embroidery and artifacts; actively participating within their ethnic community to perpetuate a Ukrainian environment for their children; contributing to the mainstream community; encouraging their children to achieve higher learning; being educated themselves and very importantly, presenting a respectable image to the host society, thereby gaining acceptance as a legitimate and deserving citizens of Canada. Savella believed that the aforementioned roles would achieve self-fulfilment for women.

4

Building Bridges

Over the years Savella kept all of her letters, articles, books and pamphlets neatly filed in the library/office of her home on Albert Avenue. In her late 80s, she decided the time had come to give her collection a new home and requested the National Archives in Ottawa to house them permanently. The archives accepted and made available her materials for research, with her permission when she was alive and after her death with the permission of her family. All letters discussed in this book are filed in the National Archives.

Ukrainian handicraft, especially embroidery, was fascinating to Savella. The two women's magazines *Zhinocha dolia* (Women's Destiny) and *Nova khata* (The New Home) were invaluable for their information and description of Ukrainian handicraft and culture.[1] She was so impressed with these two women's publication that in 1925 she began correspond with the editors, especially *Zhinocha dolia's* Olena Kysilewska. Savella realized Olena wanted to promote her publication and Canada was a country with many Ukrainians and, therefore, a good market for selling subscriptions to the women who were keenly interested in these handicrafts and could afford the subscriptions. This smart business woman wrote to Savella frequently and Savella sold many subscriptions to the magazine. Because she sold so many subscriptions, Savella's name and address appeared on the last page as the monthly magazine's representative in Canada, remaining there from the late 1920s until after World War II. Also, many UWAC branches subscribed to the magazines which were lent to members.

In a letter dated January 1, 1926, Olena Kysilevska thanked Savella for successfully encouraging Ukrainian women in Canada to subscribe to her magazine.[2] By doing so, the Ukrainian Canadian women were not only helping the magazine, but also women in Ukraine materially and morally. She also requested that Savella write about the Canadian way of life, since women in Ukraine were keen to learn about life in the diaspora.

In the spring of 1927, with the resignation of the rector Philip Halytsky, the board of directors of M. Hrushewsky Ukrainian Institute in Edmonton were looking to fill the vacancy. They were aware of Julian's success at Mohyla Institute and decided to ask him to take over so that Hrushewsky could be operated under a similar system as Mohyla. Julian agreed and went to Edmonton in April 1927, leaving Vasyl Gauk in charge of Mohyla Institute. Savella and Tolio remained in Saskatoon only long enough for her to write her final university exams, after which she and Tolio joined Julian in Edmonton.

At this time, the popular Ukrainian folk dance choreographer, Vasyl Avramenko, and his assistant, Victor Moshuk, came to Edmonton and organized a Ukrainian dance group. Yuriy Hasan, a choir director and a recent immigrant from Ukraine, came as well and organized a mixed choir. Savella spent a busy spring and summer in Edmonton singing in the choir and, always one to immerse herself in as much Ukrainian culture as possible, took dance lessons with the Avramenko School of Ukrainian Dance. Vasyl Avramenko was a celebrated dance instructor who had recently immigrated to Canada and opened Ukrainian dance schools across the prairies to teach Ukrainian folk dancing. He was so particular that he demanded costumes be authentic to each region of Ukraine for specific dances. Until his arrival, a hodgepodge of styles dominated, and many Ukrainian costumes were more a mixture of Ukrainian, Polish, Canadian and whatever styles were familiar in the local communities. Under Avramenko's influence, Savella learned the various styles of costumes relative to different regions. This was an additional stimulus for her to develop a keen interest in Ukrainian embroidery and the authenticity of Ukrainian folk costumes.

A trip to Banff, Alberta that summer with some friends and Bishop Ioan Theodorowich of the Ukrainian Orthodox Church of the United States reinforced for Savella that she belonged on the prairie. Although she was greatly impressed with the majestic sight of the mountains, she felt claustrophobic, being hemmed in by their size. She was truly a prairie woman. Bishop Theodorowich was temporarily ministering to the Orthodox flock in Canada, since the Canadians did not have a bishop of their own and, therefore, he made periodic trips to Canada for certain church occasions.

Julian, Savella and Tolia in the fall of 1927 returned to Saskatoon where she resumed her studies. The Stechishins did not want to make Edmonton their permanent home and the board of directors of Hrushewsky were able to find a permanent rector to take over from Julian now that he had implemented a good operating program. Savella continued to lead a very busy schedule: university student, national UWAC president, head of Mohylianky, teacher of Ukrainian literature twice a week at Mohyla, church choir member and community worker.

Continuing their correspondence, Kysilewska in 1927 asked Savella to write an article of interest to women such as the social activities of Ukrainian-Canadian women and on household topics in their annual *Kaliandar-almanakh* (calendar almanac). Savella was thrilled that Kysilewska considered her writing good enough to be published in a Ukrainian women's magazine. Years later Savella remembers: "I was truly elated that O. Kysilewska considered me good enough to write an article to such a prestigious publication."[3] Kysilewska was aware of Savella's writing ability through the articles she wrote for the *Ukrainian Voice*. The *Ukrainian Voice* was routinely sent to publishing houses in Ukraine. For the almanac, Savella wrote about the pioneering work at Mohyla Institute and about the young women's group, Mohylianky. A group photograph of Mohylianky was also included. Savella was published in

Kaliandar-almanakh again in 1928 and1929. A photo of her was even included with her article in 1930.

On numerous occasions Kysilevska also requested Savella to ask the Mohylianky and the youth in Canada to write to her so that she could publish their letters in *Zhinocha dolia.* It was hoped that a pen pal relationship could be established between the youth of Ukraine and of Canada.

It is obvious in perusing the collection of letters from Kysilevska to Savella that Savella was heeding the wishes of Kysilevska to increase the circulation of *Zhinocha dolia* in order to make the magazine profitable.[4] Kysilevska wrote early in their exchange: "You give our publication a lot of help."[5] This collection of personal correspondence is made up almost exclusively of letters from Ukraine to Savella; correspondence by Savella is not available.[6] Unfortunately, it was not until May 16, 1928 that Savella's correspondence to Kysilevska appears in the collection.

In this personal correspondence, Savella had been forwarding the monies for subscriptions and in some cases, the Canadian women themselves had sent a prepayment for the subscription (Kysilevska preferred prepayment).[7] Also, Kysilevska sent Savella cookbooks and almanacs to be sold in Canada. The proceeds from the sale of the books was added profit for *Zhinocha dolia* and helped Kysilevska in her work assisting women in villages. In a letter dated April 15, 1926, Kysilevska requested that various cookbooks be sold for $0.25 and $0.75 each and the enclosed articles about embroidery cost $3.00 each.[8] In September 9, 1926, she complied with a request from Savella: "Yes, a primary textbook will be sent to you".[9] Kysilevska also revealed the prevailing atmosphere in Ukraine,

> The women's organization in Ukraine has no direction, is not on the patriotic path. You help us more with the subscriptions than our own Ukrainian people. Thanks for the *Ukrainskyi holos*, we enjoy your column and kind words. We will listen to your direction.

Whether Kysilevska, an educated and dynamic woman, actually 'listened' to Savella's direction or was merely saying this for the purpose of encouraging Savella to sell more subscriptions, books and embroidered pieces for her is unknown. She does appear to be open to suggestions because she asked Savella: "How do the women like our little journal? Do you have any ideas for improvement?"[10]

Historian Martha Bohachevsky-Chomiak in her book *Feminists Despite Themselves: Women in Ukrainian Community Life, 1884-1929,* writes of Olena Kysilevska as an important feminist in the development of a higher standard of living for Ukrainian peasant women. Kysilevska was instrumental in organizing women co-operatives, where women could sell the products of their cottage industry (i.e., handicrafts, eggs, and butter). Through her magazine she provided village women with information to improve housekeeping, nutrition and to take an effective public role.[11] Olena Kysilevska became politically active and was first elected to the Polish senate in 1928 (Western Ukraine was a part of Poland at this time). In her book, Bohachevsky-Chomiak does not make any reference to the immeasurable help Kysilevska received from Savella Stechishin or Ukrainian-Canadian women.[12] Apparently unaware of the help by Canadian women, she does not acknowledge their financial contribution through subscriptions and purchase of embroideries or moral support by writing columns in their magazines and/or writing personal letters. Bohachevsky-Chomiak explains that Kysilevska introduced "home economics" to the village women in the late 1920s. This period coincides with the exchange of letters with Savella. In December 1927, Kysilevska wrote, "I would be pleased to hear further about household science. We don't have classes like that in Ukraine."[13] Presumably, Savella had written to Kysilevska about the household science classes she studied in school and that these were helpful to women in Canada and would be useful in Ukraine. A few months later, Kysilevska again reaffirmed the lack of these types of classes in Ukraine: "No one teaches our children here in Ukraine about home economics, household management, marriage relationships. There is nothing like this in our schools and universities. Again, please write about these issues and we will publish them in our almanac."[14] By December 1928, Kysilevska had become almost desperate,

> I have not heard from you. Could you please write 2 or 4 columns and put them in an envelope? I would like to publish your articles. Please write. We desperately need information about women in Canada and America. Please don't forget us. Is the *Zhinocha dolia* not helpful to your women's movement in Canada? Write about the popular home economics or about anything. You promised this.[15]

Savella greatly aided the women in Ukraine by selling their embroidered articles in Canada. In early 1927, Kysilevska suggested that "Together with *Nova khata*, we can export all kinds of embroideries: blouses, tablecloths, runners, different kinds of embroideries which are characteristic of Ukrainian designs."[16] On April 1, 1927, Kysilevska sent Savella some embroidered aprons with the hope that the Mohylianky would buy them. The cost for white aprons was $2.25 and $3.00 with gold thread. She further asked whether other women would buy these articles and whether Savella could inquire from the Canadian women what they specifically want:

> We could send you runners, aprons, curtains, for *rushnyky* icons, many patterns - Hutsul [a region in Ukraine]. Factories make some embroideries but we want to help the women who embroider handicraft. Also, blouses, men and women's shirts, pillowcases. If you like them, we can have various patterns of stitches made. We will have women embroider these specifically. Material here is not good for embroidery. It must be ordered from Czechoslovakia or Yugoslavia. The cost is expensive at $3.50. Let us know the patterns and colours you would like. I cannot send the book of patterns but we would like to send the embroidery. Sending parcels is expensive so can you advise us precisely what can be sold in Canada? We can embroider men's ties but what for women? We are pleased that there are so many young people active in Canada. This is truly

a good thing. Canada is much further ahead than America.[17]

As few Mohylianky could afford to buy these articles, Savella sold primarily to the Anglo-Canadian community and in one year was able to sell three hundred dollars' worth.[18] Violet McNaughton, who encouraged the sale of such items through the Saskatoon Arts and Crafts Council, was one of the 'English' women who bought a number of items.[19] Patriotic women, although not well off, saved enough money over time to buy these items in order to help their sisters in Ukraine. Another reason to buy the articles was that they admired the artistry and wanted these luxury items to beautify their homes.

An example of the financial assistance Savella was providing is in the December 1927 letter in which Kysilevska enclosed an invoice in the amount of $48.66 Canadian for the embroidered articles. In part, it was as follows: napkins with tablecloth (cross-stitched) - $10.92, napkins with tablecloth (*nyzynka* stitch, expensive fabric) - $13.32; cross-stitched man's shirt - $4.03; man's tie - $1.04.[20] After the sale of these items, Savella would send the proceeds to Kysilevska who had had established a women's co-operative in her district.

Ideas were exchanged. Savella suggested ideas and helped Kysilevska, and Kysilevska advised Savella. Kysilevska expresses her belief that "The material help is appreciated, but more important is the unity of all our women. We must encourage the union of all Ukrainian women regardless of their background."[21] Savella endorsed this sentiment in her newspaper articles as well as advocating this theme of unity in her vision of a national women's organization in Canada. Also, Savella in May 1928, confirmed Kysilevska's influence: "We are grateful to *Zhinocha dolia,* which has given us the inspiration to organize our women.[22] The 1928 Calendar-Almanac of the *Zhinocha dolia* carried an article with an accompanying photograph of the first organization of Ukrainian women in Canada at the Ukrainian National Convention in Saskatoon in 1926. In doing this, the publishers recognized that the new organization was important enough to inform the public in Ukraine of the advancements made by Ukrainians in Canada. Knowledge that Ukrainian women in a distant country cared deeply about and actively pursued Ukrainian interests, the publishers hoped, would give the women in Ukraine additional motivation to become more participatory in their communities.

By 1929 the letters grew few in number. This lack of correspondence was because of Savella's commitments to her university studies, her volunteer work with the UWAC and involvement with the Ukrainian community in Saskatoon. At this time Savella was studying for her Bachelor of Arts degree, bringing up her son, teaching Ukrainian literature at Mohyla Institute, singing in the church choir and serving as national president of the Ukrainian Women's Association. As president she was responsible for writing articles for and editing of the UWAC page of the *Ukrainian Voice* and preparing speeches when invited to speak throughout Saskatchewan. She also had a major role in preparing directives for the UWAC branches to follow: a program of the branch meetings had to have a lecture, a talk or reading about some Ukrainian historical event or a Ukrainian poet or some outstanding Ukrainian personality and each member was encouraged to subscribe to Ukrainian newspapers and buy selected books and read as much as possible.

Another reason for the limited correspondence was Kysilevska's illness and the death of her husband, as well as the unsettled political situation. At the beginning of the Polish "pacification" campaign against Ukrainians in early 1929, Olha Basarab, a well-known Ukrainian woman activist, was killed by the Poles (see Appendix A for more information on Basarab). Kysilevska wrote pessimistically: "Basarab is killed. I don't know what will happen next. Not many from overseas are buying our almanac. If our own don't buy it, it will be a catastrophe. We are putting our fate in your hands."[23] In desperation Kysilevska placed a heavy burden on the shoulders of 26-year-old Savella with her appeal for financial and spiritual help. By the middle of the 1930s, communication ceased as a result of the intensifying suppression of Ukrainian political and cultural activities by the Polish government and subsequent Soviet occupation.

After Kysilevska's visit to Canada and America at the end of 1929, no correspondence has been filed in the National Archives collection. However, Savella did write about the women's movement in Canada in the Calendar-Almanac of the *Zhinocha dolia* in1930. In the article, she illuminated the beginnings and direction of the Ukrainian Women's Association, the role Mohylianky played in the organizing of the Association and wrote of her proposed *"Plan roboty dlya viddiliv, Soiuzu Ukrainy Kanady"* (Plan of Activities for Branches, Ukrainian Women's Association of Canada).[24]

In late spring of 1928 Julian and Savella left Canada to visit Europe and Western Ukraine. Tolio was left with Julian's brother Michael, his wife Nastunia, and their four children in Yorkton. Savella felt that Nastunia was a maternal woman, kind and considerate that she would be the best person to look after Tolio. A group of Ukrainians from Alberta was also taking the trip to Ukraine. Among them was the owner of the Ukrainian Bookstore in Edmonton, Dmytro Ferbey, and others who were mostly prosperous Ukrainian immigrant farmers anxious to visit their homeland and see family. For the Stechishins, this was a business trip, but they also took the opportunity to visit their families. Julian had a number of business quests: to buy books and archival material for Mohyla Institute, to seek out theology students (Greek Catholic) who opposed celibacy and wanted to come to Canada to be ordained as Orthodox married priests, and to get acquainted with Ukrainian activists who were aggressively promoting nationalism. Savella took the opportunity to make contact with the leading Ukrainian women activists.

The group boarded the train in Saskatoon, stopped in Winnipeg to visit, then went on to Ottawa, where they met with MP Michael Luchkovich, the first Ukrainian member of parliament in

Canada (elected in 1926, United Farmers of Alberta). He showed them the House of Commons, the Senate and other places of interest. From Ottawa they headed to Montreal where they boarded the Empress of Scotland, which after ten days took them past the White Cliffs of Dover and on to France.

Because Julian corresponded with Ukrainian activists in Ukraine and in the diaspora, they met with many leading members of the Ukrainian society. In Paris they brought greetings to Olha, the widow of Simon Petliura, and met with political refugees and members of the government-in-exile of the Ukrainian National Republic. Savella found Olha Petliura and her daughter living in poverty and both appeared to be frail and suffering poor health. They also visited Petliura's grave in Paris. The Ukrainian emigre population in Paris was small at this time, so they did not spend much time there. Nevertheless, with the help of Mr. Honchar, a Ukrainian emigre as their guide, they did have the opportunity to visit famous places, such as Lourdes, the Eiffel Tower and the theatre.

The group travelled through Switzerland and on to Austria where Ukrainian organizations were flourishing and Ukrainian language newspapers were being published. The government-in-exile of the Western Ukrainian National Republic (WUNR) (1918-1919) was headquartered in Vienna, which was considered the centre of activities for fostering an independent Ukraine. The Ukrainian language newspapers Mohyla received and were read by the students were published here: *Prapor, Postup, Khliborobska Ukraina* and others. They tried to make contact with the WUNR's ex-president E. Petrushevych, but he was away for the summer. Instead, they looked up a younger brother of a Saskatoon friend, Dmytro Yanda who was attending Vienna University, and he acted as a guide, showing them the sights of Vienna.

After Vienna, Julian and Savella visited Prague, Czechoslovakia where a vibrant Ukrainian emigre colony of writers, poets, scholars, students, artists, and ex-politicians thrived. The Ukrainian Diplomatic Mission of the Ukrainian National Republic had been located in Prague during the brief existence of the Republic (1918-1920). Many Ukrainian students studied Ukrainian language and literature at the Prague University. In Vienna, Savella met Zinaida Mirna, the outstanding Ukrainian woman activist/feminist with whom she had exchanged letters. Mirna was active in the government of the Ukrainian National Republic in Kyiv and on the executive of the Ukrainian National Women's Council, which had been organized in Kyiv during the brief period of Ukrainian independence. Through Mirna, Savella met other outstanding Ukrainian women activists. Savella made arrangements with Mirna to sell in Canada some of the Ukrainian embroidered articles made by Ukrainian women students in Prague who were in need of financial help. Mirna offered to contribute written articles to the UWAC Women's Page in the *Ukrainian Voice* for whatever price the UWAC thought fair. Savella was pleased to meet these outstanding activists and be considered their equal.

After visiting Prague, the Stechishins were anxious to tour another city, Podebrady. When the Bolsheviks took power in Ukraine and the Ukrainian National Republic fell, many people associated with the Ukrainian national cause fled to Czechoslovakia where they were well received. To accommodate the Ukrainian emigres, Czechoslovakia financed an academy for Ukrainian students. Savella was eager to see her old friend Kharytia Konenenko, who had recently graduated with a doctoral degree in Ukrainian law and living in Podebrady. She lived here next to her aunt and uncle, who was teaching at the academy. They visited with her and saw that she was in good health but with little money. Kharytia arranged a gathering where the Stechishins met the students. News of a young Ukrainian couple from Canada spread quickly and many students came out to see them. As Kharytia took them on a tour of the university, Savella noticed that the students were not young, as in Canada, but mostly mature men who were endeavouring to finish their university degrees and other training that had been disrupted by war. It appeared that only men were students as there were no women to be seen.

The next stop in the European tour for the Stechishins was the city of Krakow in Poland and then on to Peremyshl for a short visit. Peremyshl had in the past been under Ukrainian rule, but later passed on to Poland and was in Polish hands at the time of the visit. There were many Ukrainian institutions and the majority of the population was Ukrainian. One especially interesting institution was the Ukrainian Girls' Institute where some time was spent touring the building and discussing the courses of study. It was a residential school with studies in humanities and along with it was a seminary. The school also offered courses in sewing and homemaking for girls in the surrounding countryside. Julian conducted business in this city and they met many prominent people.

L'viv was the next city on their itinerary. They stayed at the hotel *Narodna Hostynnytsid* with rooms furnished in the Hutsul style. The beautifully carved table and chairs and the *kylymy* (type of rug) on the wall and floor fascinated Savella as being unusual and beautiful. To their surprise, the Stechishins found that breakfast was not served in restaurants as everyone ate breakfast at home. Savella had to contend with a cup of coffee and a bun every morning during their stay in Ukraine. They also found to their disappointment that many people had left their city homes and retreated to the Carpathian mountain resorts for the summer. Their first visit in L'viv was to editors of the two important publications: daily *Dilo* and the monthly magazine *Literaturno Naukovyi Visnyk*. Julian was able to acquire books and other material for Mohyla Institute. They also met a few Ukrainian parliamentarians and political activists.

Savella was eager to meet the women with whom she had been corresponding over the years. She visited the offices of *Nova khata* in L'viv and members of its publishing company, the *Ukrainske Narodne Mystetstvo* (Ukrainian Folk Arts Council), and a women's co-operative. The manager, Iryna Pavlykovska, offered her a gift that she was to choose herself. Savella selected a small teacloth with tiny napkins. The napkins, to her surprise, were designed to serve as placemats for tea glasses; tea was served in glasses held in silver metal holders.

A reporter of *Nova khata*, Olena Zalizniak, interviewed Savella in her hotel room and this interview was published the following October.[25] Olena Zalizniak was also a director of a women's cooperative, *Trud* (Toil), which was similar to a technical school, as it offered courses in dressmaking, tailoring and embroidering. Savella visited it with the intention of obtaining information and writing about it when she returned to Canada. The school had been started in 1914 and it appeared to be offering good service by employing women.

Having heard and read so much about the women's organization, *Soiuz ukrainok*, Savella was anxious to meet its executive and arrangements were made for her to do so. Maria Dontsov and Olena Sheparowych, two executive members, were available and Savella spoke with them. Milena Rydnytska, the president, was away on vacation at a resort in the Carpathian Mountains. The members of *Soiuz ukrainok* requested she address their organization to describe life in Canada. An announcement of the upcoming address was published in the daily paper, *Dilo*.[26]

The time came to visit Julian's family and so they travelled to Terebovla, a small historical city with castle and monastery ruins. There Julian, with some difficulty, found a man who owned a car to drive them to the village of his family, Hleshchava. For a princely sum of $20.00 the Stechishins were driven to the village. The arrival of a car made a great sensation in the village. When they alighted in front of Julian's brother's house, they saw that his brother appeared to be fairly prosperous with a new house. By Canadian standards, the village was primitive and the standard of living low. The roads in the area were just dirt and mud.

After a ten day stay, the Stechishins left Hleshchava for Tarnopol and went on to Sokal, the closest town to Savella's village, Tudorkovychi (now Fedorivka). Vasyl Gauk, who was managing Mohyla in Julian's absence, had asked them to visit his brother, Rev.

Stepan Gauk in Wariazh, in the Sokal area not far from Tudorkovychi. Rev. Gauk, a Greek Catholic priest, met them at the train station in Sokal and took them home to meet his family and to stay for a few days. The next day Rev. Gauk agreed to have them driven to Savella's village. It was considered improper for a priest to drive a horse and wagon so he had his hired man do the driving. Savella discovered to her disappointment that her village had not been rebuilt after the destruction of the First World War. There was much devastation, as this area was on the frontline during the war.

In Kolomeiya, the Stechishins visited Olena Kysilevska, the editor of *Zhinocha dolia*. After a friendly chat, they left and went on to have meetings with well known activists and writers. One such personality was Andriy Chaykowsky, who wrote about the Cossack period of Ukrainian history and whose stories Savella had read. She also met several women writers: Iryna Wilde and Mila Dorotska-Chaykowska. With the Carpathanian Mountains so near, the Stechishins wanted to see them. They had read and heard so much about the rivers and the mountains of this region in various songs and stories that they held a lot of romanticism for the region.

Olena Kysilewska organized a group to take the trip to the Carpathians by car. On their way they stopped at a summer resort, Yaremcha, and unexpectedly they met a group of well known people: Milena Rudnytska, national president of *Soiuz ukrainok* and Member of Parliament in the Polish Sejm, writer Bohdan Lepky whose novels were read in Canada and his brother, O. Oles, a priest and poet, as well as others. Milena's ex-husband, Iwan, years later immigrated to Canada and was a professor of history at the University of Alberta. Yaremcha is still a popular tourist spot and many Ukrainian handicrafts are available there for purchase.

On their return to Kolomeiya, Olena Kysilevska informed them that the well-known Ukrainian novelist, Olha Kobylianska was visiting her relatives, the Karatnyskys, in Kolomeiya and asked if they would like to meet her. Savella and other Ukrainian Canadians, especially women, had read many of Kobylianska's books and so, of course, she would be thrilled to meet her. A number of UWAC branches had been named in her honour. Arrangements were made and in a few days they had the pleasure of speaking with this esteemed author. Savella found her to be of stately stature, slim to the point of almost being emaciated, dressed in a dark dress, her hair drawn back severely in a knot and suffering from slight facial paralysis. She walked with a cane and spoke with a feeble voice. They chatted about Canada. Years later Savella remembered that Kobylianska "was greatly surprised that Ukrainians in Canada knew about her and read her novels, and that UWAC branches are named after her." As they departed, Kobylianska gently kissed Savella and wished them success.

Kosiw, a Hutsul small resort town was the next destination on their itinerary. The hotel they stayed at was similar to all hotels they encountered in Ukraine: old with no running water. Well executed Hutsul arts and crafts produced by the peasants living in the neighbouring countryside could be purchased in many little shops along the streets. The reason for their trip to this area was for Julian to meet Prof. Dr. Iwan Ohienko in the village of Moskliwka just outside Kosiw. He lectured at Warsaw University and vacationed in his cottage during the summer. Prof. Ohienko had served in the government of the Ukrainian National Republic during its brief existence in 1918 as Minister of Religion and Education. He was a learned man with expertise on the Orthodox Church and Ukrainian language, having written a number of books on these subjects as well as serving as editor of the journal *Ridna mova* (Ukrainian Language). Julian was wishing to discuss with the professor the problem of a lack of a bishop for the Ukrainian Canadian Orthodox adherents. Bishop Teodorowich of the United States had been temporarily assigned to Canada, but he was unable to continue to cover the entire North American continent. After the death of his wife and emigration to Canada with his two sons and daughter after the Second World War, Dr. Ohienko became Metropolitan of the Ukrainian Greek Orthodox church of Canada with its headquarters in Winnipeg, Manitoba.

Julian and Savella continued on to the small mountain villages of Kuty and Zhabia. It was exciting to see the Black Cheremosh River that is glorified in many Ukrainian folk songs flow through the village of Zhabia. Since it was Sunday, the Stechishins attended church. Savella found it interesting that because the people had long distances to walk to church, they brought meals with them, so that after the church service they could sit on the church lawn and have their lunch. Meanwhile, a member of the Polish Sejm was speaking to a group of men. The church played an important social role in the lives of these mountain people. Because few immigrants from this area had settled in Canada, their particular dress and speech accent were unfamiliar to the Stechishins.

Now it was time to begin their journey back to Canada. They arrived in L'viv where Savella had to present the speech she had promised. The announcement in the daily paper, *Dilo*, read:

Ukrainian Women's Movement in Canada
Under the auspices of Soiuz Ukrainok there will be a public lecture on Saturday, August 25 at 6 p.m. in the afternoon in the Besida Hall (22 Rutkowsky) by the President of the Ukrainian Women's Association of Canada, Mrs. Savella Stechishin, about the Ukrainian women's movement among the Ukrainian immigrants in Canada. Members are requested to attend. Guests are welcome.

Another announcement appeared among news of the day in the same paper:

GUEST FROM CANADA
Visiting Halychyna during the last several weeks is Mrs. Savella Stechishin, President of the Ukrainian Women's Association of Canada, who is going to speak at the meeting of Soiuz Ukrainok on Saturday evening at 6 p.m., August 25, in the Besida Hall about the activity of Ukrainian women in Canada. As a teacher and college student she is well informed about the conditions of life of Ukrainian settlers in Canada.

Savella wrote in her autobiography, "Needless to say, I was under stress. The very idea of me speaking in L'viv to Ukrainian educated intelligentsia was frightening. There wasn't much time to prepare a speech. On top of that, Julian, on whom I counted for moral support, had to go to Stanislaviw on some of his business in connection with church and politics." Although many people were away for the summer, the hall was well attended, as the Ukrainians were very much interested in life in Canada. It was filled with mostly elderly women and a sprinkle of men. Savella's speech was well accepted and followed by questions.

During her stay in L'viv Savella purchased many exquisite embroidered articles and Hutsul crafts. With their trip coming to a close, they reflected on the great progress underway in those villages where cooperatives and improved farming methods had been introduced.

At the end of August the Stechishins bade farewell to their beloved Ukraine. Brief stops in Warsaw, Poland and then Berlin brought them closer to home. In Berlin, which they found to be an orderly and clean German city, they met with Hetman Pavlo Skoropadsky, who had been head of the briefly establish Ukrainian Hetman State in 1918. The word "Hetman" in Ukrainian means cossack commander-in-chief. This State had been sponsored by the German and Austrian governments, however, their support ended shortly after their defeat in the Great War, leaving the Hetman with few resources to combat his enemies. With defeat staring him in the face, Pavlo Skoropadsky abdicated on December 14, 1918 and fled to Switzerland, then later to Germany, where he kindly received a small pension from the newly established Weimar Republic. In Berlin, Skoropadsky was fairly active in the conservative emigre community of displaced politicians, members of the overthrown dynasties and journalists. Soon, however, his hopes of restoring Ukrainian independence faded, and with it his interest in Berlin intellectual circles. But prior to his disillusionment, he did set up the

Ukrainian Scientific Institute in Berlin, initially directed by the historian Dr. Dmytro Doroshenko with whom he had collaborated in Kyiv in 1918. Julian had been asked by the pro-Hetman organization in Canada to discuss several issues with Skoropadsky. They met Skoropadsky along with his two assistants, S. Shemet and V. Kochubey, in a restaurant. It was a memorable experience for the Stechishins. Savella received a bouquet of flowers and a box of chocolates from Skoropadsky. He impressed her with his courteous manner and aristocratic, handsome looks. She found that contrary to the rumour that he spoke Ukrainian "tainted with Russian", his Ukrainian was pure and well enunciated.

With the first week of September upon them, the trip of a life time neared its end as Julian and Savella left Europe behind them. Their first stop in Canada was Montreal. Here, both Stechishins spoke at an arranged meeting to tell of their impressions of Western Ukraine. They went on to Fort William (now Thunder Bay) and again spoke to a prearranged gathering. The train then took them to Winnipeg. By now Savella was very anxious about their son, Tolio. He was to begin school and spoke no English, only Ukrainian. Although a meeting was arranged in Winnipeg, Savella left for Yorkton leaving Julian in Winnipeg for a day. Julian arrived the next day and people gathered at his brother Michael's house to hear what they had to say. Savella recalled, "People were anxious to hear what Julian had to say about life in Western Ukraine." They arrived in Saskatoon by train during the second week in September.

To promote the talent and artistry of Ukrainians amongst Canadians, during her travels in Ukraine Savella had purchased various elegant embroidered articles and intricate wood carvings to sell in Canada. Two cooperatives in L'viv, *Ukrainske Narodne Mystetstvo* and *Trud*, carried beautifully detailed embroidered articles that Savella believed would be perfect as samples for the members in UWAC branches to copy. Savella brought a suitcase full of embroidered linens and other handicraft items. The elaborately executed designs on the embroidered women's *sorochka* (shirt/blouse) sleeves represented various regions of Ukraine. Each region had its own folk costume and its own style of embroidery designs. In the cooperatives, certain designs were selected and applied to household linens, modern blouses, handbags and other everyday articles. She came up with the idea of introducing the various designs from the *sorochky* (shirts) that the pioneer women brought with them to Canada for use on modern clothing and household items. There was need to preserve the folk costumes in Canada as an art form. What better way to disseminate the information to engender preservation and pride in these designs than through the branches of the UWAC! Women would embrace Ukrainian arts and crafts, especially since this type of handiwork was performed predominately by women.

Savella also had made copious notes of her experiences in Ukraine and about life in general there. Upon her return to Saskatoon, she shared her observations and memories with the readers of the *Ukrainian Voice* in three instalments.[27] She appealed to Canadian women to pay for *Zhinocha dolia* to be sent to their relatives in the villages of Ukraine. While visiting villages in Ukraine, Savella had discovered that most women did not subscribe to this magazine even though she was sure that it contained much advice that would benefit them.

During the years 1929 to 1931, Savella corresponded with Zinaida Mirna who she had met in Prague.[28] She thus added another source from which to purchase embroidered articles for sale in Canada. Mirna sent Savella handicraft articles embroidered by Ukrainian women university students badly in need of financial help.[29] Again, Savella sold embroidered articles to aid women abroad. To return the favour, Mirna agreed to write articles, for a fee, in the UWAC Section of the *Ukrainian Voice*. The addition of articles by an educated Ukrainian woman from overseas added prestige to this page and gave credibility to the UWAC amongst Ukrainian Canadians. At this time, because Savella's name was listed as a Canadian correspondent in *Zhinocha dolia*, she received letters from authors wanting her to sell their books in Canada and others who wanted to know about Canadians.[30]

Savella's collection of Ukrainian embroideries and handicraft bought on her trip also served to enrich exhibits in the wider Canadian community. These exquisite items were truly authentic and because her collection was varied and in good condition, they were excellent to display. In March 1929, at the Canadian Pacific Railway sponsored multicultural exhibition at the Hotel Saskatchewan in Regina, Savella's collection was accepted as a good example of Ukrainian handicraft. The UWAC was responsible for the display, which attracted a lot of interest and attention. Members of the UWAC in Saskatoon and Regina presented a Ukrainian Easter egg (*pysanky*) display and demonstrated *pysanky* writing. A Ukrainian choir and the Avremenko dance group of Saskatoon performed as well. Savella felt very proud to show off her collection as she was certain that it would be viewed as more than just provincial handicraft, it would be considered art.

There were many benefits of Savella's preoccupation with all things Ukrainian and the promotion of them, not only for herself because she became an expert on Ukrainian heritage, but also for all Canadians of Ukrainian descent. Now they would be looked upon as a cultured people.Ukrainians in the homeland benefited by the assistance given by Savella and other Ukrainian Canadians. In fact, leaders of the women's movement in Ukraine appreciated and acknowledged the generous contribution of Ukrainian Canadian women. In 1933 the president of the *Soiuz ukrainok* at a women's convention in Ukraine officially made the resolution that:

> The organized women of Halychyna (Galicia) express their warmest gratitude to their sisters, especially to the Ukrainian Women's Association of Canada, for their material assistance to our organization, for their contribution to the delegates' fund which has allowed us to maintain our ties with international organizations and propagate our cause abroad . . ..[31]

In the *Iuvileina knyzhka* (Jubilee Book, 10th Year), Zinaida Mirna of Czechoslovakia, Olena Kysilevska of Kolomyia, Ukraine and Anastasia Wagner of the United States, presidents of their respective women's organizations, brought greetings.[32] The exchange of correspondence strengthened ties amongst the Ukrainian women living thousands of miles apart – an important objective of these organizations. They were building bridges within the new land and to their homeland.

Savella pictured here at 15 years old taking her Grade 8. Her first year at Petro Mohyla Institute, 1918 and her first year in the city of Saskatoon.
Courtesy Savella Stechishin Collection.

Savella and Julian Stechishin. Wedding photo, 1921. Married to the rector of Mohyla Institute at 17 years in the Ukrainian Orthodox Church in Saskatoon. The wedding was a small affair with only close relatives.
Courtesy Savella Stechishin Collection.

Anatole, son born in 1922, with his young mother, Savella.
Courtesy Savella Stechishin Collection.

Savella, centre back row, with friends in 1928. All dressed up for a masquerade ball held at Petro Mohyla Institute.
Courtesy Savella Stechishin Collection.

The girls group, Mohylianky, are pictured here in the school year 1925-26. Some are wearing Ukrainian embroidered blouses. Savella as dean of women encouraged the girls to learn to various Ukrainian stitches. One project was to embroider a blouse.

Reprinted from "Twenty Five Years of the Ukrainian Women's Associations of Canada. 1926-1951."

In 1928 Savella and Julian returned to their homeland, Ukraine, which was under Polish rule. Here Savella was thrilled to meet in Kolomeiya activist, Olena Kysilevska (left) and writer, Olha Kobylianska (centre) whose books were read by many Ukrainian-Canadian women and many UWAC branches were in her name. *Courtesy Savella Stechishin Collection.*

In 1930, Savella graduated with a Bachelor of Arts degree, the first Ukrainian-Canadian woman to do so at the University of Saskatchewan and the first Ukrainian-Canadian woman to graduated with a major in Home Economics.
Courtesy Savella Stechishin Collection.

The above Ukrainian Easter Eggs (pysanky), were visible symbols which Savella strongly believed should be preserved and promoted as Ukrainian art treasures. *Courtesy author.*

Pictured here are runners embroidered in Ukrainian designs and a sample of wood carving. Savella encouraged Ukrainian Canadians to understand that Ukrainian embroidered linens and folk costumes were a means to retain Ukrainian culture and heritage. These were promoted as an art form to the mainstream community. *Courtesy author.*

The first English language cookbook on Ukrainian cuisine was published 1957. It took Savella six years of testing and writing to compile the cookbook. It was a very popular cookbook for many years.
Courtesy Savella Stechishin Collection.

As an authority on Ukrainian embroidery, Savella was called upon to judge the intricacies of the workmanship. Here she is explaining about the blouse embroidery at a Yorkton competition in 1961.
Courtesy Savella Stechishin Collection.

In 1974 the Ukrainian Women's Association, Kelowna Branch named their branch in honour of Savella. She attended at the special occasion and was presented with a bouquet of roses.
Courtesy Savella Stechishin Collection.

St. Andrew's College at the University of Manitoba in Winnipeg, an Ukrainian Orthodox seminary, bestowed an Honourary Doctorate of Canon Law in 1976. Savella was very pleased to receive this prestigious honour.
Courtesy Savella Stechishin Collection.

Savella is photographed in 1989 with two outstanding Saskatchewan politicians on the occasion of her appointment as a member of the Order of Canada. In the photo, left is Roy Romanow, Leader of the opposition (New Democratic Party) and right is the Premier of Saskatchewan, Grant Devine of the Conservative Party. She was appointed on April 20, 1989 and invested on October 18, 1989.
Courtesy Savella Stechishin Collection.

This is one of the last photographs of Savella. Here she is wearing three medals she received: Order of Canada, Governor General of Canada commemorating the 125th anniversary of Canada and the Learned Societies of Ukraine. Savella was the first Canadian woman to receive the award from Ukraine.
Courtesy Savella Stechishin Collection.

5

Crystallizing Goals

The optimism and prosperity of the roaring 1920s ended abruptly with the 1929 stock market crash leading to a world-wide economic crisis and depression. Saskatchewan, a mostly agricultural province, was especially hard hit when the crisis was followed by nearly a decade of drought. Crop failures gripped the wheat belt and black blizzards swept the southern plains as the depression gave way to the 'dust bowl.' The parkland belt where most Ukrainian Canadians lived was not as affected by drought as the southern plains because the woodlands prevented the wind from stirring up a frenzy of soil. Saskatchewan, like the other prairie provinces, was one of the poorest areas of Canada. Times were hard and soon federal aid was required to help the destitute farmers throughout the three prairie provinces. Social welfare programs were initiated and expanded rapidly during the 1930s. Saskatchewan's income decreased by 90 percent and two-thirds of the population was reliant on welfare. In 1931 the first rail cars arrived with relief supplies. The southwestern areas were the most severely hit with protracted drought lasting from 1929 until 1937. The following year, relief camps were set up across Canada to keep unemployed men out of the cities. They were put to work in vast public works programs run by the federal government, but they received no pay other than an allowance of 20 cents a day to buy tobacco or personal items.

Dundurn, only a stone's throw from Saskatoon, became one of the largest relief camps in Canada. Nevertheless, the city of Saskatoon continued to grow with the population in 1931 increasing to 44,439 of which 1,846 claimed to be of Ukrainian descent. On June 1, 1929 Saskatoon's first airport had opened and in March 1930 the first air mail service linking all the major cities in Western Canada had begun. But by 1932 air mail service was discontinued and did not resume until 1938, just before the outbreak of the Second World War.

The poor economic condition of the province and its people did not prevent Savella from pursuing her goals. Savella was so resolute in realizing her dream to graduate with a university degree that the inherent hardships did not deter her. Her husband Julian was very supportive of her desire. Again, she broke with tradition; few married women attended university in 1930 and even fewer Ukrainian-Canadian women had that opportunity to prove that a woman's aspiration for self-fulfilment did not have to cease upon marriage and motherhood. Savella was a 'liberated' woman, in the modern sense, well ahead of her time and that of the average Ukrainian-Canadian woman.

Prior to receiving her degree, Savella and Julian had to find other accommodation after living at Mohyla for eight years. Julian had resigned from his position as rector of Mohyla in 1929 because of a dispute over the issue of religion at the Institute. He demanded that the students devote some time to religion studies and attending church, whereas the Board of Directors disagreed. Now homeless, the Stechishins bought an unfurnished five- room bungalow at 809 Main Street in the fall of 1929 for the high price of eight thousand dollars.[1] The purchase was a hardship since they had many debts stemming from Julian's earlier university days. Also, Savella was unemployed and both were still in university (he in law school). Salvation came in the form of her parents, who unlike many Ukrainians, had enough money to be able to give them four thousand dollars towards the purchase of their home. To help with other expenses, Savella's sister Stephania and over the years other girls boarded with them. One girl from Whitkow was Mariyka Nykiforuk, who attended Nutana

Collegiate, and a year later, Jean Galonsky arrived and remained with them until she finished high school.

By the late 1920s, more young Ukrainian girls from the rural areas were flocking to Saskatoon to find work or to further their education. Most parents had limited means to pay for their board in the city, so often these girls were obliged to work for their board and room as domestic help. Savella placed some of the girls in well-to-do Anglo-Canadian homes. Also, the YWCA had a list of people wanting to hire girls, who were going to high school or university, as domestics.

Savella's friend Tetiana Kroitor asked to have her sister, Paula Shewchuk, stay with them to attend Normal School in spite of not being able to pay for her. However, Paula agreed to repay the Stechishins when she got a teaching position. Savella and Julian kindly agreed to this proposal. For a few years, there were always three girls living with them. Since the entire adult household was composed of students, a timetable for domestic chores was worked out whereby all the female members pitched in. The generosity of Savella's family meant that there was never a shortage of food. Whenever her sister Helen and her family came to Saskatoon from Krydor, they brought a load of free food from her parents' farm and from their own farm near Krydor. There were plenty of eggs, cottage cheese, potatoes, vegetables, sauerkraut and meat, including chicken and pork. Both Savella and Julian got along very well with her family; the Wawryniuk sisters were close. Savella wrote, "Our family relationship was always very good; we enjoyed visiting them in Krydor. All of us along with the grandchildren would meet at my parents' home on the farm."[2] The Stechishin household was a buzz with young people coming and going. Residents from Mohyla, which was close by, would often stop in for coffee and the girls had many friends over to visit. Savella's friends from the UWAC executive also appeared from time to time to discuss their organizational work. Among them were Anastasia Ruryk, Stephania Bubniuk, Daria Yanda and Anastasia Greschuk. These women were strong activists and leaders within UWAC; they supported education for women of Ukrainian descent and the elevation of all Ukrainian Canadians to good Canadian standards. Each of the women continued being active in her Ukrainian-Canadian community for many years.

Other matters were often discussed at the home of the Stechishins. Although the Kameniari society was established at Mohyla Institute, it was felt by a number of Ukrainian students that there should be a separate Ukrainian students' society on the University of Saskatchewan campus. In this way students of all denominations and regardless of where they lived could socialize within one ethnic club. After much discussion, "a pre-organization meeting was held in 1929 at the home of J.W. Stechishin" and the Catholic group was approached to help form this society.[3] They were very agreeable and an organizational meeting was called in November, 1930. About twenty-five students attended the meeting with enthusiasm. The executive was as follows: President, Mr. J. Hnatyshyn; Secretary, Mr. S. Mamchur; Committee, Mr. W. Yarmey, Mr. J. Ostapovich, Mr. P. Welgan, Miss S. Wawryniuk, and Mrs. J.W. Stechishin. Many of these executive members later became well know in their professions and in the Ukrainian-Canadian milieu. Savella was also elected to be on a special committee to draft a constitution, to choose a suitable name for the society, to plan its objectives and activities and to decide what language to use at meetings. With the help of Rev. V. Kudryk, the name Alpha-Omega was accepted by all members of the committee. The meaning of the name "from A to Z or from beginning to end" suited them well and would thus incorporate many activities and objectives. Savella recorded, "The main objectives of the society were: self-advancement and education in Ukrainian history, literature, general culture and traditions through lectures and discussions, acquainting the non-Ukrainian public with Ukrainian culture and general problems, preparing work for publication on Ukrainian topics."[4] The Alpha

Omega Society flourished until about 1937 or 1938. There was then a brief period of decline before revived in 1941-1942. Over the years, it has been on again and off again, depending on the interest and numbers of students of Ukrainian descent.

On April 5, the first ever pre-convocation reception given by the Kameniari Ukrainian Students Society was held for all the Ukrainian graduates at Mohyla Institute. There were six graduates in total, with Savella the only woman. The men were: William Chepil, John Hnatyshyn, Thomas Pavlychenko, Frank Zulkowsky and Michael Peech. These men later played significant roles in the Ukrainian and Canadian communities. At the banquet, the UWAC secretary, Anastasia Ruryk, presented Savella with a beautiful tray from the UWAC executive. A lovely silver vase filled with roses arrived from her Ukrainian women friends in Winnipeg. She received congratulatory telegrams and letters, which were read at the banquet. Julian and Tolio gave her a beautiful tiny wrist watch that she was thrilled with and wore for many years until it was beyond repair.

Convocation was held on May 30, 1930, at which Savella wore a white chiffon dress that she had bought in Prague. Having rarely worn it, she considered it ideal for this momentous occasion. Savella was excited and thrilled to receive a university degree and that she had obtained her post-secondary education "as a married woman, which in those days was very unusual."[5] Several of her friends came to the convocation to congratulate her. In her autobiography, Savella refers to her family: "I had a very happy marriage and a loveable son. My husband was understanding and encouraged me in my strivings to obtain a university education. Ours was a happy trio – the three of us."

At her graduation, Savella made history as both the first Ukrainian-Canadian woman to graduate from the University of Saskatchewan and the first Ukrainian-Canadian woman to receive a Bachelor of Arts majoring in Home Economics. She felt she had broken the age-old tradition "that once a girl gets married she is through with any advancement in life. Her duty is to stay home and look after the husband and children ... [I] showed the women that life does not have to end with marriage. A woman is a free individual, just like a man, and she has freedom to pursue her interests, if she so desires, combining marriage and her strivings to achieve a standing in her own right. That was my message to women."[6]

Women did recognize her achievement and acknowledged its importance in encouraging young women to assert and empower themselves, to demand success in achieving their goals and aspirations. Stephania Bubniuk, a member of the National Executive (UWAC), praised Savella's accomplishment in the *Ukrainian Voice* urging that

> Young women who have the opportunity to attain higher learning should use Savella Stechishin as an example, she as a married woman and mother, was able to cope with her obligations as wife, mother, homemaker and student .... For some time Savella Stechishin has been president of the Ukrainian Women's Association of Canada .. .[7]

She added that if more Ukrainians in Canada had higher education, then other nationalities would look upon them with more respect. Savella was deliberately put on a pedestal as a heroine for young women to emulate. She represented the embodiment of the Ukrainian-Canadian woman as prescribed by the intelligentsia. This model was used to help raise Ukrainian-Canadians women to that of the average middle-class Canadian. After the publication of this article, Savella received further congratulations from many friends who had known her over the years.

While at university, Savella learned that the Homemakers' Department, Department of Women's Work (Extension) at the University of Saskatchewan was offering, in English, an extension class in home economics for Ukrainian-Canadian women. Many of the women did not understand English at all or not well enough to completely take advantage of the class. With the constant vision of helping her 'sisters,' she offered to teach these women in their own language.[8] After the completion of her classes, Savella approached the dean of her faculty, Mrs. Ethel Rutter, with the idea of going into the rural areas where Ukrainian women resided to teach them the fundamentals of modern home economics, which they lacked. She was interested in teaching them the proper methods of food preservation, nutrition, hygiene and meal planning. Instruction in the safe preservation of meat and vegetables was especially important, as these were the staples of the Ukrainian diet in the bloc settlements. Lecturing in the Ukrainian language, she claimed, would be more beneficial because the women would have more understanding and attendance would be greater.

Mrs. Rutter enthusiastically approved the plan to help pioneer immigrant women adapt to the current Canadian methods of homemaking and together she and Savella presented it to the President of the university, Dr. Murray.[9] Dr. Murray questioned what exactly she would teach the Ukrainian women. Savella, although apprehensive, bravely answered that canning and the knowledge of nutrition for meal planning were important and that she believed the women were not getting any guidance and help in homemaking, so this help would be appreciated. He appeared favourable to her proposition and said he would speak to Miss A. DeLury, Director of Women's Work Department. Miss DeLury received Savella warmly and expressed keen interest, quickly giving Savella the responsibility and freedom to develop and carry out the program. As this was a new project, she was paid a monthly salary for the first year. A year later her transportation, accommodation and meals were also paid. On her own initiative, she created a job for herself and, at the same time, was pursuing her goal to help Ukrainian-Canadian women. She was the first ethnic homemaker in the Department of Women's Work. This proved to be quite an accomplishment for a woman in 1930, especially for a woman who was not a member of the host society, but rather a member of an ethnic minority that was a common target of many discriminatory practices in Saskatchewan.

Savella received the required material for her lectures from the Director of the Homemakers' Department, Miss DeLury, and translated it into Ukrainian. The translated material was then mimeographed and prepared for distribution to those who attended her lectures. The lectures and demonstrations incorporated topics on food, nutrition, home decoration and housekeeping efficiency. Under the theme of food and nutrition, the typical programme was as follows:

1. Nutritive elements of fruits, vegetables and milk.
2. The vitamins and their relation to health.
3. Food for the growing child and the school lunches.
4. Inexpensive, healthy and appetizing sandwich fillings (cottage cheese, carrots, etc.).
5. The use of left-over food.
6. Canning and preserving of foods.[10]

These topics were ideally suited to the Ukrainian-Canadian women living in the bloc settlements. Their contact with the world outside their settlement was infrequent and they were unaware of the current information on nutrition, techniques of preparing healthy food effectively and the correct method of food preservation.

Fifty-five sites were selected for Savella to visit and give her lectures in that first summer of 1930. This area spanned north of Saskatoon, including Meacham, Wakaw, Hafford and others, east of Saskatoon with Yorkton, Melville, Canora and area, and southern Saskatchewan taking in Bienfait, and the Moose Jaw area. The question of transportation had to be solved. How was she to get to all of those many towns and villages in one summer? Savella noted how she and Julian pragmatically tackled the problem of transportation,

"Julian bought a new coupe car for us and I was to use it for my trips. I learned to drive it without difficulty."[11] Julian was always there to help his wife not only in a supportive role, but also instrumentally in surmounting obstacles put in her path. They both proved to be unique people for the times. In 1930 it was unusual for a Canadian woman to have the determination to travel alone in the countryside teaching women the benefits of home economics. On the other hand, the average Canadian man did not regard his wife's vision important enough to warrant the purchase of a car for her exclusive use in pursuits away from the home a week at a time leaving both child and husband behind.

Another problem, which they took care of in a practical way, was child care for their son, Tolio. Julian, as a law student, was hired along with others to travel throughout rural communities in Saskatchewan for the project "Competition in Community Progress in Saskatchewan". Members of the group consisted of the president of the University of Saskatchewan, Dr. W. Murray, several professors, journalists, colonization representative of the CNR and some ethnic persons. They travelled by car to many communities checking the condition and state of development in the settlements with regard to progress in agriculture, farmyard and buildings, education of children, cultural development, ethnic heritage, etc. Since the Ukrainian population was high in Saskatchewan, it was necessary to have an educated Ukrainian in the group, which was the main reason Julian had been selected. This employment was profitable as well as prestigious. Fortuitously, a young couple, William and Helen Yarmey with whom the Stechishins were acquainted needed accommodation in Saskatoon while William went to university. The Stechishins agreed to rent them their house on the condition that Helen would stay at home to care for Tolio for the month of June. For the months of July and August, he was looked after by Savella's parents at the farm.[12] Savella and Julian along with Tolio met at weekends.

On the morning of June 3, 1930, Savella set out in their new coupe to the parkland belt of Saskatchewan. Soon, she was passing onion-domed churches and their detached bell towers and alongside were the clusters of whitewashed crosses marking the numerous graveyards. Yes, this was Ukrainian country and her first stop was Hafford. She met with some UWAC members and the secretary of the town of Hafford to make arrangements for the upcoming weeks' meetings. Time was not wasted for that day as she was able to speak to a small gathering of women and girls of Nauka School District. It was exciting for the rural women to see and hear someone they had heard of, a highly educated city Ukrainian woman. As news spread of her work, teachers invited Savella to speak to their school children. One of the schools she visited was Slawa School, where she stayed the night with the teacher, Dorothy Werezak. On June 11 a large audience gathered in the Franko Community Hall by Bilyk's farm in the Borden area to hear her lecture. Afterwards, they requested her to give a canning demonstration, which she did. Sophie Derbowka (later Wasylyshyn) was the teacher in the area and president of the UWAC branch she had organized. At the Welychko Hall, a large number of men, women and children attended and many questions were asked of her.

Canning was of interest to many, as it was something new and beneficial to good nutrition. The farming community always grew large gardens with many vegetables and had plenty of animals and poultry that could be preserved for future use, especially in winter. Proper, safe home canning procedures helped to control organisms that could cause spoilage and allowed food to be kept beyond its normal storage period. Home canning is not complicated. It is a simple procedure that applies heat to food in a closed glass jar to interrupt the natural decaying that would otherwise take place. Safe home canning requires heat processing of all foods in glass jars placed in a canner according to tested home canning guidelines. Savella demonstrated the procedure and explained the guidelines to get good results. For her June 13th canning demonstration in Hafford, local women attended and even the local high school girls were sent in the afternoon to watch the canning demonstration. Women appreciated the canning guidelines that Savella had mimeographed in Ukrainian. These had been prepared earlier at Mohyla and brought with her for distribution.

Savella received support for her home economics tour from expected places. On June 11th Anastasia Ruryk, a member of the National Executive of the UWAC, wrote in the *Ukrainian Voice* in celebration of Savella's graduation as the first woman of Ukrainian descent to graduate as a home economist.[13] She also mentioned that Savella would be visiting various districts to give lectures on nutrition, the preparation of healthy food and proper methods of preserving foods, and that the branches of the UWAC should invite Savella to lecture. The *Ukrainian Voice* upon Savella's request, published the dates and places where she was to visit. To ensure that the women in a particular area were aware of her visit, she informed the local teacher or the president of the UWAC (most often there was a UWAC branch nearby) requesting that they disseminate the news.[14] Savella was the ideal person for this work since she personally knew a great number of the teachers and members of the UWAC in the bloc settlements. A high percentage of these women had passed through the halls of Mohyla Institute; Savella would have either instructed them at Mohyla or had encouraged them to participate in the work of the UWAC. The cost of accommodation on the lecture tours was minimal since she was able to stay with friends in all the districts she visited.

Krydor and the rural schools in the Whitkow district were visited on June 24, 25, 26 and 27. In her report of expenditures to the Homemakers' Department during her first month, June 1930, she travelled a total of 869 miles, recorded the days of service as 24, and the cost of supplies bought for demonstrations as $2.66. This expense included $1.96 for tomatoes, jar rings, etc, $0.50 for writing paper and envelopes and $0.20 for stamps.[15]

Savella put a lot of miles on the coupe in July as well. Theodore, about 250 miles east of Saskatoon, was the next stop for Savella. During July, she lectured in Theodore, Sheho, Insinger and Parkerview. In Theodore she stayed at the home of Rev. Kirstiuk and he made arrangements to have her speak to the Ukrainian Girls' Club there. She spoke about character development through reading good books. Later in July and in August, she moved southwards, covering the areas of Canora and Yorkton.

Savella's lectures and demonstrations were most often held in the rural schools, but at times community halls were also utilized. Often the entire family came out to witness the sharing of ideas from a big city with Savella providing them a window on the outside world of modern ideas. For example, Savella visited the Pelly district with the following topics and number of attendees:[16]

Localities	Topics	Attendees
Preeceville (1 day)	Canning and preserving	78 men and women
Hryhoriw (2 days)	Improvement of farm yard	(first day) 85 men and women
	Home decoration	(second day)110 men and women
	School lunches	
Arran Community Hall (1 day)	Canning and preserving	
	Improvement of farm yard & home decoration	

By September of that year, Savella added the topics of "Nutritive Value of Fruits and Vegetables and Milk: Their Uses in Daily Diet," "Table Service," "Our Duties as Homemakers," and "Vitamins."[17] The areas Savella visited in September were Rosthern, St. Julian, Wakaw, Tarnopol, Yellow Creek, Cudworth, Vonda, Meacham, Prince Albert and Meath Park. All of these towns were in the parkland bloc settlements.

In response to Savella's request for information regarding alcoholic drinks, Abbie DeLury, wrote to Savella that they had no specific literature available and that she could mention the "evil effects of alcohol as well as its moral and social effects."[18] However, there is no evidence that Savella did lecture on this topic officially. Abuse of alcohol was very much in evidence amongst Ukrainians on the prairie and was considered to be "responsible for physical debilitation, material poverty, and demoralization."[19] Anglo-Canadian newspapers often printed stories of drunkenness and physical altercations because of intoxication at Ukrainian-Canadian weddings and even funerals. This behaviour was detrimental to the image of Ukrainians and the entire Ukrainian community suffered because of the bad publicity. Savella, as a member of the nationalist group that was attempting to help the Ukrainians socio-economically and to elevate their profile as a culturally developed ethnos, hoped to spread the word of the evils of intemperance so that the drinking could be curtailed.

Men attended Savella's lectures probably more due to curiosity rather than to learn firsthand the benefits of this new program and also perhaps men were the 'drivers' so needed to transport women. Children were brought along sometimes when parents attended the lectures together, since babysitters were uncommon amongst Ukrainians. An important aspect of childrearing for most Ukrainian Canadians was to look after one's own family and babysitting was a luxury practised by middle class, Anglo Canadians.[20] Many in her audience would have read her column in the *Ukrainian Voice* and she was certainly widely considered a highly educated and talented woman. Favourable comments of the lectures were published in the *Ukrainian Voice*, for example.[21] After this hectic summer, the program with the Department of Women's Work ended for the year at the end of September.

With no job for the winter, Savella made up her mind to continue her university education and obtain a Master of Arts program in English literature. Julian fully supported and encouraged her. She enrolled in a Master's program in the fall of 1930 at the

University of Saskatchewan. Although she found her classes enjoyable and interesting, the Stechishins were unable to pay the tuition fees and other expenses. She was allowed to continue into the spring with extended credit. As it was more important that Julian continue his university classes, they decided that she would drop out and when conditions improved, she would continue. These were the early years of the Great Depression when money and jobs were scarce for a great number of people. She never returned to her Master's degree studies.

Savella had admirers who believed she had accomplished a great deal, given her circumstances. Anna Chepesiuk of Finmark, Ontario was one such person who felt strongly enough to promote Savella in the Canadian arena. Anna, a former Mohylianka, who had met Savella at the Institute after she had been sent there by her parents to further her education, respected Savella for her achievements. She was originally from Fort William, Ontario and then was teaching in Finmark, Ontario. On November 23, 1930 Anna wrote to Savella in Ukrainian saying,

> "I allowed myself to write a small article about you for "Chatelaine". I see stories about different women, and I don't know why your name is not among them. I consider it my patriotic [Ukrainian] duty to introduce our educated women to the wide English audience. I know I am not a great journalist but maybe with your help we can write something wise. So, I put the following task to you: 1. Read the article, add important facts that I missed. 2. Take out what we don't need or is not important. 3. Send me your photograph that I can send it together with the article.[22]

The Chatelaine, a Canadian monthly magazine aimed at women readers, featured accomplished women as well as articles of interest to women. In response to Anna, Savella sent an improved article about herself and a 'cut' of a photo from the *Ukrainian Voice*.

Savella described her own achievements as: "As a lecturer and a demonstrator, Mrs. S. Stechishin applied very efficiently the scientific principles of cookery, diets, home decoration and home management to the needs of the Canadian rural life. This together with her eloquent speech brought her immense success and popularity among the Ukrainian women of Saskatchewan."[23] Anna replied to Savella, telling her that she had received her letter and that the article and photo had been sent to MacLean's Publishing Company for inclusion in *Chatelaine* and she hoped they would publish the article.[24] On February 1, 1931 Anna enthusiastically wrote to Savella, "Our effort is a success, we can say 'it's a triumph.' Here is what the editor wrote: 'I can't tell you how glad I was to get your letter. It is most interesting and I was very interested in your story of Mrs. Stechishin of Saskatoon. I have heard of the very wonderful work that is being done out west and I should like to run the story.' So I am very happy for the success."[25] After further correspondence, Savella was selected for the layout on 'Women and Their Work' in *The Chatelaine* in the August 1931 issue that included a write-up as well as a photograph.

Such recognition benefited not only Savella, but the entire Ukrainian community in Canada – a woman of Ukrainian descent had 'made it' on the national stage. She was seen to be an equal with other well-known women activists. Savella was one of only four women selected for the magazine as notable women activists in Canada. The other women were prominent upper middle-class older women and wives of well-heeled men: Mrs. Gould was wife of Dr. D. Gould of Ontario, her chief interest being the Women's Institute; Mrs. Pierre F. Casgrain, a well-known Quebec feminist, born to a titled family (her father had been knighted) was the wife of a Member of Parliament; and, Mrs. David Jamieson of Ontario widely known through her husband's prominence as chairman of the Mothers' Allowance Commission and the Old Age Pensions Board, was as well a member of the well-known Bradshaw family.[26] It is interesting to note the caption under Savella's photograph is "Mrs. **Savella**

Stechishin" and her accomplishments are all her own. Her husband is not mentioned, while in the other three cases, the husband's name (e.g., Mrs. **Pierre F.** Casgrain) is clearly stated. At this time, the use of the married woman's first name was a break with established tradition. Savella was less than half the age of the other three women. Editors of *The Chatelaine* paraphrased some of Savella's description and quoted her verbatim: "Canada gave her her education and now in turn she is doing her share in the building of sound and healthy Canadian homes among the Ukrainians.. . . She is also the instigator of the Ukrainian Women's Association of Canada, which has taken root and flourished progressively."[27]

Mohyla Institute was in dire financial straits in 1930. Student enrolment was low due to the economic depression and the rector resigned. The directors approached Julian to take the reins once again. He was not willing this time because he was still taking university classes towards a law degree. However, under pressure he agreed to take over as rector for a year or two until a new rector could be hired. He remained rector for two years, renting out their house and moving into Mohyla for this period.

After travelling throughout the bloc settlements as a home economist for two summers, Savella believed that there was a further need to disseminate information regarding home economics to young women who did not have the opportunity to attend her lectures. In March 1932, with the joint sponsorship of Mohyla Institute and the executive of the UWAC, she held Ukrainian cultural classes for the young women in residence at Mohyla as well as those who travelled in from the rural areas.[28] The out-of-towners were given accommodation at Mohyla for the two-week course. Along with homemaking classes, Savella instructed participants in the Ukrainian handicrafts of *pysanka* writing and embroidery. She found teaching gratifying and was pleased to educate the young women to appreciate their cultural handicraft.

In that same year, the Ukrainian National Women's League of

America invited members of the executive of the UWAC to attend its congress held in New York on May 28-30th. Their scheduled guest speaker was the outstanding Ukrainian activist, member of the Polish Parliament Sejm and President of the *Soiuz ukrainok* in Western Ukraine, Milena Rudnytska. With the ever present thought of promoting the cohesion of Ukrainian women in both the diaspora and homeland, Savella with her friends, Tetiana Kroitor and Daria Yanda, decided to drive to New York; Daria Yanda suggested they use her new car. A male friend, William Oshanek, who was at university and without a summer job, offered to chauffeur them at no charge, but declined to contribute to any expenses. Travelling thousands of miles in an automobile for pleasure was not a common occurrence for Saskatchewan women in the 'Dirty Thirties.' Although the three women were travelling with a male companion, they showed a lot of determination to participate in this adventure. Since there were no motels in those days, the quartet got accommodations in "Guest Rooms" as they drove through the various states on their way to New York. Billboards advertising guest rooms were placed in front of private homes. Savella recalled that "[t]he trip was long and slow."[29]
Upon arriving in New York, they headed first to the home of Mrs. Pauline Avramenko, wife of the well known dance instructor who had toured Western Canada and whom Savella knew. Mrs. Avramenko arranged accommodations for them at a low rate in private homes while they were in New York.

At the banquet, the Americans recognized Savella as president and she brought greetings from the UWAC to the congress. Savella found the American Ukrainians sophisticated and assimilated into American culture, even the working language at the congress was English. She remembered, "The ladies all wore low cut evening dresses. We looked like country Janes beside them in our ordinary dresses."[30] This was the first Ukrainian Women's Congress in North America. While in New York, the Saskatchewan delegation went sightseeing and visited the publishing house of the prominent

Ukrainian American newspaper "*Svoboda*" to which many in Canada subscribed.

On the return trip, the travellers drove through eastern Canada, visiting Montreal, Toronto, and other Ontario points before driving back south to the United States to take the better road home. In the Canadian cities of Montreal, Toronto, Hamilton, and Windsor, as well as in the American cities of Detroit and Chicago, the travellers stayed overnight with friends, who were all prominent activists in the nationalist cause and women's movement. In each city, meetings were arranged for the women to speak. They extolled the virtues of the UWAC and gave support and encouragement to the members of the local branches. In Detroit, they contacted the Orthodox priest who was pleased to meet them and asked them to stay a couple of days to meet his parishioners. He called a meeting at which the three women spoke. Savella recalled that "[t]o our great surprise we received very many complements. These people had never heard women speak, it was very gratifying to us." This visit from the National President and two members of the National Executive aroused interest and the meetings were well attended. By the time the four travellers reached Chicago, they were all broke. Savella wrote, "Our funds were completely depleted, so I telegraphed Julian to send us some money by wire in care of Skehar [a friend Savella knew and with whom they stayed]."[31] Chicago was the last city where they addressed gatherings.

After returning to Saskatoon, Savella resumed her work with the Women's Department and travelled in the rural areas that year by train, lecturing on topics of home economics.[32] Her presentations were called 'one-day school' since Savella as the home economist would spend one day only in each village or town. Savella was enthusiastically welcomed wherever she went. For example, in Whitkow, the women welcomed her with a bouquet of paper flowers. She was absolutely thrilled that the women would think of such a way to honour her presence during the winter season. In my interview, she fondly remembered, "Paper flowers! Wasn't that nice? In Grunlid, it was in the summer, and they also wanted to welcome me, so they scattered flowers before me."[33] In advance of the one-day school Savella asked the women to bring lunch for themselves and some for her, as there were no restaurants nearby. "All those poor women, what they didn't bring! They brought whole chickens, pies because they were so anxious to [learn]; they appreciated it."[34] Savella taught them about nutrition as she was paid to do, but on her own initiative she also taught Ukrainian embroidery. She introduced Ukrainian needle 'drawn work' (*merezhky*) and other Ukrainian embroideries and as her samples, she used her collection purchased in Ukraine. She held classes, not including Ukrainian embroidery, in English communities and again she advertised about the one-day school and asked for lunch. In my interview, she added, "They [English] would bring me lunch. There was a difference! I want to tell you about the lunch – what Ukrainian hospitality means! White bread with some bologna and tea. That's what we had. That's the difference [from Ukrainian hospitality]."[35]

Savella continued her volunteer work with the UWAC. There always was much work to be done as she was president. Milena Rudnytska, president of the *Soiuz ukrainok* again urgently appealed to her Ukrainian-Canadian sisters for funds in 1933. This time it was for aid to participate in the International Women's Council (IWC) congress to be held March 18-20 in Marseille, France. She writes:

> Thousands of kilometres and vast expanses of ocean separate you from us . . . , we are united by a common aim, a common objective which we are pursuing: a brighter future for our enslaved Ukrainian people . . . gives us the courage to turn to you, Ukrainian women overseas, with an urgent appeal to assist us in a major undertaking: sending a Ukrainian delegate to attend the International Women's Congress . . . A delegation representing Ukrainian women must not be absent from this congress, and we must travel to Marseille to strengthen our ties with foreign women, to represent Ukrainian women with dignity,

to inform the world about the plight of our people, to gain
sympathy for our Cause. . .[36]

In order to raise funds for this appeal, Savella wrote an article in the
Ukrainian Voice asking readers to donate generously to the cause.
Considering the poor economic conditions on the prairies during the
depression, the amount of $243.78 collected, although not vast, was
respectable.[37] Many women who were first born Canadians did not
feel the strong kinship to Ukraine that Savella and the nationalist
camp did. The ICW was an outlet for the women in Ukraine to gain
wider national recognition for Ukraine and they participated in every
international women's gathering possible. The Polish pacification-
terror campaigns of 1930-1931, the purges by the Soviets and
especially the famine of 1932-1933 shifted the focus of Ukrainian
women toward national rather than feminist concerns.

The dreadful famine, *Holodomor,* engulfed Ukraine, the
northern Caucasus, and the lower Volga River area in 1932-1933 as
a result of Joseph Stalin's policy of forced collectivization. Ukraine
suffered the heaviest losses, though it had been the most productive
agricultural land of the Soviet Union; more than seven million
Ukrainians died in the man-made famine. To finance
industrialization, Stalin had instituted an all-out collectivization
whereby he raised Ukraine's grain procurement quotas so high that
there was not enough grain to feed the peasants. All food had been
confiscated along with farm animals leaving the peasant destitute;
villages had been plundered by Stalin's henchmen. Stalin's policy had
condemned millions to death by starvation. Any person caught taking
even a handful of grain from a collective farm could have, and often
had been, executed or deported (usually to Siberia).[38] Under Stalin's
rule, artists and intellectuals were arrested, exiled or executed in an
attempt to eradicate every vestige of Ukrainian culture and
nationalism. In Canada at the present time, the fourth Saturday of
every November has been designated as a day of remembrance for the
victims of the famine.

Milena Rudnytska, as the representative of Ukrainians in Poland and president of the *Soiuz ukrainok*, raised the issue of the famine and famine relief at the Congress of Minorities of the League of Nations at meetings in Geneva and Berne in 1933. She received support from the Germans who were wanting to deflect interest from their anti-Semitic legislation as well as aid Germans living in Russia and Ukraine who had been hit by the famine. Little was done. The League could not interfere in the internal affairs of a non-member state (the Soviet Union) and, furthermore, a majority of its members wanted to trade with the Soviet Union.

Meanwhile, in Saskatoon Julian had been informed about the famine by some of his clients who brought him letters from their family members. He immediately called a mass meeting in the Ukrainian Community Hall on Avenue I to inform the public of the man-made famine in which millions of Ukrainians were starving to death. Several speakers whose families had died of the famine read letters they had received from relatives and friends in Ukraine documenting the horrific conditions. A protest telegram was sent to the League of Nations in Switzerland. Similar meetings were held in other centres in Canada.

To Savella's joy on May 14, 1933, Mother's Day, a baby girl was born to the Stechishins. Savella selected the name "Zenovia, Zenia for short . . ."[39] Unfortunately, Julian had a speaking engagement in Moose Jaw that day and was unable to immediately share Savella's joy of having given birth to a girl. He did arrive in the evening to visit Savella and was very happy about the baby and that all had gone well. After a week's stay at the hospital, Savella returned with her baby to Mohyla. She was fortunate that Mrs. Katherine Drul, the cook and kitchen manager, helped her by bringing her meals and generally tidying up the apartment. By the summer, Julian had resigned from his position at Mohyla to concentrate on his law practice and they once again took up residence on 809 Main Street. As usual, the fall was the start of a busy season for Savella.

She was active at the local level as well as being president at the national UWAC.

In 1934, the *Soiuz ukrainok*, to observe the Fiftieth Anniversary of the first women's convention, which had been held in 1884 in Stanislaviv, held a Fiftieth Anniversary Congress in Stanislaviv, Ukraine. The announcement of the Congress aroused the interest of the National Executive of the UWAC and it was decided that a delegate should be sent to witness this historic event. Hanka Romanchych, an activist of the UWAC from its beginning, decided she would attend and offered to represent the UWAC. Her attendance was agreed upon and a fifty dollar donation from the UWAC was given to her to present to the Congress in recognition of their support.[40] It was a wise decision not to solicit further funds from the general Ukrainian-Canadian population during the economically depressed 1930s. The UWAC's support, financial and moral, again demonstrated the close ties that the Association with Savella at its helm, wished to keep with Ukraine.

Mary Sheepshank of the Women's International League for Peace and Freedom addressed the 1934 Congress, lending credibility and prestige to the occasion. The Congress helped to congeal the solidarity of Ukrainian women throughout the world. Establishment of a world organization encompassing all Ukrainian women's organizations was the most notable outcome of the Congress. The World Ukrainian Women's Organization came into fruition in 1937 with its headquarters in L'viv, Ukraine. Savella kept abreast of this organization and their aims by subscribing to their bi-monthly newspaper, *Zhinka* (Woman*)* that began publication in 1935.[41]

At the Ukrainian National Convention in Saskatoon in December 1934, Savella resigned as president of the UWAC because she was expecting her third child. A baby boy, Myron, affectionately known as 'Ronio', was born on January 26, 1935.[42] Always the consummate Ukrainian loyalist, Savella gave her children traditional Ukrainian given names, names that she never Anglicized, as so many

Ukrainians did. Many Ukrainians chose to Anglicize both surname and first names because they were embarrassed by the 'unpronounceability.' Others were ashamed of their heritage or sought to avoid discrimination by simply adopting English names.

The UWAC, jointly with the USRL, in 1935 held their convention in July instead of the usual December. Selecting July over December proved to be a good choice. Attendance and participation were greater, as teachers, the backbone of the organizations, on their summer break were more willing to attend. The weather was more conducive to travel, as well, and owning an automobile was more common.

The year 1935 was the deepest of the depression in Canada, and it affected everyone across the prairies. By 1936, the Saskatoon population had declined to 41,734 from the high of 43,291 in 1931. The Main Street house was rented out again and Julian and Savella moved to 609 Temperance Street, where they rented a large three story house to take in boarders and in this way help meet living expenses. Julian's law practice was not making much money and Savella did not work that year for the Women's Department because she had to care for her new baby, Ronio. They took Savella's sister Helen's children, Irene, Slava and Walter and Orest Stechishin, Julian's nephew, as boarders. All were attending post secondary school in Saskatoon. Helen again helped out by providing them with produce from the farms and from the grocery store.[43]

With three children now and a busy commitment to her Ukrainian community and the UWAC, in late 1930s the Stechishins hired maids to help with the housework. One of the results of the lack of opportunity in rural areas for women, especially the young and single, was their migration to urban centres to take up domestic employment. Savella remembered, "In those days of unemployment, it was very easy to hire a maid." Their maids were Ukrainian-Canadian girls from the farms, many of whose families were acquainted with Savella. The language in the house was exclusively

Ukrainian. These girls (maids) worked for room and board, going to school during the day and looking after the children and the housework on weekends and evenings.

In an April 2005 interview, Jean Galonsky, now Matieshan, in her late 80s and living in Toronto, spoke of her residency with the Stechishins. She clearly remembered her time living with them. Jean recalled, "She [Savella] would say [in Ukrainian], 'Jean, watch out for this, for that" and then she would go out. She used to speak [at engagements]. At night she would go out and trust me with her kids." She added, "I came to Saskatoon, so what could you do, you're really green. You go to school or you go to work or what do you do? And I remember clearly that I looked after the children and she [Savella] then said, 'Jean, go to school.' I would get out of everything and go to school. She trusted me with the kids and talked to me so kindly and so I felt very good all the time. I never felt I should cry because she did something or said something ever. She was as kind to me as a mother." When asked how she felt about the Stechishins, Jean added "To be a person living with the Stechishins was a big thing because she had a big name. Savella Stechishin was a big name. I used to think where she got such a name – Savella. Her name was unusual because at that time, it [the most common names] was Maria or Hanya. And then later when I got bigger, Savella started to write and I had to read what she was saying." Proudly, she continued, "I was a teacher. That was a big thing, if you knew how poor my family was because there were ten kids. Can you feed ten kids? That's how I grew up." She attributed her becoming a teacher to the Savella's encouragement. Thus, many years later and in her advanced years, Jean had not forgotten what Savella had done for her and was still thankful that she had been given the opportunity and support to continue her education and make something of herself.[44]

Finally, in 1935 Julian qualified as a lawyer and joined the McKercher Francis law firm as a partner. The depression was still raging and the law profession suffered along with everyone.

Provincial income decreased by 90% and about two-thirds of the population were forced to rely on welfare. Drought, dust, heat, grasshoppers, western equine encephalitis and army worms drove farmers to desperation. Savella recalled in later years, "We seldom bought oranges in those days. Instead, we gathered wild fruit for home preserves – saskatoons, cranberries, chokecherries and pincherries." The Stechishens were able to survive quite well with the kindness and generosity of their relatives. Through the 1930s, her sister Helen and husband Andrew Worobetz continued to give them products such as eggs, salted cottage cheese, pork, beef, chickens and vegetables.

To ease the financial pressures in a depressed economy, the Stechishins continued to board paying students in the late 1930s. It appears that for them economic pressures were not as severe as for other Canadians since they were able to afford a non-Ukrainian housekeeper.[45] Although an exclusively Ukrainian-speaking household, the English language began to be used occasionally because of the presence of non-Ukrainian students and the non-Ukrainian housekeeper. However, the parents continued to speak Ukrainian exclusively to the children in their home. Savella believed that the children would learn English when playing with other children and at school.

The National Executive of the UWAC had been headquartered in Edmonton under the presidency of Daria Yanda in 1935 and part of 1936. Daria was unable to carry on longer to the end of her term so Savella accepted the presidency of the UWAC again in the summer of 1936. Savella's visits in Saskatchewan as president in previous years had helped to increase membership and the National Executive decided that this tactic would be tried in Manitoba, hopefully with positive results. Again in her role as president of the UWAC, to increase the membership Savella visited all the Manitoba branches in the fall of 1938. At the same time, Savella took the opportunity to promote the idea of collecting artifacts for a proposed museum. Once again, the National Executive was centered in Saskatoon keeping Savella and the other members of the Executive busy writing and sending directives to the branches springing up across Western and Central Canada.

A convention was held that year in Saskatoon. Hundreds came from across Canada. With the depression there was little money for hotels, so the convention participants stayed wherever they could without payment. The Stechishins' bungalow was overflowing with relatives and friends sleeping on the floor in the living and dining rooms and anywhere else one could lie down. Mohyla Institute was also brimming with people sleeping on floors. Youth was very well represented. Olgerd Bochkowsky, a historian from the Podebrady Ukrainian Academy in Czechoslovakia, was the guest speaker. He was touring Canada at this time, encouraging the Ukrainian Canadians to retain their heritage and take an interest in the political situation in Ukraine. Savella gave a speech at the convention recounting the activities and the achievements of the first ten years of UWAC. She again stressed the importance of preserving Ukrainian culture in Canada by collecting cultural items, and she presented a plan that items of museum value should be housed in the two prairie Institutes, Mohyla and Hrushevsky.

As president, she along with the National Executive, steered the UWAC branches within the guidelines as defined in *"Poshyrennya prohramu Soiuzu ukrainok Kanady na rik 1936-1937"* (Broadening the Program of the Ukrainian Women's Association of Canada for 1936-37).[46] These guidelines became the fundamental elements of the movement, the tenets for the women in the UWAC branches to follow. Though Savella intensified her program, it would be considered to be within narrow confines when compared to the activities performed by women in the broader society. Some of the guidelines she was instrumental in developing included establishing *ridni shkoly* (Ukrainian language schools) in community halls, celebrating Mother's Day, and teaching Sunday School, and within the home, celebrating Ukrainian holidays, subscribing to and reading Ukrainian language newspapers and magazines and keeping a 'Ukrainian' home. For many years through to the present day, branches of the UWAC dotting the prairies and the rest of Canada follow these guidelines.

Although these tenets were similar to the organizations of mainstream women, they did not encompass the contentious issues voiced by the mainstream women's organizations, such as birth control, domestic violence and poverty. The UWAC stressed the 'Ukrainian' aspect instead of the 'woman' aspect in the sphere of women's concerns always with their ethnic group in mind. Members of the UWAC agreed with the tenets prescribed by the leaders, so there was no evidence of discord amongst the membership. Women who did not appreciate the mandate of the UWAC did not join.

During the decade 1926 to 1936, the National Executive prepared the following articles listed in the *Iuvileina knyzhka* as guidelines for implementation of the tents by the branches:[47] ten articles on organizational methods (six written by Savella Stechishin), eight articles regarding the promotion of honouring mothers on Mother's Day (the first one by Savella), two articles celebrating Ukraine's Independence Day (the first contributed by Savella), fourteen articles describing the lives and work of national leaders and writers (three by Savella), seven topics on the celebration of Ukrainian literature (Savella contributed three), six directives on education (religious, Easter customs), four articles all written by Savella on Ukrainian folk art (folk costumes, pysanky and embroidery), and nine items discussing household management (six contributed by Savella). In every case, except education, Savella wrote the first article that was distributed to the branches. Collections of prepared materials for the celebration of Lesia Ukrainka (see Appendix A), Easter, Independence Day, Mother's Day, and patterns for Ukrainian embroidery and *pysanky* were also made available to the branches.

At the close of the first decade of the founding of the UWAC, Savella and her executive concluded there was need to enhance their agenda in order to more successfully achieve their aims. In 1936 Savella writes that the foregoing tenets must be "broadened" (perhaps more accurately described as intensified) to emphasize the importance of three tasks: education (Ukrainian), national folk arts and home improvement.[48] These three tasks were the responsibility of every good mother in order to cultivate Ukrainian culture within the home and thus, collectively, Ukrainians in Canada would not be lost to the dominant Anglo-Canadian society.

To achieve the educational component, each mother was to maintain in the home the Ukrainian language, religion, holidays and songs, read Ukrainian books and newspapers, retell traditional folklore and stories of national heroes and "sacrifice for good national aims."[49] Outside the home, each member was to actively participate in her immediate community by teaching *ridna shkola* (Ukrainian school), Sunday School and officially celebrating Ukrainian holidays. As homemaker, she was expected to provide a Ukrainian cultural, patriotic and religious atmosphere for her family. Savella, the members of the UWAC and the nationalist/intelligentsia community assumed that Ukrainian women were primarily responsible for family life (within a Ukrainian context). This general philosophy of the woman bearing the major responsibility for family life is still alive in many communities in the Western world. For example, Sheva Medjuck, a sociologist, contends that the Canadian-Jewish community is a still strong proponent of this conviction.[50]

Ukrainian folk arts, visible symbols of 'Ukrainianness', were also high on the list of means of improving both Ukrainians' self-perception and their image in the eyes of the world. Savella strongly urged each member of the UWAC to become aware of the authenticity of patterns and colours of embroidery for folk costumes from different regions. These patterns could be adapted also to modern household items, such as runners and pillow cases, and to modern dress emphasizing pride in her Ukrainian heritage. A collection of *pysanky* (Easter eggs) along with the embroidered linens were to be displayed as a positive sign of a Ukrainian home. Easter egg writing was encouraged since the *pysanka*, a visible symbol, was considered an important Ukrainian treasure. The folk arts of embroidery, pysanky writing and weaving were to be taught to girls and competitions held to stimulate interest amongst the girls and thus instil pride in their culture. Patterns and instructions were sent by the National Executive (written by Savella in the 1930s) to all branches to help the membership enact these suggestions.

The last task for the mother to fulfil her duties as a good member of the Ukrainian community was to improve and modernize the home. This was important so that, as Savella succinctly wrote in 1937, *nashi dity ikh ne stydalyya* (our children will not be ashamed of them).[51] Women were to conform to contemporary convention and values, abandoning primitive methods and habits practised in the old country. The good Ukrainian homemaker was to provide the appropriate physical environment together with instilling a Ukrainian *dusha* (spirit) in her children. Savella did not emphasize preparation of Ukrainian dishes and baking. Recipes and culinary practices were handed down from mother to daughter so that knowledge of these skills was taken for granted. Also, since Ukrainian dishes were fairly basic, cookery was not considered important enough to enhance the image of Ukrainians at this time.

A decade later, the National Executive of the UWAC, headquartered in Winnipeg, reinforced and expanded Savella's tenets. In 1947, they published a book titled *Na storozhi kultury* (*Guardians of Culture*), in which the themes of appropriate behaviour and activism for the Ukrainian supermom were elaborated. This book served as a guide for the members as it defined methods of preserving and promoting the Ukrainian language, culture, religion and folk arts in the home and community. Additionally, it explained the traditional customs of celebrating Christmas and Easter and included recipes and how to set a proper table for the holidays.[52]

Still involved with guiding the UWAC, Savella began work with the Women's Department at the University of Saskatchewan in 1937 with the Cooperative Schools sponsored by the Saskatchewan Wheat Pool. In exchange for the financial aid that the Wheat Pool gave to the university, professors and speakers were asked to speak to farmers on topics relating to agricultural practices. Savella was asked to lecture on topics of interest to women from October to Christmas. She elected to speak on the use of the pressure cooker in food preservation. For this work she received a wage. The designated area for her presentation was again the Ukrainian bloc settlements of Sheho, Foam Lake, Yellow Creek, Alticane, Glaslyn, Hafford, Whitkow and the surrounding districts.[53] She travelled with the professors who spoke on agriculture.

The Ukrainian-Canadian population in Saskatchewan had been gradually increasing from the arrival of the first immigrants at the turn of the century until the middle of the twentieth century. With no dramatic shift in the demographics of Ukrainian women in Saskatchewan, the location of additional UWAC branches followed the pattern of the initial ones. In 1931, 16 percent of Ukrainian women resided in urban areas while 84 percent were rural, and in 1941 the distribution was similar, with urban at 19 percent and rural at 81 percent. With the large concentration of women in the rural area, branches were not only surviving but thriving. When some became defunct, others would replaced them just a few miles away, still within the bloc settlements, as the population shifted slightly and certain communities became more vibrant. Once the economic state of the Ukrainian-Canadian rural population improved, they were able to build their own churches and *narodni domy* (community halls). Members of the UWAC then held their meetings and social activities in the newly constructed *narodni domy*, whereas previously they had been meeting at the homes of the members. Once a hall was built, sometimes two branches would amalgamate to become one, centring at the hall. The population base was thus able to sustain leaders and workers to allow the branches to fulfill their agenda and the social aspect of the women's sphere and community life.

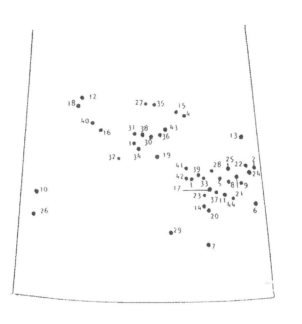

Figure 1:

Location of UWAC Branches in Saskatchewan in 1936

1 Alvena; 2 Arran ; 3 Bankend; 4 Brooksby (**2**); 5 Buchanan; 6 Calder; 7 Candiac; 8 Canora; 9 Donwell; 10 Eatonia; 11 Edmore; 12 Glaslyn; 13 Glen Elder; 14 Goodeve; 15 Gronlid (**2**); 16 Hafford; 17 Insinger (**2**); 18 Marlin; 19 Meacham; 20 Melville; 21 Mikado; 22 Norquay; 23 Parkerview; 24 Pell; 25 Preeceville; 26 Prelate; 27 Prince Albert; 28 Rama; 29 Regina; 30 Reynaud; 31 St. Julien; 32 Saskatoon; 33 Sheho; 34 Smuts; 35 Strong Pine; 36 Tarnopol; 37 Theodore; 38 Wakaw; 39 West Bend; 40 Whitkow; 41 Wimmer; 42 Wishart; 43 Yellow Creek; 44 Yorkton

During the first two decades, 1926 to 1946, the year in which the largest number of branches was functioning was 1936, with forty-seven branches. They were located almost entirely in the bloc settlements (see Figure 1). The impact of the women's movement initiated by Savella Stechishin and other women activists in her milieu was widespread in the areas inhabited by Ukrainian-Canadians, most especially in the rural areas. Women naturally gravitated to those of similar interests and bonded in their commonality of language, socio-economic background and religion.

Savella strongly urged the membership to buy books for their libraries located in the community halls and eight branches specifically stated that they had done so. The Meacham branch stated, "*A tovarystvo prydbalo svoyim koshtom knyzhok do biblioteky na 170 dolyariv*" (The branch spent $170.00 to purchase books for the library.).[54] The Gronlid branch, with a membership of only eighteen in 1929, over roughly a decade spent $753.05 for books for its library. In the *Zolotyi vinets: Pivstolittia viddilue soiuz ukrainok Kanady imeny Marii Markovych u Kanori, Saskachevan, 1926-1976* (Canora's *50th Anniversary Jubilee Book*), the Canora membership found the suggestions espoused by the National Executive as precisely fitting the path they wanted to follow. When Savella introduced the idea of honouring mothers on a special day (Mother's Day), the Canora branch responded, "When in 1928 the National headquarters of the UWAC in Saskatoon held its first Mother's Day, the Canora Branch promptly followed their example. In the Association's records we find that on 13 May 1928, the Canora Branch held its first Mother's Day."[55]

Unlike the Homemakers' Club in Canada that encouraged women to serve others, support hospitals, district nurses and child clinics and during the depression do relief work,[56] Savella Stechishin and the UWAC did not specifically promote these activities other than to merely suggest participation in their communities. However, some branches did help financially in building hospitals. Both organizations took part in charity work with the Red Cross during the

Second World War.

Savella expended much energy in defence of her ancestral home and informing the branches of the political situation of Ukraine. News of Polish abuses of Ukrainians in Western Ukraine during the late 1920s had reached Canada by 1930, and the *Ukrainian Voice* reported assorted atrocities committed by the Polish army.[57] Incensed by what Ukrainian Canadians saw as an absolute injustice, in 1938 Savella wrote in the *Ukrainian Voice* asking the branches and individuals to protest the violence by writing letters of protest to (1) the Government of Poland through the Canadian Consulate, (2) the Government of Canada, Foreign Relations Department, and (3) the General Secretary of the League of Nations, Geneva.[58] Even *Soiuz ukrainok* came under suspicion for subversive activity against the Polish government, resulting in the police in 1938 closing their offices and arresting all branch presidents.[59] The intent of writing letters of protest was primarily to inform the general Canadian public of the subjugation of Ukrainians in their own country, but only modest success was achieved. As a result, little was accomplished to alleviate the repression of the Ukrainians by the Poles.

Ukrainian-Canadian women tended to ghettoize within their own community, and the Anglo-Canadian women's organizations on the whole left them to their own people. The differences in religion, customs, tradition, language and history separated Ukrainian-Canadian women from their Anglo-Canadian sisters and other ethnic women. As the years pass, the edges of both communities, Ukrainian and Anglo-Canadian, have continued to blur as positive interactions and understandings have evolved.

6

Home for Ukrainian Treasures

In December 1922, Savella had been present when Dr. Osyp Nazaruk, a representative of the failed Western Ukraine National Republic (1918-1919), in his address at the Ukrainian National Convention in Saskatoon, suggested that Mohyla Institute house a museum. He recommended that there be an initiative to collect Ukrainian artifacts brought over by the immigrants as these artifacts were beginning to be destroyed. He added that a collection of Ukrainian books and ethnographic material be included in the museum.[1] Most of the people attending the convention agreed that this was an excellent idea. However, the poor financial state of the Institute did not permit the project to come to fruition – at that time. Savella was very enthused with the idea of a museum. Beginning in 1927, she put her heart into devising a strategy to establish a museum for Ukrainian articles and continued in this direction for a decade until personality conflicts got in the way of her participation. After a decade of hard work on her dream of a museum, Savella left the project for various personal reasons, although the project never really left her. Even though the museum steadily grew over the years, she still felt a responsibility for it, to the point of setting the record straight concerning the origin of the museum in the waning years of her life. She did so by writing in her favourite newspaper, the *Ukrainian Voice*, her version of the history of the Ukrainian Museum of Canada in Saskatoon.

To start at the beginning, Savella credits not only Dr. Nazaruk but also Rev. Kudryk for being responsible for the creation of the museum. Rev. Vasyl Kudryk, a single, well educated, Ukrainian Greek Orthodox priest, was serving in the Saskatoon Ukrainian Greek Orthodox church and in a number of churches in the outlying districts. A collector of historical items and residing at Mohyla Institute, he began encouraging people in the countryside and the cities to collect or donate various artifacts, such as embroidered clothing and linens, woodcraft and implements, to Mohyla Institute. Alternatively, members of the Ukrainian community halls located in the bloc settlements were urged to start up their own museums where items could be preserved for future generations. The collection and preservation of their artifacts would give value and pride to their heritage and in turn to themselves, the good reverend thought.

Over the years, many articles had been left to fall into disrepair, were destroyed or forsaken, as many Ukrainian immigrants and their families believed that these vestiges of their culture were now an embarrassment. This was the era of 'progress' and 'modernism,' movements that deplored antiquated forms. Also, Ukrainians were often looked upon by other nationalities as clinging to their backward and unsophisticated ways and, thus, would not be good, contributing Canadian citizens. For those Ukrainians succumbing to the humiliation engendered by such discrimination, it was paramount to adopt Canadian dress and values and even to Anglicize their names – to blend in and be unhyphenated Canadians. They decided that life would be easier if they made these changes; they could then assimilate into the dominant society, thus affording themselves more opportunity for material wealth and happiness.

In Saskatoon, the organization "Arts and Crafts Guild" in the 1920s was collecting handicrafts from as many nationalities as possible. Despite the contemporary trend towards modernism, there were still people in the influential stratum of Canadian society who placed value on traditional and old world craftsmanship. In 1923, contact was made between the Mohylianky and the Guild.[2] Savella urged the Mohylianky to begin collecting handicraft articles, such as embroidery and *pysanky*. They also set up demonstrations in

Saskatoon on how to write *pysanky* and organized exhibits of the regional differences in style of Ukrainian folk costumes. Because Ukrainians did not have a well known identity in the 1920s, Ukrainian embroidery was sometimes misrepresented as Russian embroidery. It was a difficult task for Savella and the Mohylianky to educate the Canadian public in Saskatoon. However, this challenge served to fuel educated Mohylianky to fervently pursue their mission to enlighten both Ukrainians and the general public of the importance of this skilled, beautifully executed handicraft.

In the late 1920s, Savella taught embroidery, *pysanka* writing and Ukrainian folk costuming to the girls residing at Mohyla Institute. Years later she wrote, "I felt it incumbent upon myself to pass on my knowledge about the Ukrainian folk arts to our students."[3] Savella theorized that the making of Ukrainian handicrafts and the gathering of Ukrainian 'treasures' for showcasing in a museum went hand in hand. At the national convention of UWAC in Saskatoon in 1927, in her speech, Savella stressed the importance of Ukrainian folk art, how it was not only falling by the wayside, but also how it was being misrepresented as Russian. So that the general public would be accurately informed, a collection of Ukrainian artifacts was necessary.

The germ of the idea of a museum had been planted by Dr. Nazaruk, and Savella built on it. This dream was one of the reasons for the Stechishins' trip to Western Ukraine in 1928, as she stated, "My husband was on a mission to buy books and procure archival material for the proposed museum in the Petro Mohyla Institute." But, it was the University of Saskatchewan Museum that acted as the catalyst for her resolute desire in establishing a museum, for it had determined that something had to be done to enlighten the uninformed public about Ukrainian folk costuming and handicrafts. To Savella's chagrin, a Bukovynian folk costume obtained by the University from the Sheho area had been labelled Austrian. In order for the University of Saskatchewan Museum to have an accurate and appropriate representation of Ukrainian folk art, in 1929 Savella, on behalf of the UWAC, presented the Museum Committee with a splendid authentic, hand embroidered Ukrainian linen table runner featuring a geometric design, a handmade magnificent straw jewellery case and a hand-woven delicate basket. A concerted effort was begun by the executive of the national Ukrainian Women's Association to collect authentic but good quality handicraft articles to donate to the University's museum assortment of artifacts.[4]

Savella often spoke with Rev. Kudryk and was fascinated with his idea of forming a large collection of Ukrainian cultural artifacts. Knowing her talent for writing and her tenacity, he urged her to write in the UWAC section of the *Ukrainian Voice* to encourage Ukrainians to gather various items still in good condition and to preserve them. She wrote with determination and purpose in the *Ukrainian Voice Almanac* in 1930, "About the History of Ukrainian Embroidery". Savella appealed to the readership to donate and collect various Ukrainian articles, such as folk dress, weaving, woodwork objects, *pysanky*, and embroidered articles and to store them with care in community halls. "Get in touch with Ukrainians in Canada who still live in an 'old country' manner. Gather or buy from them those items related to folk dress, weaving, wood engraving, and so forth. Every region should have something in the form of a small museum in its Ukrainian community hall which reflects the material culture of the Ukrainians who first settled there."[5] Her appeal was the first of its kind in the press for the collection and preservation of artifacts reflecting Ukrainian heritage.

From 1931 to 1933, Savella again taught a course in Ukrainian handicraft (embroidery, *pysanky*, folk costume patterns) and home economics at Mohyla Institute as she had done in the 1920s.[6] Most of the young women who boarded at Mohyla attended Normal School and enjoyed taking this course to enhance their knowledge. They then went into the bloc settlements to teach school after graduating and on the side taught the handicraft skills to the local women and girls. This was a successful method of raising awareness of Ukrainian handicrafts among Ukrainian-Canadian people, with the bonus that it might have a ripple effect touching non-Ukrainians as well.

At the time of Savella's presidency, the National Executive of the UWAC requested an annual fee of five dollars from each branch to purchase pieces of Ukrainian folk art for the University of Saskatchewan Museum's collection. However, by 1933 the branches were beginning to feel that five dollars was too much of a financial burden for their members to bear given the escalating economic depression, so the fee was discontinued. However, not to be deterred, it was decided at the 1933 national convention, spearheaded by Savella as President, that the UWAC should have its own collection of handicrafts to be based at Mohyla Institute.[7]

In 1935 the change of venue of the UWAC convention, in conjunction with the Ukrainian Self-Reliance League of Canada and the Canadian Ukrainian Youth Association (CUYA) (*Soiuz ukrainskoii molodi Kanady*), from Mohyla to a large building on the Exhibition grounds was a good choice. The turnout was excellent and well represented by all organizations in the USRL family. The executive, now under the presidency of Daria Yanda in Edmonton, set up a very large and well organized exhibit of exquisite Ukrainian handmade articles that had been collected from families across Canada. Some articles were made in Canada, but most had been brought from Ukraine by pioneers. Articles, such as beautifully and meticulously embroidered linens, blouses, dresses, woven runners and vibrantly coloured *kylymy* (tapestry/rugs), carved wooden articles, and *pysanky* were exhibited and highly appreciated by all participants at the convention and admired by the general public. Of particular fascination was the *kylym*, an ornamented woven fabric used to cover floors or to adorn walls. Peasants had used these in Ukraine since at least the 10th century. In the late 19th and 20th centuries, *kylymy* were widely used as symbolic elements for weddings and funerals and decoratively in homes, where they covered walls, benches and tables.

Originally flax and hemp were the raw materials, but later wool dominated. Savella gave a rivetting speech at the UWAC session in which she vigorously stressed the prime importance of preserving Ukrainian cultural heritage. She also earnestly encouraged the branches to begin "collecting items of museum value and store them in specially built cabinets in the local community halls."[8]

In the *Iuvileina knyzhka* (UWAC 10th Anniversary Book), Savella, in her article *Ukrainske Narodne Mystetstvo* (Ukrainian Folk Arts), argues the importance of keeping folk costuming authentic and the pride one must have in this inherited art form.[9] Also, she emphasizes ten *sposoby plekannya narodnoho mystetstva* (methods of care for folk art) that were of absolute necessity to instil pride and to enlighten Ukrainian women in Canada. These are:

1) broaden knowledge of folk art patterns;
2) relate patterns to modern household needs and dress;
3) collect *pysanky* and folk costumes and then send these to the UWAC for their collection and they will be available to all;
4) compulsory subscription to *Nova khata*;
5) organize evenings where folk costumes could be worn;
6) those individuals who can weave organize a workshop;
7) organize projects of handicrafts for girls;
8) organize a project for embroidery;
9) organize exhibitions and contests of embroidery, *pysanky*, folk costumes;
10) establish museums in Ukrainian community halls.[10]

Savella wrote many well researched pertinent articles on the foregoing ten topics in her directives to the branches across Canada during her tenure as president in the periods 1928-1934 and 1936-37.[11] She utilized the publication *Nova khata*, where articles on handicraft topics were written by experts, including historical facts together with 'how-to' instructions. Because embroidery and *pysanky* writing traditionally fell into the women's realm of activities, Savella was determined to revive interest in these age-old art forms, these treasures, amongst women. The artistically inclined women pioneers in the bloc settlements had continued to write *pysanky* for the Easter holidays and to embroider blouses and runners. However, with the burden of pioneer life on the prairies, time was precious so that some women discontinued these practices. In a few cases, women did teach their daughters handicrafts, but the general neglect over teaching the art of *pysanky* writing and embroidery stemmed from the belief that these arts were too trivial, or the younger generation showed little interested in them because they were considered old country hobbies. Women in urban settings had more leisure time and these women, along with rural women, Savella targeted and encouraged to become interested in Ukrainian embroidery and *pysanky* writing. Savella deemed it her mission to insist that this folk art be recognized as a genuine art form, similar to fine art, and, thus, acceptable to the host society at a time when the host society regarded Ukrainian embroidery and *pysanky* writing to be inferior. Many Canadians considered Ukrainians "inferior and undesirable foreigners" and by association their dress and folk art were also considered inferior.

Continuing on her path to ensure that Ukrainian artifacts were not destroyed, at the 1936 convention, Savella in her presentation underscored the importance of urgently acquiring cultural items in good condition for preservation and presented her plan to house these items at Mohyla Institute and Hrushevsky Institute in Edmonton. Her proposal was well received and in response the following resolution was passed: "This convention considers folk arts and crafts important and indispensable and we must put all our effort into their development. This convention urges us all to support the UWAC's action in setting up a museum of Ukrainian folk arts and crafts in our Institutes."[12] This resolution was the first step to specifically form a museum. The outcome, however, was that only Mohyla ended up accommodating a museum. This is most likely because Savella and the executive of the UWAC resided in Saskatoon, and they were determined to have the resolution fulfilled.

Shortly after the 1936 National Convention, Savella convened an executive meeting to deal with the resolution to establish a museum. The newly elected executive consisted of: Savella - President; Helen Hnatyshyn - Vice-President; Anastasia Ruryk - Corresponding Secretary; Anne Bilak - Recording Secretary; Mary Tkachuk - Treasurer. With the endorsement of the resolution, Savella presented her plan for a museum to follow the example of the one at the University of Saskatchewan, since she was familiar with this museum, having participated in its acquisition of museum pieces. She clearly and succinctly expressed her opinion that a collection of their (Ukrainians) own was imperative and urged that it begin immediately. The members decided to concentrate on obtaining embroidered articles, since many were available in Canada and would be the easiest to find. Hanka Romanchych of Winnipeg, a visiting friend of all those present, who had been invited to the meeting, began the acquisition process by offering to sell her album of samples of Ukrainian embroidery patterns for $27.50. The album consisted of cut-outs from old but good quality embroidered articles originally brought from Ukraine – it became the museum's first acquisition. What joy the women experienced, now that they saw their first tangible item! Savella was exhilarated to see her dream becoming a reality.

The 50th Anniversary book "A Half-Century of Service to the Community" of the UWAC states that the "first acquisitions of embroidery designs, shirts and other suitable artifacts collected by Hanka Romanchych formed the basis for the permanent museum collection of the Ukrainian Women's Association of Canada. This collection, numbering approximately 200 items, included early embroidery designs, samples of household weaving, belts, shirts and other articles, which were collected in the rural communities of western Canada, primarily in the province of Alberta."[13]

Savella and Anastasia Ruryk, the secretary, were good friends and worked well together. But, because Anastasia was not well, Savella drafted a circular letter about this new venture, the museum, appealing to branches and all other Ukrainian Canadians to comb their communities for articles in good condition brought to Canada by Ukrainian immigrants. "As president, it was my duty to start the museum project going." Continuing her quest that articles be definitively accurate and true to Ukrainian design and pattern and in order to obtain authentic written material on costuming, arts and crafts of Ukraine, Savella wrote to prominent women activists in Western Ukraine with whom she had been corresponding regularly. They were Lydia Burachynska, editor of *Nova khata* in L'viv, the Cooperative of Hutzul Crafts in Kosiw (still today, the leading centre in Ukraine for Ukrainian folk arts), the women's *Hromada* in Chernivtsi, Bukovyna, and Iryna Pavlykovska, manager-director of the Women's Cooperative of Ukrainian Arts and Crafts in L'viv. The executive then ordered that an ethnographic map of Ukraine be designed showing costumes and arts typical of a given ethnographic area. This map was made by Ukrainian engineers at the Podebrady Academy in Czechoslovakia. Not only did the executive receive material aid, but by the end of the year they received patterns of stunning handmade Ukrainian embroidery arranged in distinctive albums and an assortment of *pysanky* with many symbolic and identifiable designs. To their delight, they also received a pair of enchanting dolls in authentic Ukrainian costumes from L'viv. With no official physical storage space, some of these artifacts had to be stored in Savella's home and others in the secretary's home.

Under Savella's leadership and in her capacity as president, the National Executive officially launched the "Ukrainian Arts and Crafts Museum" in 1936. For several reasons, the ideal location for the Museum was the Petro Mohyla Institute. The Institute was already imbued with a national spirit and had become an important centre for Ukrainians on the prairies and it served as the location of the national office of the UWAC. As well, artifacts could be drawn from a large nearby pool by way of donations because of the large Ukrainian population in the surrounding bloc settlements. Having carefully conceived her strategy, Savella took her ideas on tour.

Savella was not content to have a single Ukrainian museum on the prairies. At the annual convention of M. Hrushevsky Institute in Edmonton and the Alberta provincial Ukrainian Self-Reliance League, held in Edmonton the first two days of a cold January in 1937, Savella representing the UWAC took the opportunity to speak about her pet project, the realization of a museum. She created a flurry of interest. That same year, in June she attended the CUYA convention and jamboree in Hafford, Saskatchewan, where again she spoke about the proposed museum and asked those in attendance to help by donating items that would qualify for display in a museum.

She also explained that money was needed to build up a fund for museum purposes. Continuing on this theme, she delivered the keynote speech at the UWAC national convention in Saskatoon the following month, where she stated in no uncertain terms the value of preserving the Ukrainian cultural heritage and the importance of a museum. She had samples of artifacts to show the attendees and appealed for their help in collecting articles of museum value. At this convention, the National Executive, headquartered in Saskatoon, had organized an exhibit of authentic Ukrainian folk costumes and modern dress with Ukrainian embroidery.

With momentum for the Ukrainian folk art museum growing, Savella was asked to speak at the CUYA jamboree held at Sandy Lake, Manitoba later in July. Accompanying other delegates, she travelled in the Mohyla Institute company car with John Kishchuk, the rector, with a plan to speak about her dream. The CUYA jamboree was a disappointment due to a lack of interest. Undaunted by rambunctious youth, she attended a CUYA convention in Pine River, Manitoba in October, 1938 which turned out to be well organized and fruitful for all attending. This was an opportunity to inform the younger Ukrainian-Canadian generation about her cherished project, a Ukrainian museum, and the need to collect museum articles. Beginning on September 30 and continuing almost daily until October 21, with determination, Savella travelled by train, bus and car to fourteen branches of the UWAC in Manitoba to share information on the sorts of authentic articles to gather so that they would be good enough to form a part of a museum's collection. To have a national president visit rural branches was indeed an honour and a morale booster for the UWAC members scattered throughout Manitoba, and isolated from the national office headquartered in Saskatoon. Many members did not attend national conventions, most likely because of economic and time restraint reasons, and would normally have never met Savella or anyone of her stature in the Ukrainian-Canadian community. She was the elite leadership visiting the rank and file.

Ukrainian cultural artifacts soon began to trickle in from the branches, individuals, and even from Western Ukraine. By now, there was an impressive selection of intricately designed *pysanky* and well appointed albums brimming with exquisite handmade embroidery samples. Cash donations were also increasing. Since there was no available space at Mohyla for these articles, they continued to be stored in boxes and suitcases in the homes of Savella and Anastasia Ruryk.

Although occupied with pursuing her goal of launching a museum, Savella as president, continued to participate in other activities. As a teaching aid and for general interest, in 1937 she put out a brochure titled *Ukrainskyi narodnyi stryi* (Ukrainian National Costumes). In the fall of 1937, the UWAC received an announcement that an organization of all Ukrainian women world wide had been created: the World Union of Ukrainian Women (*Svitovyi soiuz ukrainok*). It was conceived at the general meeting of *Souiz Ukrainok* in L'viv on October 9-10, 1937 with Milena Rudnytska as president. The unity of Ukrainian women in a common cause was a great achievement in Savella's eyes. UWAC sent a letter of congratulation expressing their support and willingness to join this organization. However, the euphoria and hopes and dreams of this organization were crushed by the beginning of World War II, in which Ukraine served as one of the main theatres of war.

Excitement stirred in the Ukrainian community in Saskatoon

in November of that same year because Hetmanych Danylo Skoropadsky, the son of former Hetman Pavlo Skoropadsky (1918) had arrived for a visit. As noted in an earlier chapter, Savella and Julian had met Pavlo in his Berlin headquarters in August 1928 on their way to Ukraine. In 1934, a group of Ukrainian sympathizers of the monarchic hetmanate (period ruled by a hetman) regime of Pavlo Skoropadsky had organized branches of the United Hetman Organization (UHO) in Canada and were dedicated to the restoration of a Ukrainian state under Hetman Pavlo Skoropadsky or his descendants. This organization supported the claim of Danylo Skoropadsky to the throne of an independent Ukraine and sponsored his visit to various cities in Canada. In 1940, the UHO became one of the founding organizations of the Ukrainian Canadian Committee (Congress). The movement declined after the Second World War, weakened by internal divisions and the death of Pavlo and Danylo Skoropadsky. Today, it no longer functions and has been taken over by the League of Ukrainians. Though the Saskatoon branch of the Hetman organization in the late 1930s did not have many members and the Stechishins were not members, to accord Mr. Skoropadsky the respect which Saskatchewan Ukrainians felt he deserved, he was hosted at a banquet at Mohyla Institute. Nevertheless, some criticism of him by opponents of the monarchical system he represented appeared in Ukrainian circles, but this does not seem to have brought about any discord within the Ukrainian community. His visit as prince and successor to the throne of an independent Ukraine even earned a write-up in the *Star Phoenix*.

Savella was quite impressed, as were many others, especially women, with him: "He was tall and handsome, in his thirties, polished and courteous in his manners just like a court gentleman should be."[14] At this time, he was living in London, England and spoke English fluently as well as Ukrainian, German, French and Russian. The day after the banquet, the UWAC held a pre-Christmas tea and sale of Ukrainian embroidered articles at the Elite Café on Second Avenue. Mr. Skoropadsky paid them a visit, where he drew a lot of attention. The enterprising local branch of UWAC asked him to autograph small handmade pin cushions, which they had for sale. These were then sold to the public as souvenirs at a very profitable price.

After her presidency ended in 1939, Savella stepped back from the UWAC and no longer involved herself in the running of the organization, locally, provincially or nationally. Several sources hint of personality clashes among some members of the UWAC in Saskatoon, and so she wisely decided to divert her energies towards more productive and challenging activities. Curiously, after so much enthusiasm, she also divested herself of any interest in the museum, again likely due to personality clashes.

Julian was elected national president of the Ukrainian Self-Reliance League of Canada in 1940. Savella wrote, "He was a good speaker and was in demand everywhere at Ukrainian gatherings." He, like Savella, had a love for his people and he worked tirelessly to achieve his vision of elevating them to as high a level as possible in Canadian society. This vision was at the top of his priorities, even his law practice was secondary. In conversations with the author, Savella stated rather proudly and without reservation that Julian was a scholar, more interested in working diligently in the Ukrainian community and writing about the experiences of Ukrainian Canadians than working at his profession for material wealth. "We were not well off like other lawyers." Although she was no longer national president of the UWAC, she was still in demand as a speaker at various conventions and she accompanied Julian on his engagements as national president of USRL. "I always went with him." They were a team.

Members of the National Executive of the UWAC in Saskatoon meanwhile continued the campaign for genuine articles representative of Ukrainian culture to add to the museum. As the collection grew, the executive requested the Board of Directors of Mohyla Institute for permission to store their collection at Mohyla Institute. Permission was granted and all the articles were then moved from members' houses and deposited at Mohyla. The original gallery of the Museum of Ukrainian Arts and Culture of the Ukrainian Women's Association of Canada opened its first displays in Mohyla Institute in 1941, quickly increasing its collection with donated artifacts.[15] Once the Ukrainians on the prairies became aware of its existence and became more nationally conscious, rather than throwing out "old personal Ukrainian-related possessions" they sent or took them to Mohyla. Small museums sprang up in church basements and community halls in Ukrainian communities across Canada. Items such as old folk costumes, embroidery, weaving, wood carvings, tools, small implements, books, magazines, newspapers and various ornaments found their way to Mohyla and to the small museums. On April 8, 1976 the museum at Mohyla was incorporated under the name "Museum of Ukrainian Arts and Culture of the Ukrainian Women's Association of Canada" and in 1980 the name was changed by Supplementary Letters Patent to "Ukrainian Museum of Canada of the Ukrainian Women's Association of Canada." The Museum remained at Mohyla until the construction of a new facility was completed in 1979 in Saskatoon.

With the brand new building, the museum was moved from the cramped quarters of Mohyla Institute to a home of 3,965 square metres. The new and renamed Ukrainian Museum of Canada on 910 Spadina Crescent East, owned by the Ukrainian Women's Association of Canada, was officially opened on May 24, 1980. The new facility, resembling a Ukrainian pioneer thatched roof house, was designed by Matthew Stankiewicz of Ottawa. It includes not only a permanent exhibit area, but also an activity centre, a small library, an auditorium, a special collections gallery and a gallery lounge. This new facility was designed to not only accommodate a collection of Ukrainian artifacts, but also to serve as an education centre. The Special Collections Gallery opened in October 2004 exhibiting the UWAC's valuable collection of paintings by the renown Ukrainian-Canadian painter, William Kurelek. He had been commissioned by UWAC to paint a twelve-part series entitled "Ukrainian Pioneer

Women" to commemorate Canada's Centennial in 1967.

A feature article about the museum entitled "'Visionaries' Maintain Ukrainian Culture", that the local daily newspaper, the *Star-Phoenix* carried on the day of the opening, prompted Savella to write her own article in Ukrainian to repudiate some of the information reported in the *Star-Phoenix* article.[16]   Her article was published in the *Ukrainian Voice* on August 13, 1980. Savella took umbrage at some of what she considered to have been conspicuous omissions and serious distortions about the origins of the museum in the *Star-Phoenix* article that had been based on interviews with employees of the museum at that time. Savella wrote, "The article noted: 'There were four visionaries – Mary Maduke, Rose Dragan, Mary Tkachuk and Hanka Romanchych-Kowalchuk, all members of the Ukrainian Women's Association of Canada, who were the most active when the museum first opened in 1936.' The same information was conveyed during the opening ceremonies and in two radio interviews with Marie Kishchuk and Linda Lazarowich [employees of the museum]."[17]   Savella further illuminates in her article in the *Ukrainian Voice*:

> Nothing – large or small – appears ready-made out of thin air. This certainly was the case with the Museum, which did not miraculously appear in 1936 with the wave of a magic wand or a shout of the word, "Bingo". The history of the museum has a long beginning in which the groundwork was being laid. This early history is linked closely with UWAC's work, for as the activities of the Women's Association expanded every year, the need for a museum became more obvious.   These early beginnings and the founding of the Museum took place during those years when I was the president of the Women's Association (Western President in 1927; and then National President from 1928 to 1934 and 1936 to 1939 . . .)
>
> This concerted effort over many years in the area of Ukrainian folk arts gave rise to the need for a collection of embroideries and folk dress under the auspices of the National Executive of the Women's Association. These efforts, in fact, might well be regarded as the first stage in the founding of the Museum, for

> without this popularization of folk arts it is unlikely that a
> Museum would ever have been formed.

She concludes her article with:

> It is clear from the above account (based mainly on documents
> put out by the Ukrainian Women's Association of Canada) that
> the "visionaries" of the Museum were those activists in the
> UWAC National Executive who worked hard, starting in 1927
> to popularize Ukrainian folk art among the membership and then
> establish a Museum in 1936 on this foundation. A number of the
> activists who took part in these campaigns among the
> membership of the Women's Association are still alive. Without
> their ground-breaking efforts, there would be no Museum
> today.[18]

Omission of Savella's contribution as well as the ground work
and early history of the museum upset Savella a great deal. She felt
this was unjust and conveyed those sentiments to the author during
interviews. She was adamant in expressing her version of the history
of the museum and on setting the record straight as she saw it.

In Savella's defence, there is documentation on the history of
the museum. Information about the history of the museum is
recorded in the UWAC's 1936 Anniversary Book and in a readily
available book, *A Quarter Century in the Field of Community Service*
(a 1952 history of UWAC). Both books are written in the Ukrainian
language. *Quarter Century* attributes the origins of the museum to:
"The matter of Ukrainian folk arts was formally raised for the first
time during the Ukrainian Women's Association of Canada
convention of 1927 by Savella Stechishin during a presentation about
the work of the Women's Association for the year. She openly
recognized Ukrainian embroidery as a national treasure, and then
expressed great concern that English Canadians often mistakenly
believed that these were Russian works of folk art. She emphasized,
furthermore, that this situation had to be challenged."[19]

Regarding the controversy of the museum "visionaries", it

seems that Savella had the last word in the Ukrainian sphere of the printed word in her article in the *Ukrainian Voice*. Regardless of the issue of formal recognition, the Ukrainian Museum of Canada in Saskatoon is an important asset, showcasing the contribution by immigrants of Ukraine to Canada and to Canadian culture. Because of the large number of Ukrainian artifacts in Canada, five affiliated branches of the Ukrainian Museum of Canada have been established at Toronto, Winnipeg, Edmonton, Vancouver, and Calgary. Artifacts in the museums encompass agricultural supplies, equipment and tools, clothing and accessories, ceramics and pottery, currency, coins and stamps, household supplies and equipment, icons, jewellery, musical instruments, paintings, posters, *pysanky*, ritual objects, and textiles.[20]

Subsequent generations have placed greater value on the tools and treasures of their forebears, preferring to not only retain these artifacts, but also to make efforts to keep them in the community. That way, the descendants of the Ukrainian pioneers can show off these precious artifacts to their neighbours, fellow citizens and tourists in their community, citing them as important contributions to the development of prairie Canadian society.

7

Successes and Disappointments

On September 10, 1939 as a member of the British Commonwealth, Canada declared war alongside Great Britain against Nazi Germany. Not only did Saskatchewan provide some 80,000 men and women to the Canadian armed forces from 1939 until the end of the war in 1945, the province also supplied a considerable amount of grain to the Commonwealth's military and civilians and provided manpower in armament factories across the country.

Savella was not immune to the exigencies wrought by the war years. The sudden rise in demand for rubber by war-related industries, especially for tires for war vehicles, created a scarcity of rubber rings for sealers used for canning food, which in turn affected her work as a home economist. Sugar was rationed along with gasoline, butter, coffee, meat and other goods. Despite these handicaps, she contributed to the maintenance of the Home Front, for in her capacity as a home economics teacher with the University of Saskatchewan, Department of Women's Work, she was enlisted to help homemakers adjust to these shortages and to improve diets. It remained important for homemakers to preserve the nutritional value of the food as well as stretch their household budget. Professional home economists like Savella received instruction in the process of dehydrating vegetables and fruits and they, in turn, taught the technique to women who attended their lectures. Savella carried with her a dehydrator that had been made at the university, a cabinet with screen shelves on which to place vegetables such as peas, mushrooms, and so on.[1] She also encouraged women to make their own sauerkraut, since sauerkraut contains Vitamin C and important minerals needed to maintain a healthy diet.

In 1939, Savella began giving demonstrations connected to the Co-operative School sponsored by the Department of Women's Work. These demonstrations consisted of co-operative canning, and labour saving devices, as this is what women were doing in the co-operative movement. Her work period began on October 10 and continued to December 14, 1939. She visited hamlets and towns, such as Hafford (30 attendance), Redberry (70 attendance), Krydor (attendance 60), Glaslyn, Martin, Whitkow (attendance 150), Alvena, West Bend, Jedburgh (attendance 150), Insinger (attendance 170), Preeceville, Canora, Yorkton, Drebot, and her alma mater Mohyla Institute. During the summers of the 1940s, Savella continued to work for the Department of Women's Work, at agricultural field days, driving out with professors of agriculture from Saskatoon. These field days were held in the communities where government experimental farms were located (e.g., Swift Current and Melfort). She lectured on home economics or judged exhibits of cooking and sewing. As part of her work with agriculture, she was an invited speaker on February 1, 2, and 3, 1944 at the Ladies' Programme of the Interprovincial Dairy Conference at the Bessborough Hotel in Saskatoon. She spoke on "Home Dehydration of Vegetables." Savella no longer lectured in Ukrainian in the villages and towns in the bloc settlements, as that programme had been discontinued by the University of Saskatchewan.

As the war raged on, imposing rationing and causing many shortages, Savella felt it incumbent to try to help by offering her expertise on nutrition and experience by working for the Women's Department in rural Saskatchewan to a wider audience. She approached the *Ukrainian Voice* to write a column on nutrition, and in 1941 she began a popular series of articles on nutrition. This was an appropriate time to inform Canadians of the nutritive value of consumer goods, because of the war a number of basic foods were not available. Disseminating information of this type was not altogether unprecedented, as newspapers and magazines throughout Canada were already carrying advice on healthy and nutritious foods and the best means of their preparation. When Savella heard that the Saskatoon Council of Women was offering special classes in nutrition, she suggested to her friend, Helen Hnatyshyn, who was on the executive of the Council, that she, Savella, could teach classes on food and nutrition in the Ukrainian language for Ukrainian Canadian women who might not be very well versed in English. Helen took the suggestion to the Council that Savella volunteered to teach similar classes, without pay, in the Ukrainian language in consultation with the Council. When they enthusiastically accepted this plan, Savella offered a one-month class that was well attended by approximately one hundred women. Classes were held Monday, Wednesday and Friday evenings at the Princess Alexandra School.[2] With the intent of helping her Ukrainian-Canadians sisters, Savella seized the opportunity of giving them the opportunities that were already available in the broader community.

With the hardships of war continuing, the Wartime Services Department of the Canadian government believed it important to disseminate information regarding the significance of nutrition and good health in newspapers of all languages in Canada. Savella, always the opportunist especially in the field of journalism, wrote to Ottawa offering her services to fulfill this commitment in Ukrainian language newspapers. Her offer was accepted and she began working for the Wartime Services Department in December 1942 with Dr. Kaye (Kysilewski), the son of her former Ukrainian correspondent, Olena Kysilewska, as her superior.[3] Knowing Dr. Kaye personally and her success in the *Ukrainian Voice* were contributing factors to this decision. The Department prepared press releases for her use, which she incorporated into a column along with her own ideas. These were then sent to Dr. Kaye who, after checking them, sent them to Ukrainian language weeklies in Canada to be placed under the heading "*Vid informatsiynoi usluhy konsumeriv Ottavi*" (Consumer Information Service, Ottawa).[4] She wrote the column until the end of the war in 1945 and was paid the standard rate by the word.[5]

In 1942, Savella discontinued writing articles for the UWAC page because of personality clashes with the National Executive of the UWAC based in Saskatoon. Four years later, with a new executive in Winnipeg, Savella was asked to write her column again. In early 1946, Savella began her column that she named *"Dovkola Domy"* (Around the Home), for the *Ukrainian Voice*, addressing topics such as philosophy, health, homemaking, family life, recipes and subjects that she considered to be of general interest to women. She was paid twenty-five dollars per month for four weekly issues by the UWAC executive. The salary from her writing contributed to the family's household operations. Olha Woycenko was secretary of the UWAC and the bookkeeper for the publishing company, Trident Company that published the *Ukrainian Voice*. Her husband was the editor. Olha and the UWAC president, Natalia Kohuska, were Savella's good friends. It was Olha who suggested that Savella write a weekly column for the UWAC page. A couple of years later, she mentioned to Savella that readers from the Ukrainian Catholic community were now subscribing because of the homemaking topics and recipes in her column. Women subscribers in the Ukrainian communities across Canada and especially on the prairies looked forward to receiving the *Ukrainian Voice* and reading her column. Her column was popular and her name became well known and synonymous with interesting articles that helped her sisters to cope in the ways of everyday life with dignity and enrichment. Writing this column made her a kind of a celebrity amongst Ukrainian Canadians.

These years boosted Savella's journalism career. In December 1945, she received a telegram from the President, Olena Lotosky, of the Ukrainian National Women's League of America (UNWLA) asking her to be the editor of their monthly magazine *Nashe zhyttia* (Our Life). Savella had been suggested by the editor of *Amerika*, a Ukrainian daily newspaper based in Philadelphia, who had read her column in the *Ukrainian Voice*. He had been so impressed with her writing ability that he suggested her as a possible editor of *Nashe zhyttia* to Olena Lototsky. This was indeed very complimentary to Savella. Lototsky did ask her to edit this American magazine, which had a large number of subscribers, and Savella was both surprised and delighted to be asked. An honorarium of $35.00 a month was offered. Although Julian encouraged her to accept, she felt that she was not qualified for the position of editor-in-chief; she believed her skills were not good enough and also, as she replied to Lototsky, "I am not totally familiar with American life."[6] Thus, because of the large responsibility for the entire magazine, she declined the position but agreed to write editorials and other articles of interest to women. An agreement with the Americans was reached and she was paid by the word.

Savella's new job began in January 1946. As she had in her columns in the *Ukrainian Voice*, Savella encouraged Ukrainian-American women to preserve and promote their culture; she believed that women were best suited to do this important task. She urged women to join their UNWLA organization regardless of political or religious affiliation so that together they would be empowered to develop pride in their ethnicity and gender. Savella urged women in both the United States and Canada to be self-sufficient and independent, and work more cooperatively within their organizations. Women should, she told them, establish their own identity, take their place in society and be recognized as equals. In other words, in *Nashe zhyttia*, she was promoting gender equality for "[a]ny work is impossible without women's cooperation as one-half of the population. Only that nation whose women are conscious of their obligations, side by side with men, has a future."[7]

At the end of her assignment with the American magazine in 1950, she wrote, "Today nobody has any doubt that a woman has been born with a mind equalling that of a man."[8] She put forward the theory that although women are born as equals, women cannot reach their potential academically or creatively because they have an enormous responsibility as guardians of the family. Men are recognized as having genius, she argued, because women have many obligations to the family and cannot devote time to pursue their chosen interests exclusively as men can. According to Savella, women have an inherent quality in caring for the family that men do not: "The family was and will be the centre of life. A woman is endowed by nature with a well-balanced mind and an inborn concern for her family. This is the survival of mankind and more important than a one-sided genius."[9] Savella was attempting to inspire her readers and to help them develop self-worth and dignity. She was demanding equality while at the same time espousing maternalistic ideas. Savella continued her contributions to 1950, when Lidia Burachynska, a former editor of *Nova khata* in L'viv, settled in the United States and became editor of the American magazine.[10] From the end of the war and until 1950, Lidia had been living in a displaced persons camp in Germany.

In 1940, the Canadian government wanted Ukrainian Canadian organizations to unite to form a single organization "to act as an authoritative representative for the Ukrainian Canadian community before the people and Government of Canada."[11] From the early 1900s, the Ukrainian community in Canada was divided into two camps: one group consisted of Ukrainian organizations associated with Ukrainian patriotism and church and the other group associated with socialism/communism. At the beginning of World War II, the Canadian federal government became interested in the internal developments of these two groups. Because they suspected the pro-communists of disloyalty, in June 1940 they banned their organizations and interned their leaders.[12] The Canadian government then decided to help the first group that consisted of five organizations (the Brotherhood of Ukrainian Catholics of Canada, the Ukrainian Self-Reliance League of Canada, the Ukrainian National Federation, the United Hetman Organizations and the League of Ukrainian Labor Organizations) to form an umbrella organization. Julian was deeply involved in this process, since he was national president of the Ukrainian Self-Reliance League.

The new umbrella organization took the name Ukrainian Canadian Committee (UCC). One of the first tasks given to the UCC by the Canadian government was to assist in the settlement of displaced persons of Ukrainian ancestry in Canada. Ukraine was devastated during the Second World War and many Ukrainians were scattered across Europe as refugees, prisoners-of-war, political exiles, and forced labourers. At the end of the war, many Ukrainians were forcibly repatriated or willingly returned to their homes to suffer under the yoke of the Soviet Union. Ukrainians from western Ukraine, many fiercely nationalistic, were granted refugee status, and rather than return to their homes chose to stay in displaced persons camps in western Europe. The UCC, in cooperation with the Ukrainian Canadian Relief Fund, helped these refugees and displaced persons settle in Canada. UCC changed it name to Ukrainian Canadian Congress in 1989, with headquarters in Winnipeg and an office in Ottawa.

At one of the UCC's congresses in the early 1940s, the idea of teaching the Ukrainian language in high schools and universities was brought forward. Ukrainian-Canadian activists recognized the need to teach Ukrainian in schools, since there were so many Ukrainian Canadians who did not know how to read or write in the language of their ancestors. It was necessary to preserve and promote the language and make it available to all who would be interested. There was one obstacle however – no textbooks. Julian was well aware of the problems with the lack of textbooks to teach the Ukrainian language, as he had taught the subject at Mohyla Institute in the 1920s and 1930s. During these times, he noticed that many students required translations and explanations of idiomatic grammar structures and orthography, and so was compelled to make notes of these problems in his lesson books. Because Julian was well qualified to teach Ukrainian studies, he was asked by the UCC executive to take on the task of immediately preparing a textbook of Ukrainian grammar. Julian accepted the assignment. With no example to guide him and no Ukrainian-English dictionaries in existence, he had to overcome many hurdles and use his own judgment in this difficult task. The printing of a textbook was a priority, as Dr. C. H. Andrysyshen at the University of Saskatchewan was to begin teaching Ukrainian classes in 1945 and he had no textbooks. In the meantime, lessons were mimeographed and distributed to the students in lieu of textbooks. Julian received some assistance at the beginning of this endeavour from Rev. E. Hrytsyna, Dr. P. Macenko and W. J. Sarchuk who were highly literate in the Ukrainian language. Later he received assistance from others in order to produce a well-rounded text.

Savella, knowing the urgency of completing the textbook, also gave her time to it. She helped with the typing using two typewriters, switching between the English typewriter and the Ukrainian one. Accuracy of the accented words emerged as an important issue, since several Ukrainian dialects existed. Standardized Ukrainian as developed in the 19th century was a conscious amalgam of Taras Shevchenko's Cherkasy dialect and the central Galician dialect Ivan Franko used.

To ensure the accuracy of the textbook, Julian enlisted the assistance of Professor Dmytro Kyslytsia, a displaced person newly arrived in Canada, to review the manuscript. The book, published in 1950, was immediately embraced by the teaching profession. It was the first Ukrainian grammar book to be used in high schools and universities in Canada and the United States and is still in use today.

Shortly after completing her contribution to the grammar textbook, in 1948 Savella agreed to prepare a manuscript on Ukrainian embroidery. Throughout the years she had lectured on Ukrainian embroideries at Mohyla Institute and in her work with the Women's Department. Also, she had taught embroidery to girls when she lectured at the One Day Schools in the Ukrainian bloc settlements in Saskatchewan. Mrs. Olha Woycenko, UWAC national secretary, knowing of Savella's work suggested that she write a book by compiling her lectures on embroideries. Mrs. Woycenko informed Savella that the UWAC would publish the book at their expense and they would be responsible for the sale of the book. In hindsight, Savella was not pleased with the published book, stating "I prepared the manuscript somewhat haphazardly without spending enough time on the contents."[13] The book of 136 pages, in the Ukrainian language, *Mystetski Skarby Ukrainskykh Vyshyvok*, (Treasures of Ukrainian Embroidery) was published in 1950 by the UWAC. It aided women who were interested in making Ukrainian folk costumes for themselves and their families, and the patterns were often used for costuming of performers in Ukrainian folkdance ensembles. There were also ideas for stitching Ukrainian embroidery patterns on household linens, such as tablecloths, napkins and modern clothing. Today, over fifty years later, the book is out of print though it still can be found in women's home libraries across Canada as a resource for good patterns and ideas for embroidery.

However, Savella did not just write about embroidery in her book; she included, at the beginning, a history behind the ornamentation of Ukrainian handicrafts, which includes embroidery, wood carving (*riz'ba*) and *pysanky*. She stated that Ukrainian art is inspired by daily life and done by the 'common people' because they needed decorative designs to enhance their homes and to satisfy their creativity.[14] Ukrainian embroidery, she wrote, was the most important 'art' for Ukrainians because it identifies a country, with different compositions and techniques as indicators of each region. As years advanced, so did the intricacy of the embroidery stitches and patterns. There is a description in the book of embroidery styles by region in Ukraine. For example, Poltava shows a richness in flowers; Hutsul region uses mostly rich, colourful wool reflective of the mountainous region, freedom and the raising of sheep; Podilia uses little colour, with just red and black mirroring hard work and closeness to the flat land and designs of rows and simplicity; Central Ukraine, the old Cossack heartland, uses delicate light colours; Bukovyna preferred black highlighted with rich colours. A photograph of beautifully embroidered linens that were sold in Saskatoon for the war effort in the 1940s was one of a number of photographs of embroidered articles and drawn illustrations of costumes and stitch patterns included in the book. Although Savella claimed that she was dissatisfied with the book, it contains well researched historical support for the artistry of Ukrainian handicraft. Of course, her own views and opinions are very much part of this book.

In 1940, the Stechishins bought a three bedroom bungalow at 604 Albert Avenue in Saskatoon. The house had a room just off the living room that they used as a library and as an office for both of them to work on their various projects. They needed to continue to board students in their home through the 1940s, however, for financial reasons and to help with housework. Usually, the boarders as in previous years numbered from two to four at any time. Olha Chimy (now Cikalo) stayed with them for two years and one summer in the early 1940s while attending university. In April 2005, Olha wrote her thoughts on her stay with the Stechishins. "Boarders were well treated and respected; in turn the boarders were well behaved and respectful and generally on time for meals. Mr. and Mrs. Stechishin's relationship was respectful and consistent. No anger was shown and if disagreeing [occurred], it was done in a quiet way." Olha's parents paid for her room and board, but "[w]hile living with them one year, I had only one class early in the morning one day a week, so it was arranged that I would do ironing for the family, and thus reduce my rent. If Mrs. S. was involved with community work, writing or whatever, she would leave instructions, i.e., meal preparation."

After having a housemaid most of the late 1920s and through the 1930s, Savella writes, "To save money I did not keep a housemaid when I was home. Besides, I did not want to have a non-Ukrainian maid because of the language problem."[15] Presumably, Ukrainian-Canadian young women were no longer interested in full time domestic work. Employment in the service industry, factories and stores was not only more lucrative, but the hours were shorter so that the women were afforded more leisure time. War industries absorbed much of the surplus labour on the prairies until 1945, mainly in eastern Canada and on the west coast, and the post-war boom starting in 1947 offered more opportunities for women, especially for the many who now had experience in skilled work.

Despite the hard times of the 1930s, by 1941 the Saskatoon population had recovered to the pre-depression level of 43,027. The Ukrainian population rose to 2,499 (6 per cent of the total Saskatoon population), most likely caused by wartime and post-war migration from rural area to urban. Also, the 1941 census reveals that the province remained Canada's third most populous.

In the late 1940s and early 1950s, Savella was a stay-at-home mom, though busy with journalistic endeavours and volunteer work in the Ukrainian community. Unbeknownst to the Stechishins, their new next door neighbour in 1950 was a *Star Phoenix* reporter, Grant Maxwell. In general conversation with them, he found out that the Stechishins were "a distinguished author-team." He coaxed them to give an interview and talk about their accomplishments and current projects; their story was published in the *Star Phoenix* along with their photograph. The reporter learned that "Julius Stechishin has published a history of the Ukrainian Institute here and more recently finished a Ukrainian-English grammar, the first book of its kind to be published in Canada. He is now working on Ukrainian-Canadian history in English. Savella Stechishin has published a profusely-illustrated book on Ukrainian needlework. She is at present writing a Ukrainian cookbook in English."[16] It was a good human interest story for the general Saskatoon public.

By the middle of the 20th century, the Ukrainian community in Saskatchewan was being accepted into the mainstream of local Anglo society. In Saskatoon the Ukrainian Canadians were recognized by their unsolicited favourable reports in newspapers and attendance at establishment venues. At this time, Savella had been accepted in the mainstream community as evidenced by the report in the local daily and requests to speak at various mainstream clubs. In February 1952, on the invitation of the University Women's Club at the University of Saskatchewan, Savella spoke on Ukrainian arts and crafts. She began her address with a brief overview of Ukrainian people and the history of Ukraine. She emphasized that "Ukrainians were not of Russian origin."[17] Her displays of various embroideries accompanied her address. She also explained the symbolism of the Ukrainian Easter egg. Her address was met with much enthusiasm and she was (again) written up in the *Star Phoenix* as an authority on Ukrainian arts and crafts. She was the only member of Ukrainian descent in the University Women's Club.

The UWAC in 1952 celebrated its 25th anniversary. A convention of the USRL with UWAC sessions was held in Winnipeg. Savella spoke about the beginnings of the Mohylianky Society and the important role they played in the early stages of the Ukrainian women's movement in Canada. She also presented a paper on Ukrainian women in community work in Canada. At the convention, four prominent UWAC activists, who had been instrumental in founding the UWAC, were honoured with honorary life memberships. They were Leonia Slusar, Maria Maduke, Daria Yanda, and Savella Stechishin. They were presented with certificates and a copy of the newly published history of the UWAC entitled *"Chvert' Stolittya na Hromadskiy Nyvi"* (A Quarter Century in Community Work), authored by Natalia Kohuska of Winnipeg.

Savella's summer employment in 1952 kept her busy judging women's work along with Mrs. T.A. Johnson at several fair exhibitions in central and northern Saskatchewan. In the spring of 1951 and 1952 John Rayner, Director of the Extension Department of the University of Saskatchewan, had requested that Savella judge at exhibitions during July and August. She had agreed to do this, indicating her preference to judge needlework. The towns listed were Outlook, North Battleford, Prince Albert, Glenbush, Yorkton, Melfort, Lloydminster, Nipawin, Silver Stream, Kelvington, and Invermay. As Savella no longer had a car, she was obliged to accompany the other judges in their cars to the fairs or travel alone by bus or train. Her expenses, for instance, to Prince Albert were:

train fare return - $5.60, hotel - $2.50, meals - $2.70, totalling $10.80. The women she encountered did beautiful handwork such as embroidery, crotchet, tatting, and knitting which they entered in different classes at the local annual fairs. As a judge, Savella's duty was to look for expert workmanship, harmony of colours, material, design suitability and general appearance. The Prince Albert exhibition was particularly of interest to Savella, as there was a special section of Ukrainian needlework. There were many entries and the competition was keen. Beautiful articles in *nyzynka* and *yavorivka* stitches, used effectively on runners and cushion tops especially caught Savella's eye.

To promote the arts in 1948, the provincial government created the Saskatchewan Arts Board in Regina, benefiting many artists and highlighting the presence of Saskatchewan's culture. It was the first such organization in North America. On July 9, 1953 Savella received a letter from Miss Norah McCullough, Executive Secretary, Saskatchewan Arts Board (SAB), reading in part as follows: "From Mrs. A.H. Morton of Saskatoon I have learned of your remarkable work on the history and culture of the Ukrainian people. For this reason we would ask you to consider accepting our invitation to serve voluntarily on a "standards" committee of the Saskatchewan Arts Board to represent the Saskatchewan Ukrainians. The purposes of this committee are varied."[18] The SAB proposed a "sales catalogue" of Saskatchewan handicrafts, with a small listing to eventually offer for purchase a wide variety of excellent handmade articles. A number of 'appropriate' members were selected for the standards committee to select suitable articles for inclusion in this catalogue. To attend meetings Savella travelled to Regina most often by train. Expenses for travelling and subsistence were met by the SAB.

Beginning in the fall of 1953, the SAB advertised in the public arena for articles for the Board to sell in its catalogue. By the end of November, when little Ukrainian embroidery had come into the office of the SAB, Miss McCullough became concerned. She requested Savella's help in acquiring more embroidery or at least "addresses of people to whom we could quickly apply for handwork to include."[19] A couple of months later, Savella was able to supply the names of two Saskatoon women, Mrs. J.A. Doktor and Mrs. J. Turetski, who agreed to write Ukrainian Easter eggs and whose work Savella respected. She also suggested, "If your plan of work in handicrafts would allow for short courses in native [Ukrainian] stitchery, then, I think, the visits would accomplish something more definite.... I think a short course may turn out to be very stimulating and encouraging."[20] She advised that she could write up a circular letter to Ukrainian women's organizations and write an article for Ukrainian language newspapers in which she would advertise the workshops. Miss McCullough was pleased with the suggestion and Savella went ahead with her idea. Her article appeared in four Ukrainian language newspapers, explaining all about the workshops, places and times. On examining the files, there are articles in newspapers, but evidence of the outcome is not available.[21]

The committee examined the handicraft articles that were sent in from many areas of Saskatchewan and then selected ones that they considered appropriate for the sales catalogue. These included leatherwork, knitting, weaving, lace weaving, spinning, woodwork, and cross-stitching. The Board then gave the handicraft women suggestions of items to produce in order to enhance sales: "over-shoulder bag - canvas, lined, shorter and longer straps as desired, $35.00 (suggest less design - say only one side - and sell for $20.00)." Prices varied as the following examples show: men's evening scarves with pheasant eye design, cream, fine mercerized cotton at $3.50; woven peasant skirt lengths at $12.50; supplied wool spun at $2.00 per pound.[22]

Savella continued to maintain relations with the Saskatchewan Arts Board and went as far as to get involved with the plans for Saskatchewan's golden jubilee celebration in 1955, often travelling to Regina for meetings. She was assigned to organize the handicraft festivals held beginning in 1954 throughout rural

Saskatchewan. One of the objectives of the festivals was to encourage the preservation and development of handicraft heritage and to encourage younger people to maintain this practice. The provincial government gave financial assistance to any group of adults engaged in serious community handicraft projects. When asked by Mrs. Jean Howard, Director of Handicraft Festivals, SAB, to send her beautiful Ukrainian embroidery samples to exhibitions, Savella was always proud and pleased to do so. The SAB and the local Golden Jubilee Committee in Prince Albert held a handicraft heritage festival (handicraft demonstration-exhibition) in celebration of Saskatchewan's 50th anniversary as a province in 1955. Being on the Standards Committee of the Arts Board, Savella was asked to attend this festival. She spoke about Ukrainian embroidery and presented samples that she had brought with her to use as illustrations. She also encouraged women to pass this folk art on to their children. Two more festivals, one in Yorkton and the other at Craik, were held that year.

In 1954, Milena Rudnytska, the renowned Ukrainian political personality, was the guest speaker at the national USRL convention held at the Bessborough Hotel in Saskatoon July 2-5. She drew a large crowd. After the war Rudnytska, had emigrated to New York from L'viv, where she had been president of the *Soiuz Ukrainok*, editor of a Ukrainian newspaper *Zhinka* (Woman) and member of the Polish Seym (parliament) in Warsaw representing the Ukrainian National Democratic Union. As an activist in the national movement in Western Ukraine and an MP, she defended the Ukrainian cause at International Women's Congresses and international meetings of parliamentarians. At the 1954 convention, she was invited to speak at the general session on the topic of the current situation in Ukraine under the yoke of the USSR. As this UWAC convention marked the 70th anniversary of the Ukrainian women's movement in Ukraine, Rudnytska was the ideal person to speak on this topic. An article on the convention appeared in the Saskatoon *Star-Phoenix*, accompanied by photographs of Milena Rudnytska, Olha Woycenko (UWAC president) and Savella Stechishin. Savella, one of the pioneers and founders of the UWAC, as a guest speaker reviewed the Ukrainian women's movement in Canada. The article stated of Savella, "She has contributed significantly towards the recognition and preservation of the richness and beauty of Ukrainian traditions, language, and handicrafts in Canada."[23] The writeup further stated that the UWAC "has some 150 branches from coast to coast, the majority of which are also the Women's Auxiliaries of the Ukrainian Greek Orthodox Church."

In 1950 Olha Woycenko again approached Savella about an idea she had; she asked Savella to compile a Ukrainian cookbook in the English language. Such a thing had been unheard of. As Olha worked at Trident Press, which published Ukrainian language periodicals and books, she had her finger on the pulse of Ukrainian activities in Canada. She often helped her husband, Peter, who was the manager of Trident. In the late 1940s Olha had been asked by a number of people whether there was an English language cookbook on Ukrainian cuisine. This issue had arisen often after the war, when many Ukrainian-Canadian and Ukrainian-American soldiers returned home from overseas, bringing British and European wives with them who, of course, were unfamiliar with the cuisine of what seemed to them to be an obscure, eastern European nation. While the men wanted their wives to cook as their own mothers did back home, they found it difficult to teach their new brides how to cook *borsch*, *varenyky*, *holubtsi*, and other common Ukrainian dishes. Grandmothers and mothers had learned the traditions through demonstration and oral explanation, and passed the recipes on in the same fashion. Letters to Trident Press requesting a cookbook on how to prepare Ukrainian dishes began to pour in from across Canada, as well as from Britain, United States and later from Australia, where a number of displaced people had settled and where some Ukrainian men had married Australian girls. Requests for the cookbook also came from Canadian wives of Ukrainian-Canadian men and granddaughters who were not fluent in the Ukrainian language yet desirous of retaining the cooking traditions of their ancestors.

With her experience in the food preparation area, Savella was an ideal candidate to take charge of compiling an English language Ukrainian cookbook. Olha asked Savella to tackle this large task by compiling the recipes she had featured in the *Ukrainian Voice* in her column "Around the Home". Savella declined, since she felt that it was too big an undertaking for her. Olha then suggested that this project be made a national UWAC organizational project, whereby UWAC members of the affiliated branches throughout Canada would be asked to contribute tested recipes. They would then send them to Savella for compilation.[24] Olha also suggested that Savella ask two other home economists of Ukrainian descent in Saskatoon to share the work on this project. Savella chose Johanna Michalenko and Lesia Ewasiuk to work with her, but they declined on the grounds that they were busy with other obligations. Undaunted, Savella decided to forge ahead on her own. Other obstacles arose. For example, the majority of the recipes received from the UWAC members were Canadian, or more precisely not Ukrainian, such as chiffon cakes, pies and dainties, and so were not suitable for a Ukrainian cookbook featuring only traditional Ukrainian recipes. Other than the contributions, Savella received no offers of help. Years later, Savella wrote, "I was ready to abandon this project, but Olha Woycenko encouraged me to work at it, step by step, by myself, even though it might take a number of years. A cookbook was a necessity for the prestige of Ukrainian people in Canada, she said. It would be worth the effort and morally satisfying for Ukrainians. The encouragement and continuous support given me by Olha Woycenko and Natalia Kohuska sparked in me a new desire to continue this project."[25]

Fortunately, over time Savella had already collected most of the available cookbooks printed in Western Ukraine before the Second World War. She was unable to get any from the Soviet Ukraine because she had no communication with anyone there. The

Ukrainian cookbooks she owned used metric units or a "pinch of this" and a "handful of that." The European weights and measurements had to be converted to Canadian standard measure, using cups, tablespoons, teaspoons, ounces and pounds. Time was yet another factor that she had to edit. Some bread recipes stressed the importance of kneading the dough for one hour. However, from her own experience she knew that ten minutes of kneading was usually sufficient to develop the necessary elasticity in yeast dough. After discussing this issue with Johanna Michalenko, they came to the conclusion that perhaps the Ukrainian flour had a different gluten content. She studied the recipes from her collection and selected certain ones to experiment with. Like her book on embroidery, her plan was to include recipes from different parts of Ukraine, which meant that she particularly needed recipes from Central Ukraine, of which she had none. Few immigrants had come from that part and because it was under Soviet rule, communication with residents was almost non-existent. Fortunately, she was able to enlist the help of Mrs. Efrosyna Rudewska, a displaced person living in Saskatoon. As Efrosyna was from near the city of Kyiv in Central Ukraine, Savella turned to her for information on typical recipes from her former home. Although Savella received help from Efrosyna she wanted to check with a cookbook from Ukraine to ensure that her cookbook did not exclude recipes which were specific to Central Ukraine. When she heard that her old friend, Wasyl Swystun, was going to visit Ukraine, she asked him to bring back a cookbook. To her disappointment he informed her on his return that no cookbook was available. Savella also asked for specific recipes from a number of her Ukrainian friends in various parts of Canada, friends she knew were good cooks.

Savella wrote,"Working on the cookbook tired me so much that I used to dream about cup and spoon measurements! At times I would suddenly wake up realizing that some specific recipe has too much flour or the temperature is not right, and I would rush to make the corrections or make a note about it to be looked into. There was always fear and worry – what if some recipe fails!"[26] Three copies were typed of each recipe. She obtained a book from a home economics lecturer, Miss Wilmot, entitled "How to Write Recipes for Publications." This book was very useful as a guide in using clear terminology. The author stressed the importance of using plain kitchen language and to forego using words such as mince and sauté and substituting well known English words like chop and pan-fry. After perusing the book, Savella noticed several mistakes in her recipes and rewrote some of them with more clarity.

After the initial typing of the recipes, they had to be validated by other women. Savella created a detailed form, listing instructions on how to test a recipe and asking the tester to give a critical appraisal of the finished product on a questionnaire. For added measure, the tester was asked to test the recipe several times, ensuring that perfect results were attained. Savella asked several of her friends and a select group of younger members in branches of the UWAC to do the testing. With the inclusion of so many recipes in this cookbook, testing took many months and required a great deal of correspondence. Savella made sure to review all the questionnaires and make modifications in measurements, temperature or methods as suggested. Then, for the final proof, the recipes had to be retested by her. Savella acknowledged the tester by printing her name below the specific recipe. This explains why some of the recipes in the book look as it they had been contributed by a specific person when, in fact, the reference was to the tester for that particular recipe, not the contributor.

Wanting to give the book authenticity and uniqueness, Savella retained the original Ukrainian names for most of the well-known dishes and pastries. However, this transliteration presented a problem, since the Ukrainian language uses the Cyrillic alphabet, which is not entirely compatible with English. After several attempts to do this herself, she asked Dr. Andrushyshen of the Slavic Department of the University of Saskatchewan to help. He did so quite willingly, and thereby became yet another unnamed contributor to the project. To make the book even more unique and charming as a resource book, Savella decided to include descriptions of select customs, traditions and festive ceremonies. Many of the dishes included are associated with specific traditions and holidays. Each section opens with a lengthy introduction explaining the traditions associated with the recipes that follow. For example, page 15 has a commentary on "Who are the Ukrainians?" The next section heading is "Christmas, New Year, and Jordan Holidays" with an explanation followed by "Suggested Dishes for Christmas Eve Supper," "Easter" and "Suggested Dishes for Easter Breakfast" follow. Even the humble borsch earned two pages of description. About poultry and game, she wrote, "Because poultry is a faithful standby in the average Ukrainian family, ingenious cooks have developed a variety of choice chicken dishes to avoid the monotony of serving poultry the same way day in and day out."[27] Many recipes are not only accompanied by instructions, but also an annotation of the people of the particular region where the recipe originated. For the *Hutsulian Kuleshka* (Hutsul Corn Meal Mush) recipe, the introduction states that "The Carpathian Mountain strip of Ukraine is the home of the Ukrainian Hutsul tribe known for its proud and independent bearing. These Ukrainian highlanders engage mainly in sheep-raising and wood-cutting. Corn is their native cereal and a staple part of their diet. It is used in the form of corn meal and coarsely ground hominy. The following is the Hutsul way of preparing their traditional corn meal dish called "kulesha"."[28] The recipe was tested by Mrs. O. Arsenych of Winnipeg, Manitoba. The book contains twenty-two sections with recipes for a great variety of delectable foods: appetizers, soups, meats, *holubtsi* (cabbage rolls), 'starchy food', desserts, pickles and even 'Crystallized Rose Petals' that call for "a fresh rose of a deep red color" that could be used for decorating the top of a cake.

Once the typing of the recipes was completed, Savella asked Johanna Michalenko to proofread the recipes. Johanna Michalenko was paid $300.00 (1956-57) and given ten complimentary copies of the book. Her help was a great relief to Savella in taking to completion her arduous project – the manuscript was ready for printing. An artist by the name of Wadym Dobrolige of Edmonton was suggested to her to do the illustrations for the book. She contacted him and he agreed to illustrate the cover and provide some illustrations for inside of the book; she paid him $100.00 for his work. Savella was very pleased with the cover, "very traditional and symbolic" was her opinion.[29] However, the inside illustrations she felt could have been better. A university professor who edited publications of the University of Saskatchewan was brought on board to perform the final editing. Savella also paid him $100.00.

Savella sent the manuscript to Trident Press in Winnipeg for publication and then received printed galleys for proofreading. The question of financing the publication of the book arose. In her autobiography, Savella explained that Trident Press informed the UWAC executive, who had actually initiated the cookbook, that the book would be printed on a "job printing", which meant that a payment of $20,000 in advance was necessary before they would even consider printing. After printing, all the books would have to be taken and marketed by the UWAC executive. However, the executive was unable to agree to these conditions. Because they did not have the funds, the storage or anyone willing to take charge of the sale of the book, the executive of the UWAC decided against undertaking the publication and marketing. Trident Press then agreed to take over the project. Savella, as the author, with the help of her friends, Olha Woycenko and Natalia Kohuska, as well as Julian, who gave legal advice, entered into a satisfactory legal arrangement with Trident Press regarding the expenses she had incurred in the preparation of the book.[30]

The book, Savella stated in her autobiography, had taken six years to write, including researching, interviewing selected women, supplying ingredients, purchasing books, stationery, paying helpers, testing recipes and arranging to have other women test certain recipes. Since the UWAC had not invested any money or provided help in the preparation of the book, Savella felt they had no claim to the royalties from the book. Trident Press credited the UWAC for the first stage because they had announced the project in their circular letter asking branch members to send in recipes. Their compensation was in the form of a generous discount on the sale of the books to the branches. A number of books were eventually even sent to the branches for sale at a discount and at no shipping cost. The 500–page book was priced at $5.50 per copy.

The cookbook, titled *Traditional Ukrainian Cookery*, was finally published in 1957. It met with great enthusiasm, which translated quickly into good sales. Savella aptly dedicated the cookbook to, "The women who treasured and practised the rich traditions of their homeland and thereby preserved them for posterity in this fair and free land of their choice."[31] It was the first cookbook in the world featuring Ukrainian dishes and explanations of Ukrainian traditions in the English language. And the demand was enormous. Savella received excellent press reports and even Canada's McLean's magazine reviewed the book. To promote the cookbook in Saskatoon, she asked a friend, Mary Cherneskey, who was a member of the Canadian Federation of University Women in Saskatoon, to have Savella speak about the cookbook at a meeting of the club.[32] Proudly, she collected the many favourable press reports about the book into a scrapbook. As a result of several positive write-ups about her cookbook in the Saskatoon *Star Phoenix*, Savella was invited to join the Saskatoon Women's Press Club in the fall of 1957. She gladly accepted as she felt comfortable with the women, especially since she knew a number of them.

In 1959 Dr. Edith Rowles Simpson, Dean of the College of Home Economics invited Savella to speak to her university class about her experience in writing a cookbook. Savella was pleased to be asked to share her experiences. Being a member of the Saskatoon Home Economics Club Savella was acquainted with many of the members. It was very exciting to be able to be a guest lecturer at the university where she had been a student herself thirty years ago. Following her talk at the university, she was asked to address the

Saskatoon Home Economics Club and again she accepted with delight. The title of her address was: "How I Came to Write a Cookbook."

Savella did not restrict herself just to Saskatoon and Canada in advertising her cookbook. She wrote to Volodymyr Sichynskyi, a prolific scholar of Ukrainian architecture, art and graphics, who had taken up residence in New York after the Second World War. He had been working on his doctoral degree in Prague when the Stechishins visited the city on their trip to Ukraine in 1926. It can be presumed that Savella had met him at that time. The Sichynskyi Collection at the Ukrainian Research Institute, Harvard University in the United States reveals that "[o]ne interesting letter is from Savella Stechishin who wrote to Sichynskyi regarding her cookbook *Traditional Ukrainian Cookery.* She explained to him the politics behind writing a Ukrainian cookbook in English, and that her goal was to educate North Americans about national customs and to elevate Ukrainian cuisine to the rank of that of other cultures."[33] Within two years the cookbook made its way to the United States, garnering very positive responses. Women were pleased to have a cookbook of Ukrainian cuisine available in the English language

A second edition was printed in 1959; in 1963 a third edition came out, and so on, so that by 1989, the mighty cookbook was in its 15th printing and still selling well. Although now out of print, Savella's cookbook is still considered a 'must' for anyone interested in cooking authentic Ukrainian cuisine or learning about Ukrainian culture. Her cookbook has been passed down to generations and shared amongst family members and friends. Presently, in 2009 there are approximately fifty entries about the cookbook and various recipes from it on the Internet. These range from the best borsch recipe to the hunt for the delectable mushroom and to how to prepare them.

Despite all this success, or perhaps because of it, dark clouds of scandal began to form over the new cookbook. Discord regarding the copyright of the cookbook amongst some members of the UWAC arose and continued to be a bone of contention for many years. Some members believed that because the project had been started by the UWAC, Savella was not entitled to royalties and that the National UWAC executive was the rightful owner of the book. Rumours and gossip reached Savella over the years and finally in 1975 she confronted the National Executive of the UWAC in Edmonton. Savella saw these reproaches as unjust, unfair and untrue, and she dealt with them with her usual directness and assertiveness. On December 3, 1975 she wrote a letter to the National Executive informing them that she was aware that "[s]everal women from the national executive and others on the executive of the Ukrainian Museum in Saskatoon are spreading malicious accusatory rumours about me: that I am receiving royalties for my cookbook "Traditional Ukrainian Cookery" which according to them, rightfully belong to the national organization because, they say, this was a project of the Ukrainian Women's Association and the branches provided the recipes for the book." She went on to say, "Ladies, allow me to refresh your memory that U.W.A.C. gave up the publication of this cookbook for justifiable reasons. . . . the branches did not shower me with tons of recipes as is being inaccurately presented. I searched for them alone. The organization did not assist me in this search. . . The National Executive did not contribute any money to this project   . . . U.W.A.C did not conduct the cultural research, did not compile the recipes, did not prepare them for publication, did not invest any money into it, and yet earned some profit as well as undeserved recognition for it."[34] Controversy over ownership of the cookbook continued for many years .

In the fifties, the Stechishin's two younger children attend university. Zenia graduated in 1955 with a degree in Home Economics. Meanwhile, Myron enrolled in the Arts faculty at the University of Saskatchewan. After two years he decided to pursue dentistry and left Saskatoon for Edmonton, since Saskatoon did not have a dental school.

Savella did not work away from her home in the fifties other than writing articles for the *Ukrainian Voice*. She and Julian enjoyed an almost idyllic life without children at home. During the summer months their favourite pastime was picking wild mushrooms that grew in the bluffs around Saskatoon. Julian would leave his office at about 4 o'clock in the afternoon to rush home to change out of his work clothes. Then they would be off in the car westward around Grandora area or south to Dundurn farms. They would come home with baskets of delicious wild mushrooms that Savella cooked in butter and cream. Like most Ukrainians and descendants of Ukrainian immigrants, they found mushrooms a wonderful and much sought-after delicacy. Savella had learned the art of differentiating between edible and non-edible mushrooms from her mother as a young girl. Favourite mushroom spots were and even today are jealously guarded and never revealed to anyone other than one's own family.

In 1958, Savella unexpectedly landed a job with the federal government. It was a part-time, which suited her very well. The Progressive Conservative party was in power, the party that the Stechishins supported. A friend of Julian's asked Savella whether she would be interested in taking an easy job enumerating the labour force for the Bureau of Statistics of Canada. She jumped at the offer. The job entailed visiting homes in an assigned area in Saskatoon, taking down the names and ages of the adult members of the family and noting their employment, number of hours at work, the type of dwelling they occupied, owned or rented. Over the period of one week of each month, the schedule was set for the same family to be interviewed once a month for six months. After the six months were complete, another set of homes was assigned in another area. Savella worked at this job for about a year and received over one thousand dollars in salary, at that time a substantial amount of money for a part time job.

When a teaching job came up, Savella decided to quit her part time work and re-enter her former profession. She had not considered going back to teaching after such a long lapse; however, at a regular monthly meeting of the Home Economics Club in December 1959 the shortage of qualified home economic teachers in Saskatoon was discussed. Although there were a number of graduates available, they did not possess the required teacher training or a teaching certificate. One teacher, Helen Craik, who worked at Princess Alexandra School, had to leave for surgery, and had no one to replace her from January to June. The only woman at the meeting who had a teaching certificate was Savella and so she offered to teach the remaining months. The school was a central school, where grades 7 and 8 girls from various schools took home economics classes half a day each week. Savella also taught a couple of classes of exceptional children. She found teaching nutrition, food selection and practical lessons in cooking an easy task. Lessons for the second term consisted of textiles and sewing: aprons for grade 7 and peasant skirts or blouses for the grade 8 girls.

After her six month contract, she did substitute teaching in 1960 and 1961. In 1962-63 she taught the entire year at Caswell School and for the next two years she substituted at Mount Royal High School on occasion. By the mid 1960s, Savella retired from teaching at public schools, but she did not retire from teaching altogether. When a large number of students enrolled for Ukrainian language at the University of Saskatchewan, she was asked to serve as a sessional lecturer teaching Ukrainian language classes from 1964 to 1967. She confessed that she was very pleased to be able to spend the last years of her teaching career at the university where she had started back in the 1920s. What a fitting way to end her professional career, a career she demanded for herself in spite of the norms of the day in the 1920s when she was in her 20s and a young married mother!

In the 1960s, a lifetime membership in the Canadian Association of Slavists (CAS) was awarded to Savella and Julian, he for his *Ukrainian Grammar* and she for her commercially successful *Traditional Ukrainian Cookery*. The CAS had been organized in

1954 by a number of scholars of Slavic-related disciplines at a convention in Winnipeg. It brought into its fold Slavic scholars from all the Canadian universities where Slavic studies were on the program calendar. The participating universities were: Universities of British Columbia, Alberta, Saskatchewan, Manitoba, Western Ontario, Toronto, Ottawa, Montreal and McGill.

In spite of her many interests, her love and pride in Ukrainian embroidery never waned and Savella continued to give talks and demonstrations of the art whenever possible. In celebration of Saskatchewan's 60th Anniversary as a province, the Saskatchewan Arts Board again held festivals across the province, as they had on their 50th anniversary.

The first Ukrainian-theme workshop, held in Yorkton on September 22, 1965, was an introduction to the "Saskatchewan Festival of the Arts", which was to begin in Yorkton on October 15-20. Savella conducted a "Ukrainian Handicrafts and Stitchery Workshop" sponsored by the Ukrainian Women's Association of Canada, Yorkton Branch, at the Coronation Hall, with registration fee at $5.00 and $2.00 for students. It included lecture-demonstrations on: 1) historical background of Ukrainian arts; 2) Ukrainian designs (Easter egg and embroidery designs-characteristics and symbolisms); 3) Ukrainian embroidery designs and stitches (regional differences, adaptation to modern items, selection of pattern and color harmony, mistakes to be avoided); 4) and Ukrainian folk dress (classification and characteristics, mistakes made in costumes used in Canada, children's costumes). Participants were asked to bring their own supplies of linen or cotton panama embroidery material, white, black and red embroidery thread (D.M.C. or Clarke's), embroidery needles, a thimble, a small pointed scissors, a small box to hold sewing supplies, a notebook and a pencil. A social hour was held at which tea/coffee and delicious sampling of pastries was offered, and where everyone was invited to attend in pioneer or national costumes. The SAB hoped that this workshop would generate interest and enthusiasm for the festival in October. Yorkton's Mayor, W.E. Fichtner, officially opened the workshop.

The Regina *Leader-Post* stated: "Mrs. Savella Stechishin, well-known Ukrainian home economist from Saskatoon is conducting the two-day workshop... . Mrs. Leo Collins of the Saskatchewan Arts Board in Regina commented on the beautiful display of Ukrainian embroidery. She said this is the first workshop of its kind to be held by the board ... " The *Yorkton Enterprise* wrote: "The Yorkton workshop, she [Mrs. Collins] said, constitutes another first for the Saskatchewan Arts Board."[35] An announcement in the *Star Phoenix* began with the headline "Ukrainian stitchery, handicraft workshop" and explained Savella's professional background and printed a photograph of her.[36] And so Savella received yet more recognition for her years of interest and love in Ukrainian embroidery.

When Savella was informed by the National Executive of the UWAC that they were intending to publish a monthly magazine, she wholeheartedly support this new venture. To fill the pages of the new journal, branches would be encouraged to submit articles about their activities, women's issues would be discussed and promoted, and recipes and articles about Ukrainian folk art and history would be included. The first issue of *Promin* (translated into English as *Sunbeam*) was published in January of 1960 as the official monthly journal of the Ukrainian Women's Association of Canada. Since then, the journal has gone through various stages of development to best serve the membership. *Promin* is now bilingual (English/ Ukrainian) and is received both by the members of UWAC in Canada and by women of Ukrainian descent beyond Canada. The aim of *Promin* is to inform and serve as a communicative link for Ukrainian women throughout the world and to ensure that the journal serves as the voice of its membership and reflects contemporary women's issues. This national women's periodical keeps Ukrainian women in Canada informed of current events, both within the Ukrainian community and around the globe, and features various issues and events of cultural interest. Nevertheless, it still contains recipes for holiday occasions and ordinary meal preparation. Its distribution is approximately 1600, with 90% of readers in Canada and 10% in the USA and abroad.[37] Savella was proud of the journal and submitted articles when she deemed it necessary. Recognizing her achievements and her place within the UWAC, articles of her accomplishments and honours were carried in the journal. Although she had no direct role in the founding of *Promin*, she strongly encouraged women to subscribe and support it.

Savella's 'celebrity' within the Ukrainian-Canadian community led to her being solicited by the Dauphin Chamber of Commerce (Manitoba) in 1965 to play a key role in the creation of an annual festival to celebrate Ukrainian culture in Dauphin. Many Ukrainians had settled in this area, making it a large bloc settlement. The festival now known as Canada's National Ukrainian Festival, has enjoyed an unbroken record of annual celebration since its inception. The Chamber made plans to have an advanced recipe contest with original recipes using ingredients contained in Ukrainian cookery, with the winning recipe to be used as the trademark of the festival. Savella, as an authority on Ukrainian cooking, was asked to give sound advice on suitable recipes for the contest, and went as far as to suggest using recipes from her cookbook. At the first National Ukrainian Festival, recipes for traditional ritual breads – Christmas kolach and Easter paska – were taken from *Traditional Ukrainian Cookery* and acknowledged.[38]

The Ukrainian Self-Reliance League at this time put into action a concept they had planned for many years. Theodore Humeniuk of Toronto, the president of USRL, initiated the SUS (*Soiuz Ukrainskyiv Samostiynyk*) Foundation with the initial donation of $50,000.00 in 1965. Savella was asked to be one of the seven founding members. The foundation was established to generate revenue to provide for cultural, educational and community programmes within the Ukrainian Orthodox community and so "would obviate the need for constantly recurring appeals and campaigns for funds."[39] By 2004, the foundation had donated over one million dollars to its various organizations: St. Andrew's College in Winnipeg, St. John's Institute in Edmonton, St. Petro Molyla Institute (formerly Petro Mohyla Institute) in Saskatoon, St. Vladimir Institute in Toronto, Ukrainian Museum of Canada in Saskatoon and its branches, National Ukrainian Orthodox Youth, as well as to such Ukrainian interest groups as Ukrainian Canadian Research & Documentation Centre and the Society of Ivan Franko, and to universities (the Ukrainian Studies Centre at the University of Manitoba, the Ukrainian Studies Centre at York University, and the Ukrainian Folklore Endowment at the University of Alberta).

The year 1965 was also the 80th anniversary of the Ukrainian feminist movement, initiated by the writer Nataliya Kobrynska and her Society of Ruthenian Women. Kobrynska had arranged the first public session in 1884 in Stanislaviv, Western Ukraine at which she called on all Ukrainian women to join together to create a unified force in support of the rights of Ukrainian women and to encourage women from different social classes and political camps to understand and accept the benefits of education and modernization. Another important event in Ukrainian feminist history is her publication of the Almanc, the *Pershyi vinok* (The First Wreath) in 1887 (with Olena Pchilka) in which she espoused her feminist view.[40] To commemorate the 80th anniversary in the province of Saskatchewan, four Ukrainian women's organizations in Regina held a joint convention: the Ukrainian Women's Association of Canada, the Ukrainian Women's Organization, the Ukrainian Catholic Women's League and the Women's Association of the Canadian League for Ukraine's Liberation. Savella was invited to speak at the convention, as the Regina *Leader Post* reported, describing "the sharp contrast between the vitality of Ukrainian culture, flourishing today in Canada, and the declining national heritage of the Ukrainian peoples of the U.S.S.R . . ."[41] This was the time of the Cold War when communication between Soviet Ukraine and the rest of the world was restricted. Savella, always the Ukrainian patriot, kept abreast of what was happening in the world concerning Ukraine.

In summary the Second World War and post-war years found Savella taking a proactive involvement in helping her sisters in Saskatchewan and throughout Canada by doing something she enjoyed and was talented at – writing beneficial articles. At the end of the 1960s, now middle aged and not quite as full of vitality and with the changing times, she continued to be assertive and a credit to her community. She was now recognized and appreciated in both the Ukrainian-Canadian and mainstream communities for all her knowledge and accomplishments.

8

Life Without Julian

Savella's beloved Julian unexpectedly died of a heart attack on February 24, 1971, cutting short his most prolific writing period. He had been absorbed in writing the history of Ukrainians in Canada in the Ukrainian language, documenting their socio-cultural development, and had completed only the first volume. After his death, while devastated and in mourning, Savella took upon herself the task of editing his manuscript, retyping most of the chapters and filling in what she considered to be conspicuous gaps. She also had to organize the bibliography.[1] Savella wrote the foreword for the book, explaining the condition of the manuscript at Julian's death and her own contributions to complete the manuscript for publication. The book, titled "*A History of Ukrainian Settlement in Canada*", was published in 1971 by the Ukrainian Self-Reliance League of Canada, an organization he had helped to found many years ago. In 1992, the book was translated into English so that it would be accessible to more people. Although this period was a very sad and difficult time in her life, she also had to wind up his law practice.

Savella's continuation of Julian's project was possible because the couple had worked together in harmony for many years and all his documents were in the study of their home together with her papers. Many years later, one of their boarders stated, "When either one was working on some project or writing, they would discuss it with one another. They were on the same wavelength, respected each other's opinion and were willing to listen to suggestions and accept or not as it affected their projects."[2]

In the 1970s and now in her 70s, Savella slowed down her activities allowing her to reflect on her life. Her children now lived far away: Anatole in Atlanta, Georgia; Myron and his family in Edmonton; and, Zenia in Toronto. All of them were pursuing their own careers. Savella's siblings and their children did not reside in Saskatoon either. She was quite alone in the prairie city, living in the same house on Albert Avenue for many years.

Not one to remain idle or brood because she was alone, in her usual exacting way, Savella embraced projects that appeared on the horizon and called for her full and undivided attention. The Olha Kobylianska Branch in Saskatoon, of which Savella has been one of the founders, was celebrating its 50th anniversary in 1973. She had been its first president 1923-24 and again for the years 1926, 1928, 1934 and 1936 and with all her journalistic experience and skills, Savella was a good choice to write the history of the branch. The result was a 220 page book, *Pivstorichya 1923-1973 Zhinochoho Tovarystva Imeny Olhy Kobyblianskoi v Saskatuni, Saskachevan Pershoro Viddily Soiuzu Ukrainok Kanady* (Fifty Years of the Olha Kobylianska Branch of the Ukrainian Women's Association of Canada, Saskatoon, Saskatchewan. The First Branch of the Ukrainian Women's Association of Canada 1923-1973) published in Ukrainian in 1975 by the branch and printed in Saskatoon. Photos depicting certain aspects of its history accompanied the text.[3] There is no English translation.

An important recognition for Savella occurred in 1973. She was selected to be in the directory, *Ukrainians in America.* A decision had been made by a group of men of Ukrainian descent in North America to write a biographical directory of noteworthy men and women of Ukrainian origin in the U.S.A. and Canada. They requested her permission to include her in their compilation of names, which she gave.[4] The directory was published in 1975 and contained 2000 biographies. It is now out of print.

Accolades followed both Stechishins. Saskatoon's population continued to rise so that by 1971 it had risen to 126,449, including

14,390 Ukrainians. As a result, there was the need to open new subdivisions to accommodate the growing population and, of course, to name them. With this in mind, the Ukrainian Self-Reliance League of Canada in 1973 submitted names of four men of Ukrainian descent whom they felt contributed "significantly and conspicuously in community and educational services and as such should be recognized by naming streets, avenues, crescents and parks [after them]"[5] in the new subdivision of Silverwood Heights. The subdivision was completed in about five years. On February 9, 1978 Savella received a letter from Mayor Clifford Wright, that said, "I can think of no one who more aptly suits this criteria as much as the late Mr. Stechishin. His contribution to the Ukrainian community and this City has been truly remarkable and worthy of more recognition than merely having a street named after him."[6] There are three designations named after Julian: Stechishin Crescent, Stechishin Way and Stechishin Terrace.

Savella always kept abreast of what was happening with the UWAC nationally, provincially and locally. In her archives, she kept all the newsletters put out by the provincial and national UWAC. Although she had no longer been in the leadership elite of the UWAC for many years, she wanted to know what was happening in this organization at all times and felt that she had the right to give criticism and advice. The local UWAC was still of interest to her and she attended as many meetings as possible, but did not to serve on the executive or any committees. However, she willingly advised and guided when necessary and gave speeches when asked. Since the meetings were held Sunday afternoons after the church service, it was easy to stay behind and attend these meetings.

Savella's fountain of knowledge was recognized and appreciated by many who were interested in the subject of Ukrainians, with the result that she received requests for information and interviews. She was the authority on the Ukrainian women's movement in Ukraine and in Canada from the early 1900s. Her knowledge encompassed not only that of Orthodox women, but all

Ukrainian women's organization. One organization that she believed all Ukrainian women's organizations should belong to was the World Federation of Ukrainian Women's Organization (WFUWO) (*Svitova federatsiia ukrainskykh zhinochykh orhanizatsii*).

In 1948, the World Federation of Ukrainian Women's Organization (WFUWO) was formed mainly by Ukrainian women who had immigrated from displaced persons camps after World War II. It was and continues to be headquartered in the United States with membership in Canada, the USA and the rest of the world. The organization was formed to strengthen and coordinate the political and cultural-educational work of the Ukrainian women outside the Soviet bloc. Prior to the war, the World Union of Ukrainian Women (*Svitovyi soiuz ukrainok*) was formed in 1937 with headquarters in L'viv, Halychyna (Western Ukraine) with Milena Rudnystka as president[7] and the UWAC became affiliated with it. However, in 1939 the women's movement was suppressed after the Soviet occupation of Western Ukraine, ending the contacts with Ukrainian-Canadian women. After the war, female activists in the displaced persons camps began to organize, but because of some disagreement, a splinter group broke away from the World Union of Ukrainian Women, and formed the World Federation of Ukrainian Women's Organization (WFUWO). Savella's former correspondent, Olena Kysilewska, who had immigrated to Ottawa, Canada in 1948, became the first president of the WFUWO. The World Union of Ukrainian Women with Rudnystka as president lasted only for a few short years before the WFUWO quickly became the preferred organization of Ukrainian women worldwide. Although both the Ukrainian Catholic Women's League of Canada and the Ukrainian Women's Organization of Canada became charter members, the UWAC did not, since many of its members' sympathies were still with the ideals of Rudnytska. Savella believed that since Canadian women were not privy to the machinations in the displaced persons camps, the UWAC should become a member of WFUWO, as it was the world organization of all Ukrainian women. After many years of debates at

UWAC conventions, delegates at the 2003 convention finally voted by secret ballot to join the WFUWO.

Savella had always felt it important to belong to the WFUWO for the sake of the unity of Ukrainian women worldwide, but could never persuade the executive of the UWAC to become a member. By the late 1940s, she had stepped back from the UWAC and had little influence. However, she did take out individual membership in the WFUWO and attended a few of its conventions and kept up correspondence with the executive. In 1968 Savella, wrote to Mrs. Olena Zalizniak, president of the WFUWO in Philadelphia, expressing her regret at not seeing her at their convention. She went on in her letter, "It would have been delightful to meet with you again, even for a few minutes. I often remember our meeting in L'viv [Ukraine]. I was then very green, but full of energy to do work. The years have passed so quickly."[8]

Leaders of the WFUWO knew Savella and her work and respected her. On occasion they asked her to write articles for their journal or send them her published articles for reprinting in their journal. She was also asked to review books that they thought were important to their work. In 1965, the executive requested that she review the book *Vukhovantsia pokolin* (Bringing up Generations), advising her that the review when published in their journal would be a kind of advertising to help sell this excellent book that they were promoting amongst their membership. Correspondence was kept up over many years with requests and sundry communication. For example, in 1968, the president of the WFUWO wrote Savella telling her she enjoyed reading Savella's articles in *Ukrainian Voice* and also her regret at not chatting with Savella at the last annual congress because of her busy schedule with convention organizational work.

In the 1960s, when the executive of the WFUWO decided to update its archives their archivist appealed to Savella to send copies of speeches, books and articles that she had written. The executive recognized her contribution to the betterment of women of Ukrainian descent in Canada and they also thought highly of her cookbook.

The archivist, who was located in Winnipeg, Manitoba wrote, "I have given your cookbook to seven brides this summer and they are delighted with it. They have had good success in baking."[9]

Savella's correspondence with other Ukrainian women's organizations, found in her files at the National Archives, consist of requests and general enquiries about her health and her activities. Another women's organization with which Savella kept up long time correspondence was the Ukrainian National Women's League of America. These American women recognized her writing ability, her knowledge and her devotion to her Ukrainian heritage. In 1962, for instance, the editor, Lidia Burachynska, requested permission to reprint in *Nashe zhyttia* Savella's article on [Ukrainian] Christmas traditions that Savella had written in her column "Around the Home" in the *Ukrainian Voice*. Savella was pleased to consent to reprinting the article.[10] At the time of the 50th anniversary of the Ukrainian National Women's League of America in 1975, the executive asked her to write and submit her recollections of the first Women's Congress in 1932, which she attended along with the other Canadian women. They were planning to have their history written and published. Savella agreed.

Although Savella slowed down with her writing in the 1980s, she wholeheartedly accepted a request from the national executive of the UWAC in Edmonton to participate in a project to write works on Ukrainian culture. They approached various writers and translators to fulfil this project. "Essays from the History of Ukrainian Culture" was published in 1984 in three volumes in both Ukrainian and English: Book One was, "Prominent Figures in the History of Ukraine" by Dr. Savella Stechishin and "Selected Luminaries of Ukrainian Literature" by Natalia Kohuska; Book Two was, "Ukrainian Composers" by Serhiy Eremenko and "Ukrainian Drama and Theatrical Arts on a Historical Path" by Valerian Revutsky; Book Three was, "Ukrainian Fine Arts" by Ivan Keywan. Savella wrote short biographies in Ukrainian on notable historical figures who were rulers of early times. This latter work was her last significant journalistic effort.

Still being acknowledged for her activism in the Ukrainian Canadian sphere, in 1984, Savella was invited by Victoria Symchych to be one of "twelve people of outstanding merit" [of Ukrainian descent in Canada] in a book she was writing: *What Canada Means to Me*. Mrs. Symchych explained by letter that photographs and short biographies were to be included in this book and believed that it was important to have Savella as one of the twelve. Savella complied, adding that she believed it would be an important contribution to the history of Ukrainians in Canada. The book was readied for publishing, but Mrs. Symchych who was in advanced years, became ill and sadly the project was never completed.

Savella was invited in 1985 to be a presenter at the Second Wreath Conference in Edmonton, Alberta on October 11-14. This conference was named after the Nataliya Kobrynska and Olena Pchilka's 1887 women's almanac *Pershyi vinok (First Wreath)*. To mark the centenary of the almanac, the conference was organized by Ukrainian-Canadian feminists outside the Ukrainian establishment circles. By the 1980s, Ukrainian studies had emerged as a respectable academic pursuit in Canada, particularly in Edmonton, Winnipeg and Toronto, with the result that Savella's pioneering work in community activism was starting to receive more critical and intellectual attention. The purpose for the conference was to examine women's position in contemporary Ukrainian society and community structures. In the 1970s and 1980s, Ukrainian-Canadian feminists were seeking to make their ethnicity compatible with their feminism. They had concerns with improving their position in mainstream society, while simultaneously wanting to improve their position within their ethnic group. They felt suffocated by what was expected of them, i.e. preserving their heritage and identity as prescribed by members of the Ukrainian-Canadian nationalist camp. Many feminists believed that they were expected to marry a Ukrainian professional, produce children who promoted Ukrainian culture, and work in the kitchen to finance "Ukrainian" buildings while the men led the community – women worked and men played politics! Of the conference, historian Frances Swyripa states, "Despite involvement by other ethnic women, particularly Jewish feminists, dialogue with and participation by women from traditionalist Ukrainian-Canadian women's organization was limited and strained."[11] However, the organizers valued Savella's work in the field of Ukrainian women and so they invited her to speak at this conference. She presented a paper called "The Formation of the Ukrainian Women's Organizations in Canada." Years later, her verbal response to the author about the theme of the conference was only that she found it interesting – she did not elaborate. Savella was not involved in the broader feminist community in the 1950s and 1960s and she did not concern herself with the contentious issues of the feminists. While she was well read, she does not seem to have had a sophisticated grasp of the feminist debates, even in the 1920s. Since her activism was now over and she was elderly, it appears that she did not want to get into the fray of these discussions. After all, she had been one of the architects of the 'blueprint' that Ukrainian-Canadian women were to follow.

Savella's paper at the 1985 conference was comprehensive and fair to all the women's groups but one. She would not give any credit to Ukrainian women involved in left-wing politics for their contribution to the Ukrainian women's movement in Canada. They were conspicuously omitted.   Savella was vehemently anti-Communist and anti-Russian and did not hesitate to admit it. Her beliefs were formed in the 1920s with the rise of socialism amongst Ukrainians living in urban centres and mining towns.   Their organizations, Ukrainian Labourer and Farmer Temple Association and the Workers Benevolent Association of Canada later became known as the Association of United Ukrainian Canadians (AUUC). Savella refused to give the pro-Communist AUUC any credit for positive contributions to the building of Canada or to the elevating of Ukrainian Canadians. If anything, she considered this organization a detriment and an embarrassment to Canadians of Ukrainian descent.

When the author discussed with her Frances Swyripa's statement in her book *Wedded to the Cause* that the Women's Section of the ULFTA was organized in 1922, prior to UWAC, Savella responded by letter: "Frances Swyripa gives the Can. [Canadian] Communists first place in Canada – their organization was first and also their women's journal *"Robitnytsia"* (Woman Worker) was first – but it was ordered and paid for by Moscow – Communist propaganda. They had nothing to do with the Ukrainian cause. They opposed any nationalistic projects. . . The women in this group were not interested in promoting Ukrainian."[12] The Women's Section was guided by male organizers of the AUUC and did not organize independently of the male-dominated AUUC. The authors of *Canadian Women, A History* confirm that the Communist Party of Canada in the 1920s took up the "woman question" and inaugurated a women's department "with the object of advancing communism among women. . . Finnish, Jewish and Ukrainian leagues predominated. . ."[13]

Savella's strong anti-Russian/Communist sentiments had been longstanding and continued throughout her life. In 1954, she wrote to Norah McCullough of the Saskatchewan Arts Board that she did not think it a good idea to ask the Ukrainian Orthodox or Catholic groups to sponsor an exhibition of Byzantine icons. She writes in part:

> For your information the Ukrainians have no friendly feeling towards the Russians and anything that is Russian. It is a long standing feud between the two countries dating to the Treaty of Pereyaslaw of 1654, when Russia broke the treaty and mercilessly subjugated the Ukrainians; wiped out its leaders and intellectuals; forbade the use of Ukrainian language; took control of the church and appropriated priceless art treasures of Ukrainian churches including valuable Icons. The oppression continued throughout the centuries to this very day. The animosity towards Russia has been intensified with the communist regime. The Ukrainians cannot forgive the Russians for exterminating nine million Ukrainians by a deliberately planned famine in the thirties, and for sending fifteen million Ukrainians into slave labor camps in Siberia. There are hundreds of Ukrainian D.P.'s (mostly intellectuals) in Canada who have

witnessed the planned famine and have worked in the Siberian
slave camps.

Into the 1980s and early 1990s, Savella continued to write,
although with less energy and commitment, to Ukrainian newspapers
and the UWAC journal, *Promin*. It may have been to submit an
article or simply give her opinion on something she saw not to her
liking. A lecture that Savella gave on behalf of the Ukrainian
Canadian Committee, Saskatchewan Provincial Council in Saskatoon
in 1989 was published in *Promin*.[14] She spoke on Ukrainian national
dress and its contribution to sustaining Ukrainian culture in Canada.
About two years prior to the 100th anniversary of the arrival of
Ukrainians in Canada (1991), various organizations held meetings
and workshops to discuss ways to celebrate this momentous occasion.
She agreed with the path that the UCC had taken in helping the
various dance groups by providing directions and funding to ensure
the authenticity of their costumes. Authenticity of costumes had been
dear to Savella's heart since the 1920s and she continued to promote
this throughout her life. She further added that the "masses" can
understand better what they see and that the visible symbols of
Ukrainian dance, folklore, song, embroidery, national costumes, and
food can be easily appreciated and identified as part of Ukrainian
culture. This visibility develops a deeper understanding of the
culture, as well as interest in one's roots, and in this way history is
cultivated. One effect is that it even increases the desire to see the
country of Ukraine. Therefore, she stated, the visibility of Ukrainian
culture is a good start and plays an essential role in the preservation
of the culture. One of the last articles she wrote for *Promin* was in
1993 on the occasion of the 70th anniversary of the Olha Kobylianska
Branch in Saskatoon, explaining the beginnings of the branch.[15]

Savella was of strong character. In her interviews, it was
abundantly clear that she was mainly interested in retelling her story
and had no desire to talk about anything that portrayed Ukrainian
Canadians unfavourably. She showed little regard for books or
newspaper articles that discriminated against Ukrainians. She did

approve of Paul Yuzyk's history on Ukrainians, which showed Ukrainian Canadians in a admirable light, but she did not take kindly to sections in contemporary scholar Francis Swyripa's book that included the negative elements of Ukrainian-Canadian women. According to Dr. Swyripa, there was "[t]he ignorant and apathetic peasant immigrant woman and her rebellious rudderless daughters. . ."[16], women who believed in early marriages for their daughters and did not express a desire for self-education or higher education for their daughters. Savella spoke and wrote about the early Ukrainian leaders, men and women, who promoted the policy of self-reliance, self-respect and pride in one's national origin and that they encouraged the younger generation to strive for higher learning. She did not readily acknowledge that women had to endure multiple births of children, death of children at birth, their own death during delivery of children, hardships of physical labour while pregnant, abortions, no available methods of birth control, physical abuse and male chauvinism. These topics rarely entered public discourse in the first half of the 20th century, and they were conspicuously absent in the discussions within the Ukrainian-Canadian community.

Savella never moved in the poor lower class circles of Ukrainian Canadians, but that did not mean she ignored them or trivialized their hard life. On the contrary, her program for uplifting the Ukrainian-Canadian community, whether socially or culturally, focused on the uncultivated and disadvantaged Ukrainian immigrant woman. Savella was well aware of the mind set of those who believed that women should marry, bear children and work in the home and in the fields alongside their husbands, and who further believed that education was not necessary for daughters. However, desiring to combat these prejudices, she never thought it necessary to discuss them because they represented aspects of the Ukrainian pioneer culture that she believed needed to be overcome. In this, she was at one with the early Ukrainian intelligentsia. And this is one of the reasons she proselytized to women in the bloc settlement that there was more to life than early marriages and having children.

Mary Harbus, an acquaintance of Savella's recently said, "Savella woke up the women that there was more than just marriage, children and hard work. They should be educated and learn about Ukrainian culture." Mary went on to say that her own mother and other older women in the Whitkow area where Mary's parents lived did not know how to embroider and were delighted to learn and also pleased to have their daughters taught this folk art form.[17] When Savella travelled to the bloc settlements teaching home economics and Ukrainian embroidery in the 1930s, the village of Whitkow was one of her stops. Her niece, Jean Meketiak, Michael Stechishin's daughter, who was originally from Yorkton, remembers the reaction of the women in the bloc settlement, "They respected her very much. They used to talk about her and they really looked up to her, mostly because she had more education and she gave the lectures and they were learning from her. It was like an aura – they really respected her."[18] Although some women did not appreciate Savella because she did not participate in mundane chores of fund raising, meal preparation and so on, choosing only to give advice and speeches, they did respect her for her determination to become educated.

Jean Meketiak added that Savella's greatest achievement was "[t]he fact that she was one of the women who started the Women's Association way back in 1926. These were forward looking women and they started the museum way back . . . I admire them incredibly because they had the foresight to do this, to think of it." Jean also stressed, "She really felt that the women really needed help and she dedicated all that time to teaching women and she really pushed education. She believed that the mother was the important person in the family and she should have an education. I remember that very well throughout the years I've known her. She felt it was very important for women to have an education."[19]

Savella was always available to help her family – kind and giving. The wife of her nephew, Myron Warnick, Stella, spent two weeks in 1973 with Savella in Saskatoon researching for her master's dissertation on the history of Ukrainian costume. In the memorial for Savella Stechishin that Stella wrote at the time of Savella's funeral, she recalled, "By the time I arrived in Saskatoon [from Seattle, WA], Savella had made contact with all the key people, had a lovely room ready for me in her home, and during the next two weeks accompanied me on my visits to the [Ukrainian] Museum, waiting patiently as I photographed for hours. She was so instrumental in helping me to achieve an accurate and quality thesis, and for that I will be eternally grateful. But what was so precious to me were the evenings we shared as we relaxed and visited with one another."[20]

Both of Savella's brothers changed their surname: Eugene to Warnick and Apolonius to Warnock early in their careers. Her response to these changes is not documented and is not known. Being so adamantly opposed to changing Ukrainian names, what did she think about her own brothers anglicizing their surname!

In her senior years, Savella had to deal with the death of her son, Anatole. He had suffered a heart attack in the summer of 1986 in Atlanta, Georgia where he worked as a city planner. He died on December 3, 1986. She brought his body home to Saskatoon and buried him next to his father.

An important facet in Savella's life, especially in her senior years, was gardening. She loved to garden and compost, believing that plants and leaves as well as household waste should be returned to the earth, not only eliminating waste, but also recycling and replenishing the soil. Apple trees in her back yard provided filling for the pies she enjoyed baking and the raspberries bushes provided fruit for fresh consumption and for freezing to be used in the winter. Savella was a considerate hostess and always enjoyed serving her baking along with tea to anyone who dropped in for a visit. The back yard was host to a bountiful vegetable garden along with approximately 75 species of flowers, of which she knew each name. Her neighbours appreciated her sharing her knowledge of gardening and the compost heap she kept on her property near the back lane. They were encouraged to dump their waste into the heap and even help themselves to the end product, fertile soil. She shared her harvest of fruit and vegetables with her neighbours of over fifty years, Gordon and Bea Clarke. Recently Bea Clarke reminisced, "She was a good neighbour, very helpful, very knowledgeable and well educated. She taught me a lot about planting and gardening, weeds and pruning trees and [how to grow] tomatoes."[21]

Savella had definite ideas about the way she lived her life. She believed in prayer and prayed often. Her prayers were answered many times, she said to her friends, and she would pray for other people when she felt there was a need. She was spiritual and shared her thoughts on the subject with others by writing to them and suggesting books and articles. Also, her good health was vitally important; she took control by concocting her own home remedies for minor ailments – and they appear to have worked! When in 1990 she discovered she had heart problems, because of her thirst for knowledge, she immediately sought out chelation therapy that she had heard about. She travelled a number of times to Kelowna, British Columbia to receive this therapy and then continued in Saskatoon when a chelation clinic was set up there. Keeping fit and exercising was something else she held strong beliefs in. She would exercise with an exercise program on television almost daily, especially in the winter when the climate prevented her from working in her garden or walking a few blocks in her neighbourhood. She continued this practice into her 90s.

In the last twenty years of her life, Savella was unable to be as independent as she would have liked. With no transportation of her own and no immediate family to assist, she had to often rely on the kindness of friends to go shopping, visit the doctor and go to church. Mary Cherneskey was one friend who at least once a month took her shopping for groceries and visited her. Her friends, the Savitskys, the Chomyns and others, all retired for many years, often extended a helping hand.

Both the Ukrainian- and Anglo- Canadian communities have acknowledged Savella's pioneering and outstanding contributions to her people by way of profiles in magazines, newspapers and books, and numerous citations and awards. Some of these honours are: Honorary Member of the Ukrainian Women's Association of Canada (1956); Taras Shevchenko Medal (1962); "The Struggle of a Pinetree" a poem by poet Larysa Murovych dedicated to Savella Stechishin and arranged for a women's choir by composer Serhiy Yaremenko (1969); the UWAC Branch in Kelowna named in her honour (1974); Honorary Member of Saskatchewan Home Economics Association (1975); Woman of the Year, nominated by the Ukrainian Canadian Committee, Saskatchewan Provincial Council (1975); Outstanding Saskatoon Woman nominated by the City of Saskatoon and Civic Committee on the Status of Women (1975); Honourary Doctorate of Canon Law, St. Andrew's College, University of Manitoba (1976); Notable Saskatchewan Woman, government publication, 75th Anniversary of Saskatchewan (1980); Century Saskatoon award for journalism and multiculturalism (1982); plaque from the Mohylianky at Petro Mohyla Institute, as initiator of the Ukrainian women's movement, Ukrainian Women's Association of Canada (1983); medallion commemorating the 70th Anniversary of Petro Mohyla Institute in recognition of being the first Ukrainian woman graduate of the University of Saskatchewan and as initiator of the UWAC (1985); medallion celebrating the 25th Anniversary of Promin for journalism (1985); the Ukrainian Women's Association of Canada Medal (1985); Ukrainian Self-Reliance League of Canada Certificate of Honour (1985); University of Saskatchewan Faculty of Home Economics, Member of the Living Hall of Fame (1989); appointed to the Order of Canada (1989); medal celebrating Ukrainian Centenary in Canada (1992); Governor General of Canada medal commemorating the 125th Anniversary of the confederation of Canada (1992);   and, the Ukrainian Canadian Congress, Saskatchewan Provincial Council, Nation Builders Award (1995).

On May 15, 1997, Savella received the most prestigious award, crowning her efforts of the many years of dedication to her gender and ethnicity. Ukraine acknowledged Savella for her contributions in perpetuating Ukrainian culture. Although unable to attend the ceremony in Kyiv, she was the recipient of an award from the Learned Societies of Ukraine in recognition for the betterment of the Ukrainian nation. The Learned Societies of Ukraine and the Taras Shevchenko Institute of Literature in the City of Kyiv sponsored a series of evenings honouring five outstanding Ukrainian women that year. Savella was the first Canadian women to ever receive such an award; the other women now deceased lived in Ukraine. Each of the honourees had an assigned day of honour. President Leonid Kuchma of Ukraine was to be present at the evening reception.[22] A special exhibit of Savella's written work (4 books, newspaper column samples, and pamphlets), an enlarged photo along with family photographs and a special presentation on the life and readings of Savella consisted of the program. This award mainly recognized her *Traditional Ukrainian Cookery,* which was at that time in its eighteenth printing.[23]

Also in 1997, the author successfully completed a Master of Arts degree with Savella as the subject matter of the dissertation, at the University of Regina, Regina, Saskatchewan, titled "Savella Stechishin: A Case Study of Ukrainian-Canadian Women Activism in Saskatchewan, 1920-1945." The Saskatchewan Order of Merit was bestowed on Savella in 1998, the last honour awarded to her. In 1999, Savella's friend, Mary Cherneskey, nominated her in the culture/community category of the Women of Distinction Awards sponsored by the Saskatoon Young Women's Christian Association. Although the nomination was accepted, she was not selected as one of the winners.

The Institute where Savella formulated many of her goals did not forget her. The Mohylianky Society invited her as a special guest at their Annual Charity Ball, *Chervoni Maky* (Red Poppies) at Mohyla Institute on January 29, 2000. She was honoured as having founded the Mohylianky seventy-seven years earlier in 1923. What a wonderful moment of history for the young Mohylianky present to witness! "Seeing Zenia Stechishin leading her wheelchair-bound mother Savella in a dance was heart-touching. Even at 96 years of age Mrs. Stechishin still enjoys the beauty of Ukrainian dance!" announced the *Holos Institutu* (Mohyla Institute Newsletter).[24]

Because Savella was so serious and determined much of the time, little is known of her 'fun' side. She enjoyed taking part in an occasional prank and hearing a good joke. She was very curious and disciplined all her life and remained so until her last breath. World news and community news were of great interest to her and she kept abreast of current events until the end. Almost every detail about her grandchildren was important and she always kept in touch with them. In her 90s, she wrote out instructions for the disposal of her material possessions and made provision for donations of her liquid assets. Everything was to be in order at the time of her death.

Savella died on April 22, 2002 at the age of 98. Savella had remained in her beloved home on Albert Avenue until she became immobile in 1999 moving to the Lutheran Sunset Nursing Home in Saskatoon (across the street from Mohyla Institute) and she remained there until her death.

Savella Stechishin dedicated her life's work to the retention and promotion of her Ukrainian heritage within the woman's sphere; she urged her Ukrainian sisters to realize self-enlightenment. As a feminist, she organized women by unifying their interests, thus enabling them to strive for equal rights within their ethnic group and mainstream communities. Many of these women, illiterate or semi-literate, with century-old attitudes, had to reform in order to grasp Canadian societal values. Savella empowered the transformation of Ukrainian-Canadian women from 'peasant' into 'modern' women and, therefore, identifies her as a social reformer. The feminist principles Savella espoused were not only social, but equally maternal. She emphasized the importance of motherhood and the belief that the mother was the key to family unity and prosperity. Children were to be the main focus for the woman as mother. At the same time she emphatically states in her writings that women should not be confined to the 'kitchen.' She acted as a role model for young women to emulate: she was educated, knowledgeable about her heritage, a community activist, who impressed the importance of education onto her children and who was an equal workmate with her husband. Upwardly mobile, she was and remains respected as a Canadian as well as an esteemed member of her own ethnic group, the Ukrainian Canadians.

Her contributions merit historical documentation as a leading figure in the Ukrainian-Canadian women's movement. In consideration of the dedication she extended to her people, it is clear that Savella Stechishin should take her rightful place alongside other female activists in Canada. She was a liberated woman, liberated in the sense that she successfully opposed the oppressive aspects of the traditional role of a married woman, freeing herself to spread her wings and fly in any direction she wished.

APPENDIX A

Notable Authors and Activists of Ukraine

NATALIA OSARKEVYCH KOBRYNSKA (1851-1920), born in Carpathia, Galicia (Western Ukraine), is considered the founder of the women's movement in Ukraine.[1] She was the first outspoken theoretician of feminist thought among Ukrainians and the first to organize secular Ukrainian women's associations. She was one of the first women in Europe to "advocate the fusion of feminism with socialism."[2] Her most important aim was to advance education amongst Ukrainian women to increase their socio-economic status and self-worth within Ukrainian society. Having founded the **Society of Ruthenian Women** with the initial meeting on 7 October 1884 with 95 women in Stanislaviv, she then arranged the first public session on 8 December 1884 calling on all Ukrainian women.[3] Another important event in Ukrainian feminist history is her publishing the Almanac, *Pershyi vinok* (The First Wreath), in 1887 (with Olena Pchilka) in which she espoused her feminist views.[4] The Almanac had three main goals: to serve as a literary aid to women, to develop their self-confidence, and, by publishing works of Ukrainian women from the Russian Empire in tandem with Western Ukraine, to stress the solidarity of Ukrainian women. With her own funds, she published a magazine aimed at women, *Nasha dolia* (**Our Fate**), in 1893, 1895 and 1896.[5] Through the magazine and through personal appearances, she attempted to popularize the idea of the organization of women for self-improvement and fuller participation in the life of the community. Another high priority with her was the practise of good nutrition by women. She was the first to advocate that educated women made better mothers.[6] Kobrynska, born to a Catholic priest and married to one, came from an intellectual family. So dedicated to her vision, her husband and she decided not to have children so that she could devote herself to the cause of women.

===

OLHA KOBYLIANSKA (1865-1942), born in Bukovyna, Western Ukraine, of a German-Polish mother and Ukrainian father, wrote the first and most popular feminist novel in Ukrainian literature, *Tsarivna* (The Princess) published in 1896.[7] She began to write in Ukrainian upon becoming friendly with Natalia Kobrynska and published her first short stories in Ukrainian. Originally, she wrote in German since German was spoken in her parents' home. She became a close friend of both Kobrynska and Lesia Ukrainka, another famous woman writer.[8] Her popularity grew as a writer and she became one of the most widely read Ukrainian authors in Ukraine, Canada and the diaspora.[9] Although she disclaimed her feministic views, her fiction spoke to generations of Ukrainian women and even men.[10] Her fiction inspired a feminism championing freedom and independence for the woman.[11]   Kobylianska believed in the independence of Ukraine but did not actively participate in the political arena. She did not publicly advocate socialism as Kobrynska and was more popular with the pioneering Ukrainian-Canadian women activists who tended to be fiercely anti-Bolshevik and anti-Communist and equating socialism with the left wing in Canada. Kobylianska remained unmarried.

===

LESIA UKRAINKA (Larisa Kosach-Kvitka) (1871-1913), a second generation "feminist", was the daughter of Olena Pchilka, a feminist in her own right and an ardent Ukrainian nationalist and staunch supporter, along with her husband, of the Ukrainian cultural movement.[12]   Ukrainka is considered the greatest Ukrainian women writer and poet, one of the most cultured women of her time, well versed in the literature of the world.[13] She mastered eight languages besides Ukrainian which was invaluable in her studies of world history and literature.[14] At the age of nine, she had her first poem published and at 21 years her first collection of lyrics was published by the eminent poet, Ivan Franko.[15] She was prolific in that she wrote plays, poetry, and novels. Her inspiration was drawn from classical antiquity, early Christian, Western and Eastern Middle Ages, and European literature.[16]   Her most influential teacher was her uncle, Professor M. Drahomaniv, a prominent radical political emigre in Bulgaria. Drahomaniv was active within the democratic Ukrainian movement and together with other radicals aspired for national, social and political freedom for Ukraine.[17] These aspirations are reflected in her works. In her writings, she also portrayed strong individualistic characters and advocated education of Ukrainian women. Ukrainka almost always chose subjects for her poetry which had at least some indirect signifance for Ukraine and the cause of its people. In the following example, she compares an orgy in the Roman period to the raping of Ukraine and its confinement of women:

> And why can't I go?
> The Roman women can go everywhere,
> Why can we not follow their sample?
> I'll go and say "My husband is unwell,
> But so as not to disappointment Maecenas
> He sent me, being his wife, to the reception?"[18]

She married but did not have children. Coming from a close knit family, she often took care of her younger sisters, and yet having grown up surrounded by independent women she, in typical female fashion, sewed and embroidered well[19]. Her fame was almost entirely posthumous having died at an early age due to contracting tuberculosis in her youth.[20]

==

OLENA PCHILKA (Olha Drahomanov Kosach) (1849-1930), is important in the development of the Ukrainian women's movement. She was energetic, dedicated and actively involved in all aspects of Ukrainian cultural and political life.[21] Her husband was a judge and they were members of the upper middle class 'cultured' circles in Kiev and in other centres they lived. Adamantly believing in nationhood and solidarity for Ukraine, she took every opportunity to foster close co-operation among Ukrainians in both the Russian and Austrian Empires.[22] She resisted the social pressures to use Russian as a language which enhanced upward mobility and insisted her children learn Ukrainian and Ukrainian was spoken in the home exclusively. All six of their children received their education at home from hired teachers, rather than at the Russified schools in Ukraine.[23] Since her style of writing was similar to Jane Austen, which was not fashionable at the time, her body of work was not popular. Her advocacy of Ukrainianism was embraced by Ukrainian women and Ukrainian-Canadian women. Besides being well know as "mother of Lesia Ukrainka", she is equally famous and respected as a Ukrainian woman activist.

==

OLHA BASARAB (1889 - 1924), was one of the leading women in the secret organization known as Ukrainian Military Organization (UVO) in the interwar years. The UVO was dissatisfied with the Polish domination of Western Ukraine after WW I and attempted to throw off the Polish yoke.[24] Basarab was also active within the Ukrainian women's movement and became the first treasurer of the Union of Ukrainian Women (Soiuz Ukrainok) in 1922.[25]   She is considered a Ukrainian Joan of Arc because she gave up her life for the Ukrainian independence cause. Arrested by the Polish police for activities as an intelligence courier for the illegal UVO, she was brutally killed in jail without betraying her comrades or the cause.[26] Her martyr's death had an aura that inspired the activities of women in Ukraine and in the diaspora.

MARKO VOVCHOK   (Mariia Vilinska Markovych Zhuchenko) (1834-1907) was born to a Russified landowning family. Upon her marriage to Markovych, a member of the Cyril-Methodius Brotherhood (the Brotherhood fostered a federation of Slavic peoples whereby each nation would be virtually independent) and due to her husband, she became converted to Ukrainianism. All the members were sent into exile by the Tsar for sedition in 1847. Vovchok met her husband when he was exiled to the town in which she lived.[27] Although she did not espouse direct feminism in her writing, she drew on history and contemporary life. Vovchok's life spanned the period of the renaissance of Ukrainian national spirit and the birth of Ukrainian literature based on lives of real people.[28] One of her many books, *Marusia*, a popular novel, was eventually made into a movie in North America becoming popular in Canada with Ukrainian Canadians in the 1940s and 1950s. Vovchok became a popular and wellknown author who appealed to the masses earning the praise of being the outstanding prose writer of her period.[29]   Taras Shevchenko, the national bard of Ukraine, saw her as his heir in the literary field. She had spent several years in St. Petersburg and was known in Russian literary circles.[30] In fact, Turgenev (an eminent Russian author) learned Ukrainian to translate her stories into Russian.[31]

TARAS SHEVCHENKO (1814-1861), the foremost and revered poet of Ukraine born a serf in the region of Kiev, is often compared to Robbie Burns of Scotland. Not only was he a poet, but also, a respected painter having studied painting in St. Petersburg and having lived there a number of years. He was not only the greatest of Ukrainian poets, but was the first writer who was purely Ukrainian and believed in an independent Ukraine with its own language and literature (separate from dominant Russia)[32]. His first collections of poems was published in 1840 under the title *Kobzar* (Folk Minstrel) and is collected and read to the present time.[33] Shevchenko encapsulated Ukraine's thousand years of history and vicissitudes in his *Kobzar.* He idealized and glorified the Cossack period of Ukraine and became recognized as a powerful spokesman of Ukrainian nationhood. With his pen, he fought for the rights and freedom of the Ukrainian peasantry, vigorously protesting the injustices administered by the ruling classes. Through his poetry, he also admonished his own people for their past and present errors, and urged them to rise to the numerous challenges facing them to secure their freedom. "He is unique among world poets in that he restored single-handed a submerged folk's consciousness of its separate identity and roused it to assert itself supremely as a nation."[34] Because he was sympathetic to the Sts. Cyril and Methodius Brotherhood, he was arrested, along with the members, by the tsarist police in 1847 as a subversive and exiled. He was meted out the harshest punishment due to his ridiculing the family of Tzar Nicholas I in his poem, *The Dream*, and his condemnation of the Russian aggression against his people in his writings. In 1857 he was given amnesty by Nicholas' heir, Alexander II, a broken man. However, he was able to return to St. Petersburg to complete his studies in art and was given the title of academician at the Imperial Academy of Art.[35] He died at the age of forty-seven and was buried in St. Petersburg, but in his poem *My Testament* he wished to be buried in his beloved Ukraine. A few months later, his remains were transferred by his countrymen to his chosen place on a hill at Kaniv overlooking the Dniper River. Immediately his burial-mound became a place of pilgrimage for Ukrainians from all over the world and remains so to this day.

==

IVAN FRANKO (1856-1916), is second only to Shevchenko in importance, but he is even greater as a complete humanist - his interest and knowledge covered a broad spectrum from poet, dramatist to sociologist and politician. His radical views curtailed his ambition to enter politics and further, due to his agnostic beliefs, he was unable to secure employment for which he was easily qualified. This caused him to eke out a miserable livelihood for many years.. In 1894 he had earned a doctorate from the University of Vienna in literature.[36]   Franko's poetry raised him to eminence above all his contemporaries. One of his famous poems, *Ivan Vishensky*, concludes that the freedom of his countrymen is more important than his own soul.[37] Lesia Ukrainka respected Franko and often sought his advice, sending him her manuscripts for his comments.[38] Born in Galicia (Western Ukraine), to a poor village blacksmith, his chief concern was dedicated to the material betterment of Ukrainians in the left bank. [39] The socialism he advocated was to uplift the socio-economic strata of his people. For a number of years, his people did not readily accept his methods and he battled the prejudices and animosity hurled at him. After twenty-five years of public and literary activities, the Ukrainians in Galicia accepted Franko as their leader on the road to freedom and an independent Ukraine.[40] Through his famous poem, *Kameniari* (The Stonecutters), he illustrated the plight of his people.[41] He was studied by all Ukrainians as well as Ukrainian Canadians. The students at Petro Mohyla Institute adopted the name of this poem for their students' club, demonstrating their reverence for Franko and his teachings.

Notes

Chapter 1–A New Beginning

1. Savella Stechishin, unpublished autobiography, 5.
2. John-Paul Himka, "The Background to Emigration:Ukrainians of Galicia and Bukovyna, 1848-1914" in *A Heritage in Transition, Essays in the History of Ukrainians in Canada*, ed. Manoly R. Lupul (Toronto: McClelland and Stewart Ltd., 1982), 15.
3. Frances Swripa, *Wedded to the Cause: Ukrainian-Canadian Women and Ethnic Identity, 1891-1991* (Toronto: University of Toronto Press, 1993), 24.
4. *S.S. Barcelona*, ship's manifest, Archival Microfiche Reel No. T4799.
5. Orest Martynowych, *Ukrainians in Canada, The Formative Years 1891-1924*, (Edmonton: Canadian Institute of Ukrainian Studies Press, 1991), 66.
6. Petryshyn, *Peasants in the Promised Land: Canada and the Ukrainians, 1891-1914*, (Toronto: James Lorimer & Company, 1985), 11.
7. William Darcovich and Paul Yuzyk, eds., *Statistical Compendium on the Ukrainian Canadians, 1891-1976*, (Ottawa: University of Ottawa Press, 1980), Series 50.24-38, 506-507.
8. Saskatchewan Archives, Homestead Microfiche, Registration No. 3002330.
9. Ibid.
10 .Petro Mohyla was born in Moldavia, son of a Moldavian nobleman and the Hungarian princess Margareta. He studied in Lviv Dormition Brotherhood School and pursued education in theology in Holland and France and then returned to Ukraine to pursue an ecclesiastical career. In 1631 Mohyla created a college which eventually became the largest centre of education in Eastern Europe, the Kievan Mohyla Academy. Printing flourished under his guidance bring in the best scholars, master printers and engravers to work at the press. In 1634 at the age of 36 he was appointed metropolitan of Kiev (Orthodox). Mohyla donated substantial amounts of money to supporting various Orthodox churches and he bequeathed most of his estate to the Mohyla College. **Source:** *Ukrainian Encyclopedia*, 432-433 and Orest Subtelny, *Ukraine, A History.* Third Edition (Toronto: University of Toronto Press, 2000, 120-1).
11. John E. Lyons "Savella Stechishin and the Redefinition of Ukrainian Culture in

Canada", *Vitae Scholasticae*, Fall 1994, Caddo Gap Press, San Francisco, California, 29.

12. Candace Savage, *Foremothers, Personalities and Issues from the History of Women in Saskatchewan*, (Saskatoon, 1975), 52.
13. Savella Stechishin interview.
14. He was the brother of Olena Kysilevska, a well-known activist and writer living in Western Ukraine at the time. In the 1920s, Savella Stechishin corresponded with her and this will be discussed in Chapter 4.
15. Autobiography, 19.
16. S. Stechishin interview and autobiography, 18.
17. Hryhory Udod, *Julian W. Stechishin, His Life and Work*, (Saskatoon: Mohyla Institute, 1978), 22.
18. S. Stechishin interview, January 21, 1995.
19. S. Stechishin interview; autobiography, 22.
20. *Chvert stolittia na hromadskii nyi: Istoriia Soiuzu ukrainok Kanady (1926-1951) (Twenty-Five Years of the Ukrainian Women's Association of Canada)* (Winnipeg: Ukrainian Women's Association of Canada, 1952), 17 and Udod, *Julian W. Stechishin*, 25.
21. Frances Swyripa, "From Princess Olha to Baba: Images, Roles and Myths in the History of Ukrainian Women in Canada" (PhD dissertation, University of Alberta, 1988), Chapter 7.
22. Cited in Udod from J. Stechishin's Archives, Memorandum of the Peter Mohyla Institute, 21.
23. Autobiography, 18.
24. Stechishin, autobiography, 17. There is no record of the contents of the essay and when asked, she said that she does not remember what she wrote about "so long ago."
25. Udod, *Julian Stechishin*, 22.
26. Autobiography, 20.
27. Autobiography, 29
28. S. Stechishin, interview

Chapter 2–With Her Husband's Encouragement

1. Stechishin, unpublished autobiography, 32.
2. Autobiography, 36.
3. Nancy Russell, *Saskatoon Star Phoenix*, Saskatoon, October 18, 1976.
4. Savella Stechishin, *"Tovarystvo mohylanok - uholynyi kamin Soiuzu ukrainok Kanady"* (The Mohylianky Society - The Cornerstone of the Ukrainian Women's Association of Canada) in *Iuvileina knyha 25-littia Ukrainskoho instytutu im. Petro Mohyly v Saskatuni 1916-1941*, *(Jubilee Book of Twenty-five Years of the Petro Mohyla Ukrainian Institute in Saskatoon, 1916-1941)* (Saskatoon: Petro Mohyla Institute, 1945), 298.

Notes / 203

5. D.E. Yanda, "*Yak Divshlo do Zasnovannia Soiuz Ukrainok Kanady*" (Events Leading up to the Ukrainian Women's Association of Canada) in *Iuvileina Knyzhka, Soiuzu ukrainok kanady z nahody 10-litnoho isnovannya, 1926-1936 (Jubilee Book of the Ukrainian Women's Association of Canada Commemorating 10 Years, 1926-1936)* (Winnipeg: Ukrainian Women's Association of Canada, 1937), 9.
6. Savella Stechishin, "*Tovarystvo mohylanok - uholynyi kamin Soiuzu ukrainok Kanady*" (The Mohylianky Society - The Cornerstone of the Ukrainian Women's Association of Canada) in *Iuvileina knyha*, 300.
7. Martha Bohachevsky-Chomiak, *Feminists Despite Themselves: Women in Ukrainian Community Life 1884-1929* (Edmonton: Canadian Institute for Ukrainian Studies, 1988), 159.
8. Savella Stechishin, "*Tovarystvo mohylanok - uholynyi kamin Soiuzu ukrainok Kanady*" (The Mohylianky Society - The Cornerstone of the Ukrainian Women's Association of Canada) in *uvileina knyha*, 302.
9. Ibid.
10. D.E. Yanda, "*Yak Divshlo do Zasnovannia Soiuz Ukrainok Kanady*"
11. M.H. Marunchak, *The Ukrainian Canadians. A History*, (Winnipeg: Ukrainian Academy of Arts and Science, 1982), 411.
12. Stechishin, "The Formation of the Ukrainian Women's Organizations in Canada", 5; Savella Stechishin *Iuvileina knyha*, 300; autobiography, 38.
13. Autobiography, 38.
14. Olha Boychuk, compiler, *Zolotyi vinets: Pivstolittia viddilu Soiuzu ukrainok Kanady imeny Marii Markovych u Kanori, Saskachevan, 1926-1976 (The Golden Jubilee Book of Maria Markovych Branch of the Ukrainian Women's Association of Canada, Canora, Saskatchewan 1926-1976)* (Canora: Maria Markovych Branch of the Ukrainian Women's Association of Canada, 1981), 198.
15. Natalia Kohuska, *Pivstolittia na hromadskii nyvi: Narys istorii Soiuzu Ukrainok Kanady (A Half Century of Service to the Community: An Outline History of the Ukrainian Woman's Association of Canada, 1926-1976) (Winnipeg: The Ukrainian Woman's Association of Canada, 1986),* 922-971.
16. National Archives, MG30 D389, Vol. 1, File 2,16.Stechishin, "The Formation of the Ukrainian Women's Organizations in Canada", 5; Savella Stechishin, *Iuvileina knyha 25-littia Ukrainskoho instytutu* 3, Savella Stechishin Papers, Outline Sketch of her autobiography, entitled "Savella Stechishin."
17. Frances Swyripa, *Wedded to the Cause. Ukrainian-Canadian Women and Ethnic Identity, 1891-1991* (Toronto: University of Toronto Press, 1993), 14.
18. Autobiography, 40; Natalka L. Kohuska, *Chvert stolittia na hromadskii nyvi: Istoriia Soiuzu ukrainok Kanady (1926-1951), (Twenty-five Years of the Ukrainian Women's Association of Canada 1926-1951)* (Winnipeg: The Ukrainian Women's Association of Canada, 1952) 16-17.
19. Savella Stechishin, "*Pochatky zasnovannya Soiuzu ukrainok Kanady*" (The Beginning of the Foundation of the Ukrainian Women's Association of Canada) in *Iuvileina Knyzhka, Soiuzu ukrainok kanady z nahody 10-litnoho isnovannya, 1926-1936 (Jubilee Book of the Ukrainian Women's Association of Canada Commemorating 10 Years, 1926-1936)* (Winnipeg: Ukrainian Women's Association of Canada, 1936), 5.

Canadians, Multiculturalism, and Separatism: An Assessment (Edmonton: The Canadian Institute of Ukrainian Studies, 1978), 94.

22. Paul Yusyk, "Religious Life"in *A Heritage in Transition: Essays in History of Ukrainians in Canada* (Toronto: McClelland and Stewart, 1982), 150.

23. Oleh W. Gerus, "The Reverend Semen Sawchuk and the Ukrainian Greek Orthodox Church of Canada,"in *Journal of Ukrainian Studies*, (Summer-Winter, 1991), 63.

24. *Ukrainian Voice*, 3 June 1914, cited in Ol'ha Woycenko, *The Ukrainians in Canada* (Ottawa: Canada Ethnica IV,1967), 93.

25. Darcovich and Yuzyk, *Statistical Compendium*, Series 32.1-12, 273.

26. Darcovich and Yuzyk, *Statistical Compendium*, Series 22.17-56.

27. Autobiography., 46.

28. Ibid.

29. Kharytia Kononenko, President and Savella Stechishin, Secretary, *"Do Ukrainiskukh Zhinok v Kanady i Ameritsi"* (To Ukrainian Women in Canada and America), *Ukrainskyi holos*, 18 February 1925, 4.

30. Martynowych, *Ukrainians in Canada*, 82.

31. Martynowych, 137.

32. Savella Stechishin, *Ukrainskyi holos*, 1 April 1925, 4.

33. Stechishin, *Iuvileina knyzhka*, 7.

34. Savella Stechishin, *Ukrainskyi holos*, 29 July 1925, 4.

35. Autobiography, 56; Stechishin interview.

36. Autobiography, 37.

37. Savella Stechishin, *Ukrainskyi holos*, 6 January 1926, 5.

38. Savella Stechishin, *Ukrainskyi holos*, 17 November 1926, 5.

39. Autobiography, 59.

40. The Ukrainian students' circle in Saskatoon met on March 4, 1916 to discuss the establishment of an educational institution to suit the needs of Ukrainians. An Initiative Committee was elected and shortly thereafter, they published an appeal to all Ukrainians in the *Ukrainskyi holos*, the only independent Ukrainian weekly in Canada, for moral and financial support. On August 4 and 5, 1916, the Initiative Committee called the first Ukrainian National Convention in Saskatoon to address this issue. This began the annual conventions of all Ukrainians in Canada. Within ten years, it was exclusively attended by members of the Ukrainian Orthodox faith. **Source:** Hryhory Udod, *Julian W. Stechishin. His Life and Work* (Saskatoon: Mohyla Institute, 1978), 20.

41. Yanda, *Iuvileina knyzhka,* 9; autobiography, 60.

42. Autobiography, 59. Savella had been Olha Swystun's bridesmaid and was a close friend of Olha Sawchuk and her husband as well. Olha Swystun's husband, Wasyl, was the first rector of Mohyla Institute, one of the main initiators in the formation of the Orthodox Church and Ukrainian Self-Reliance League and a practising lawyer in Winnipeg. **Source:** Orest Martynowych, *Ukrainians in Canada*. Olha Sawchuk's husband, Semen, was also a member of this group and the first ordained priest of the Orthodox church and the first priest to use the Ukrainian language in any Ukrainian Orthodox church. **Source**: Oleh W. Gerus, "The Reverend Semen Sawchuk and the Ukrainian Greek Orthodox Church of Canada,"in *Journal of Ukrainian Studies*. Olha Arsenych's husband was an active promoter of these beliefs in Winnipeg, a

charismatic leader in the Winnipeg Ukrainian community, the first Ukrainian lawyer in Canada, the first Ukrainian judge in Canada (1948) and the president of the Ukrainian Publishing Company of Canada Limited that published the *Ukrainskyi holos*. **Source:** Ol'ha Woycenko, *Ukrainians in Canada*, 91.
43. Swyripa, *Wedded to the Cause*, 11.

Chapter 3–Daring to Achieve

1. Stechishin,"*Tovarystvo mohylanok*" in *Iuvileina knyha Ukrainskoho instytutu im. Petra Mohyly*, 303.
2. Cited in Frances Swyripa, "Nation-Building into the 1920s: Conflicting Claims on Ukrainian Immigrant Women," in *Continuity and Change: The Cultural Life of Alberta's First Ukrainians* (Edmonton: University of Alberta Press, 1988), 148.
3. Olha Swystun, *Ukrainskyi holos*, 5 February 1919.
4. Stechishin, "*Tovarystvo mohylanok*" in *Iuvileina knyha Ukrainskoho instytutu im. Petra Mohyly*, 303.
5. Herstory, An Exhibition. Agriculture: Violet McNaughton. http://library.usask.ca/herstory/ mcnaugh.html.
6. Ibid. There was direct contact with the Local Council of Women in 1930 but Mohylianky may have had knowledge of the Council in 1926.
7. Personal correspondence, January 20, 1997.
8. Bohachevsky-Chomiak, *Feminists Despite Themselves*, 152.
9. Stechishin, "*Tovarystvo Mohylyanok -Uholinia Kamiin Soiuz Ukrainok Kanady*" in *Iuvileina knyha*, 304.
10. Autobiography.
11. Kohuska, *Pivstolittia na hromadskii nyvi*, 605.
12. Most of these young women were taking classes in higher learning and were much more educated than the average Ukrainian-Canadian woman. **Anna Stasiv** (nee Chepesiuk) of Fort William was an active and supportive Mohylianka of a national women's organization and in teacher training. **Maria Maduke** was a former student of Mohyla Institute, had been a member of a women's society in Keld, Manitoba where she had taught school and now was teaching school in Vonda, Saskatchewan. At this time her husband was boarding at the Institute taking an agriculture course at the University and she visited him on weekends. **Source:** Savella Stechishin, Autobiography, 58.
13. Autobiography, 64.
14. Rev. Vasyl Kudryk was one of the founders, and the first editor of the *Ukrainskyi holos*, one of the founders and ideologists of the Ukrainian Orthodox Church of Canada, one of the first priests ordained in this church and for many years editor of the official church organ, *Pravoslavnyi vistnyk* (*The Orthodox Herald*). **Source:** Olha Woycenko, *The Ukrainians in Canada*, 91-92 and Orest Martynowych, *Ukrainians in Canada*, 501.
15. Autobiography, 66.
16. Stechishin, *Iuvileina knyha Ukrainskoho instytutu*, 304.
17. Kohuska, *Pivstolittia na hromadskii nyvi*, 604.

18. Natalia Kohuska became an active member of the UWAC in 1934 when she organized the Lesia Ukrainka branch of the Association in Sioux Lookout, Ontario. She established a close contact with the executive of the Association by often writing to the Association's page in the *Ukrainskyi holos*. In 1942 she was elected president and remained president until 1948. Taking a journalist role in the literary works of the organization, she edited the *"Chvert stolittia na hromadskii nyvi,"* "Forty Years in Retrospect", "Twenty-fifth Jubilee Book for CYMK" (Ukrainian Canadian Youth Association) and other publications. In 1960 she became the long time editor of the UWAC magazine, *Promin*.

19. Kohuska, *Pivstolittia na hromadskii nyvi*, 606.

20. From the paper by Savella Stechishin cited in Kohuska, 605.

21. Autobiography, 57

22. Autobiography, 64; *Iuvileina knyzhka*, 89; Kohuska, *Forty Years in Retrospect 1926-1966* (Winnipeg: Ukrainian Women's Association of Canada, 1967), 7; Kohuska, *Chvert stolittia na hromadskii nyvi*, 31. Kohuska, *Pivstolittia na hromadskii nyvi*, 606, states that the Kniahynia Olha Women's Association of Winnipeg was one of first branches and omits the Whitkow branch. However, the first four sources listed above state Whitkow Branch and do not make mention of the Winnipeg branch.

23. Olha Woycenko, published in *Multilingual Press in Manitoba* (date unknown), reprinted in *Promin*, (3) March 1996, 24.

24. *"Idealnay Muzhyna"* ("The Ideal Man"), *Ukrainskyi holos*, 29 May 1929.

25. Kohuska, 608.

26. Martynowych, *Ukrainians in Canada*, 495.

27. Anonymous, *Pivstolittia na hromadskii nyvi*, 930.

28. Kohuska, *Pivstolittia na hromadskii nyvi*, 611.

29. Ibid., 612.

30. Stechishin, *Iuvileina knyzhka*, 15. Savella mentions Onufrey Ewach and John Danylchuk, members of the intelligentsia, helped to type and duplicate material for dissemination of information of the UWAC.

31. Autobiography, 67.

32. Daria Yanda, *"Vplyb mohylyanky na ukrainskyi culturno-organizatsinyi zhyttya v Kanadi"* (The Influence of the Mohylianky on the Cultural Lives of Ukrainian-Canadian Women). In I*uvileina knyha 25-littia Ukrainskoho instytutu im. Petro Mohyly v Saskatuni, 1916-1941* (*Jubilee Book of Twenty-five Years of the Petro Mohyla Ukrainian Institute in Saskatoon, 1916-1941*) Saskatoon: Petro Mohyla Institute, 1945, 315.

33. The USRL ideology embodies the following slogans:
"a) SELF-RESPECT, which means exemplary and worthy of respect conduct of each individual in all phases of life.
b) SELF-RELIANCE which means that each individual, each community and each racial or ethnic group, and particularly the Ukrainian group, should learn to rely upon its own human, intellectual, spiritual and material resources, and to develop them to the fullest extent for the common good. Only such development can lead to a mutual friendly interdependence without servility or a feeling of inferiority.
c) SELF-HELP, which means that an individual or the group he belongs to is truly free and deserving respect only when, individually and collectively, they have initiative

and dynamic will to plan, and to carry out those plans without coercion or outside help." **Source:** W. Burianyk, *S.U.S. Its Meaning and Significance* (Ukrainian Self-Reliance League of Canada, 1967), 14.

34. Ol'ha Woycenko, "Community Organizations," in *A Heritage in Transition: Essays in the History of Ukrainians in Canada*, ed. Manoly R. Lupul (Toronto: McClelland and Stewart Limited, 1982), 181.

35. Stechishin, 190.

36. The Ukrainian Self-Reliance League of Canada, Circular #2, April 1978.

37. The following organizations became a part of the USRL and affiliated with the Ukrainian Orthodox Church of Canada: Ukrainian Women's Association of Canada (1926), the Canadian Ukrainian Youth Association (1931), Ukrainian Self-Reliance Association of Canada (1938), the Ukrainian Museum of Canada (1936), the Union of Ukrainian Community Centres and the Ukrainian Self-Reliance League Foundation. Two residences were also associated: Petro Mohyla Ukrainian Institute of Saskatoon and St. John's Ukrainian Institute of Edmonton and in the 1960s, St. Vladimir's Ukrainian Institute of Toronto was built to round off the entire USRL family. **Source:** W. Burianyk, *S.U.S. - Its Meaning and Significance*, 13.

38. Ibid.

39. Archives of the Ukrainian Women's Association of Canada, Daughters of Ukraine, Regina. *Persha Recordova Knyzhka, 1927-28 (First Record Book 1927-28)*, 6.

40. Kohuska, *Pivstolittia na hromadskii nyvi,* 616. Kohuska omitted Mother's Day in May, but this was an important occasion.

41. Bohachevsky-Chomiak, 194.

42. NAC, Savella Stechishin, letter to branches, 4 May 1928.

43. NAC MG30, D389, Vol. 7, File 12. Savella Stechishin, letter to Orthodox parish priests in Canada, 6 May, 1928.

44. NAC MG30, D389, Vol. 7, File 12. Savella Stechishin, letter to the National Executive namely, Mrs. Kroitor, Swystun, Sawchuk, Maduke, Slusar and Miss Romanchych, 14 May 1928; Kohuska, *Chvert stolittia na hromadskii nyvi,* 47-48.

45. *Ukrainskyi holos,* 9 May 1928, 19.

46. Kohuska, *Pivstolittia na hromadskii nyvi,* 608.

47. Kohuska, 743; Redfield-Richard history, 929 and *Zolotyi vinets (Kanori)*, 218 - record Savella's visits.

48. NAC MG30 D389 Vol 6 File 8, Report by Savella Stechishin to Ukrainian Orthodox National Convention, 28-30 December 1927.

49. Stechishin interview.

Chapter 4–Building Bridges

1. Stechishin, autobiography, 69

2. NAC, MG30 D389, Vol. 4, File 13, Olena Kysilevska letter to Savella Stechishin, 1 January 1926

3. Stechishin, autobiography, 70.

4. NAC, MG30 D389, Vol. 4, File 15. Savella Stechishin, Directive to all Branches to

subscribe to the *Zhinocha dolia*, 30 May 1928.
5. NAC, Kysilevska letter to Stechishin, 9 September 1926.
6. In my personal communication with Savella Stechishin (1 February 1997), she stated that she did not keep copies of her early letters to the women in Ukraine.
7. NAC, MG30 D389, File 15, Olena Kysilevska to Savella Stechishin, personal correspondence. Letters dated 4 April, 15 April, 20 August, 9 September, 10 October 1926; 29 February, 1 April, 22 April, 8 August, 20 September, 14 October, 12 December 1927; 8 May 1929. NAC, MG30 D389, File 13: 18 December 1928; 18 March, 25 May, 6 June 1929.
8. NAC, MG30 D389 File 13, Olena Kysilevska, 15 April 1926.
9. Ibid., 9 September 1926.
10. Ibid.
11. Bohachevsky-Chomiak, 159-161.
12. Dennis Sowtis and Myron Momryk, "Biographical Sketch of Olena Kysilewska (1869-1956)," in *The Olena Kysilewska Collection*, Research Report No. 12, Canadian Institute of Ukrainian Studies, University of Alberta, Edmonton, 1985, 7. Kysilevska was decorated with the Cross of Merit by the Red Cross for her work with the Red Cross during the First World War. Writing under a pen name, her first book was published in 1910. She published a Ukrainian women's monthly magazine, *Zhinocha volia* (Women's Will), and visited many European countries to study the development of women's movements. In 1948, she emigrated to Canada and was elected first president of the World Federation of Ukrainian Women's Organizations and held this position until her death. She remained in Canada until her death.
13. NAC, MG30D389, File 15., 12 December 1927.
14. NAC, File 15. Ibid., 8 May 1918.
15. Ibid., 18 December 1928.
16. Ibid., 29 February 1927.
17. Ibid., 1 April 1927.
18. Stechishin, *Iuvileina knyha Ukrianiskoho instytut im. Petro Mohyly*, 301.
19. Emmie Oddie of Regina, a former home economist and a sister of one of McNaughton's secretaries, inherited these exquisite items which I was able to see in her home.
20. Ibid., 12 December 1927.
21. Ibid., 20 August 1926.
22. Stechishin, letter to Kysilevska, 16 May 1928.
23. Kysilevska, 18 March 1929. Bold by author.
24. NAC, Vol. 6, File 13. Savella Stechishin, *"Zhinochy rukh v Kanady"* (The Women's Movement in Canada) in the Calendar-Almanac of the *Zhinocha dolia*, Kolomeiya, Ukraine, 1929.
25. NAC, Vol. 1, File 2. Olena Zalizniak, *"Zist z Kanady"* (Visitor from Canada) in *Nova Khata*, Lviv, Ukraine, October 1928.
26. NAC, MG30 D389 Vol. 4, File 13. *Dilo*, Lviv, Ukraine, August 1928.
27. Stechishin, *"Uruvku Spomyniv Podorozhi do Ridnoho Krau"* (Experiences on the Road to the Homeland) in *Ukrainskyi holos*, 29 May, 6 June and 13 June 1929.
28. Zinaida Mirna, an activist and a member of the intelligentsia, was descendant of the

Kuban Cossacks. She was a board member of the Kiev Branch of the Russian Society for the Protection of Women, founded in 1900. The Kiev branch was composed of members of the intelligentsia dedicated to helping the poor.

29. NAC, MG30 D389, Vol. 4, File 13. Savella Stechishin letter to Zinaida Mirna, 6 June 1929; Zinaida Mirna to Savella Stechishin, 20 January, 2 April, 22 May 1929, 19 July 1931 and one postcard undated.

30. NAC, MG30 D389, Vol. 4, File 13. I. Zubenko, Kolomeiya, Ukraine, 5 August 1927; Khartia Hrynyvychova, Lviv, Ukraine, 10 November 1928, 18 February 1929, 14 April 1929, 27 January 1931; Ostap Bondarovich, 18 October 1927.

31. Milena Rudnytska, Lviv, 1933. Cited in Natalia L. Kohuska, *Pivstolittia na hromadskii nyvi*, 603.

32. *Iuvileina knyzhka*, 39-56.

Chapter 5–Crystallizing Goals

1. Stechishin, autobiography, 125.
2. Autobiography. 126.
3. Savella Stechishin, "How Alpha-Omega Came About in Saskatchewan." n.d.
4. Ibid.
5. Autobiography, 134.
6. Ibid. 134-135.
7. Stephania Bubniuk, "*Konvocatsia na Universuteti Saskachevanu*" (Convocation at the University of Saskatchewan) in *Ukrainian Voice*, 30 July 1930, 11.
8. Stechishin, personal interview, Saskatoon, Saskatchewan, 21 January 1995.
9. Ibid.
10. NAC, Vol. 8, File 1.
11. Stechishin, autobiography, 138.
12. Ibid., 140.
13. Anastasia Ruryk, *Ukrainian Voice*, 11 June 1930, 11.
14. Autobiography, 140-141.
15. NAC, Vol. 8, File 1. Expenditure Report to Homemakers' Department, University of Saskatchewan.
16. NAC, Vol. 8, File 1. Report to Bertha Oxner, Director, Homemakers' Department, University of Saskatchewan, Saskatoon.
17. Ibid.
18. Ibid. Letter from Abbie DeLury to Savella Stechishin, 21 June 1930.
19. Swyripa, *Wedded to the Cause*, 45.
20. Anna Supynuk, personal interview. 13 November 1994, Regina, Saskatchewan.
21. *Ukrainian Voice*, 12 November 1930, 11; 24 December 1930, 11.
22. NAC, MG30 D389, Vol. 1, File 2. Anna Chepesiuk letter to Savella Stechishin, 23 November 1930.
23. NAC, MG30 D389, Vol. 1, File 2. Sheet "Mrs. Savella Stechishin".
24. NAC, MG30 D389, Vol. 1, File 2. Anna Chepesiuk letter to Savella Stechishin, 30 January 1931.
25. NAC, MG30 D389, Vol. 1, File 2. Anna Chepesiuk letter to Savella Stechishin, 1

February 1931.

26. *The Chatelaine*, August 1931.

27. Ibid.

28. Autobiography, 151; Udod, *Julian Stechishin*, 29; UWAC Archives, File #18.

29. Ibid. Savella does not write in the autobiography the number of days it took to arrive in New York. No other sources were found in relation to the trip.

30. Ibid.

31. Ibid., 157-158.

32. Savella does not explain why she travelled by train instead of by car. Presumably Julian needed the car for his use.

33. Savella Stechishin, personal interview, 21 January 21 1995, 27.

34. Ibid.

35. Ibid., 28.

36. Natalia L. Kohuska "A Half-Century of Service to the Community", 644-645.

37. Ibid., 162.

38. http://www.ibiblio.org/expo/soviet.exhibit/famine.html. Accessed November 11, 2006.

39. Autobiography, 160.

40. Ibid., 168.

41. Ibid.

42. Ibid., 173.

43. Ibid., 178.

44. Jeanne Matieshan, personal interview. Toronto, Ontario, 7 April 2005.

45. Autobiography, 204.

46. Stechishin, *Iuvileina knyzhka Soiuzu ukrainok Kanady z nahody 10-litnoho isnovannia, 1926-1936*, 81-84.

47. *Iuvileina knyzhka*, 97

48. Stechishin, *Iuvileina knyzhka*, 81.

49. Ibid.

50. Sheva Medjuck, "If I Cannot Dance to It, It's Not My Revolution: Jewish Feminism in Canada Today," in *The Jews In Canada*, ed. Robert J. Brym, William Shaffir and Morton Weinfeld (Toronto: Oxford University Press, 1993), 333.

51. Stechishin, *Iuvileina knyzhka*, 84.

52. *Na storzhi kultury*, 45-111.

53. NAC, Vol. 8, File 1.

54. *Chvert stolittia na hromadskii nyvi*, 420.

55. Boychuk, *Zolotyi vinets: Pivstolittia viddilu Soiuzu ukrainok Kanady*, 206-7

56. Georgina M. Taylor, "'Should I Drown Myself Now or Later?' The Isolation of Rural Women in Saskatchewan and Their Participation in the Homemakers' Clubs, the Farm Movement and the Co-operative Commonwealth Federation 1910-1967," in *Women: Isolation and bonding. The Ecology of Genders*, ed. Kathleen Storrie (Toronto: Methuen, 1987), 82.

57. *Ukrainian Voice*, "The Tragedy of The Ukraine. A Polish Terror," 5 November 1930 (reprinted) by a special correspondent to the Manchester Guardian. More articles followed weekly for several weeks.

58. Stechishin. *Ukrainian Voice*, 8 June 1938.
59. Bohachevsky-Chomiak, *Feminists Despite Themselves*, 233.

Chapter 6–Home for Ukrainian Treasures

1. Stechishin, *Iuvileina knyha Ukrainskoho instytut*, 301.
2. Ibid., 302.
3. National Archives, MG30 D389, Vol 4, File 18. Translated from *Ukrainskyi holos* (Ukrainian Voice), 13 August 1980 by Andrij Makuch.
4. Kohuska, *Pivstolittia na hromadskii nyvi*, 726
5. Stechishin, *Ukrainian Voice Almanac*, 1930.
6. Udod, *Julian W. Stechishin, His Life and Work*, 29; Savella Stechishin, *Ukrainskyi holos,* 13 August 1980
7. Stechishin, *Ukrainskyi holos*, 13 August 1980.
8 Stechishin, autobiography, 177.
9. Stechishin,*"Powurennya prohramy Soiuzu Ukrainok Kanady na rik 1936-37"* (The Broadening of the Program of the Ukrainian Women's Association of Canada for 1936-37) in *Iuvileina knyzhka,* 82-83.
10. Ibid., 83-84.
11. National Archives, MG30 D389, Vol 6, File 8.
12. Ibid., 182
13. Mary Tkachuk, translated by Marie Kishchuk, "The Ukrainian Museum of Canada of the Ukrainian Women's Association of Canada. Historical Highlights - 1927-1977" in *Pivstolittia na hromadskii nyvi,* 977.
14. Autobiography, 190.
15. Mary Tkachuk, translated by Marie Kishchuk, 977-980.
16. Eva Schacherl, Accent on the Arts, Saskatoon *Star-Phoenix*, Saturday, May 24, 1980.
17. National Archives, MG30 D389, Vol 4, File 18. Translated from *Ukrainskyi holos* (*Ukrainian Voice*), 13 August 1980 by Andrij Makuch, p. 2.
18. Ibid.,11.
19. Natalka L. Kohuska, *"Narodne mystetstvo i muzay Soiuzu ukrainok Kanady"* (Folk Art and a Museum of the Ukrainian Women's Association of Canada) in *Chvert stolittia na hromadskii nyvi*, 61.
20. www.ukm.sk.ca

Chapter 7–Successes and Disappointments

1. Autobiography
2. Ibid., 208.
3. Autobiography, 209.
4. Stechishin, *Ukrainian Voice,* 23 December 1942, 3.

5. Savella in the autobiography states she cannot remember the amount.

6. Savella Stechishin letter to National Office, UNWLA, 20 January 1946, National Archives, Vol. 6, File 1.

7. NAC, Vol. 7, File 12. Stechishin, *"Shto Dalyshe Pered Name"* (What is Our Future?), *Nashe zhyttia*, September 1948.

8. Stechishin., *"Zhinka yak henii"* (A Woman As a Genius), *Nashe zhyttia*, January 1950.

9. Stechishin, "A Woman As a Genius," 6.

10. Autobiography, 214.

11. Ukrainian Canadian Congress, Purposes and objects. http://www.ucc.ca/Section_1/PurposeObjectives.

12. Ukrainian Canadians: A Brief History. http://collections.ic.g.c.ca/plast/ukrcan/ukrcan4.

13. I bid., 219.

14. Savella Stechishin *Mystetskyi Skarby Ukrainskyikh Vyshyvok*, Trident Press Ltd. (Winnipeg, 1950), 7.

15. Ibid., 210.

16. Saskatoon *Star Phoenix*, 7 July, 1951.

17. Saskatoon *Star Phoenix*, 21 February, 1952.

18. National Archives, Vol. 4, File 7, Saskatchewan Arts Board 1953-66. Letter dated 9 July 1953.

19. Ibid. Letter dated 24 November 1953.

20. Ibid. Letter dated 14 January 1954.

21. Ibid. *Ukrainian Voice*, 27 January 1954.

22. Ibid. Selection document.

23. Saskatoon *Star Phoenix*, 30 June, 1954.

24. Autobiography, 235.

25. Savella Stechishin, letter to National Executive UWAC, December 3, 1975, p. 4.

26. Autobiography., 236.

27. Savella Stechishin, *Traditional Ukrainian Cookery*, Trident Press Ltd. (Winnipeg: Trident Press Ltd., 1957), Second Edition 1959, Third Edition 1963, 123.

28. Ibid., 227.

29. Autobiography, 236.

30. Ibid. Savella does not state the amount of money she was compensated

31. Savella Stechishin. *Traditional Ukrainian Cookery*, 5.

32. Mary Cherneskey, personal interview, Saskatoon, Saskatchewan, 11 February 2005.

33. http://www.huri.harvard.edu/lib/archives/sichynskyi. Accessed December 2005.

34. Savella Stechishin, letter to National Exeuctive, UWAC, 3 December 1975, 8.

35. *Yorkton Enterprize*, 22 September, 1965.

36. Saskatoon *Star Phoenix*, 22 September, 1965.

37. Http://www.infoukes.com/uwac.

38. National Archives MG30D389, Vol. 8, File 17.

39. SUS Foundation of Canada, 2004 Annual Report, Toronto, ON.

40. Lydia Burachinska, et al., *Woman of Ukraine, Her Part on the Scene of History, in Literature, Arts, and Struggle for Freedom*, (Philadelphia: Ukrainian National Women's League of America, 1955), 12.

41. *The Leader Post*, Regina, Sask. 30 November, 1965, 6.

Chapter 8–Life Without Julian

1. Julian V. Stechishin, *A History of Ukrainian Settlement in Canada*, translation by Isidore Goresky, Ukrainian Self-Reliance League of Canada, Saskatoon, 1992, xiii.
2. Olha Cikalo, letter, April 2005.
3. Savella Stechishin, *Fifty Years of the Olha Kobylianska Branch of the Ukrainian Women's Association of Canada, Saskatoon, Saskatchewan. First Branch of the Ukrainian Women's Association of Canada 1923 - 1973*. Olha Kobylianska Branch, Saskatoon, Saskatchewan, 1975.
4. National Archives, MG30 D389, Vol. 1, File 9.
5. Ukrainian Self-Reliance League of Canada letter to Mr. B. Sears, Mayor, 27 July, 1973. National Archives, MG30 D389, Vol. 1, File 9.
6. Clifford Wright, letter to Mrs. J.W. Stechishin, 9 February, 1978. National Archives, MG30 D389, Vol. 1, File 2.
7. Savella Stechishin, "The Formation of the Ukrainian Women's Organizations in Canada", Second Wreath Conference, October 11-14, 1985, Edmonton, Alberta, p. 12.
8. Savella Stechishin, letter to Mrs. Olena Salizniak, 5 February 1968. National Archives Vol. 7, File 3.
9. Ivanna Zelska, letter to Savella Stechishin dated 26 Apr il 1965.
10. Lidia Burachynska, letter to Savella Stechishin dated 30 November 1962. National Archives Vol. 7, File 4.
11. Frances Swyripa, *Wedded to the Cause*, 209.
12. Personal communication, not dated.
13. Alison Prentice, et al., *Canadian Women. A History*, (Toronto: Harcourt Brace Jovanovich Canada Inc., Second Edition, 1996), 278.
14. *Promin*, No. 6 May 1989, 11. Published in Winnipeg, Manitoba.
15. Savella Stechishin, "70 Anniversary of the First Branch of th the Ukrainian Women's Association of Canada", *Promin*, Winnipeg, Manitoba, No. 10 October 1993.
16. Swyripa, *Wedded to the Cause*, 101.
17. Mary Harbus, personal interview, Saskatoon, Saskatchewan, 11 February 2005,
18. Jean Meketiak, personal interview, Calgary, Alberta, 13 June 2005.
19. Jean Meketiak interview.
20. Stella Warnick, Memorial for Savella Stechishin, April 2002.
21. Bea Clarke, letter dated August 27, 2005.
22. Jason Warick, "Toast of Ukraine," *The Star Phoenix*, 16 May 1997.
23. Savella Stechishin, *Traditional Ukrainian Cookery*, (Winnipeg: Trident Press Ltd., 1957).
24. Mohyla Institute Newsletter, Vol. XXXVI, Number 1, April 2000, 6.

Appendix A - Notes

1. Ukraine. A Concise Encyclopedia, 332.
2. Martha Bohachevsky-Chomiak, Feminists Despite Themselves, 75.
3. Maria Oryschuk, "Women's Rights and Women Journalists," Promin, Vol 5 (6) June 1964, 15-16; Bohachevsky-Chomiak, Feminists Despite Themselves, 75.
4. Lydia Burachinska, et al, Woman of Ukraine, Her Part on the Scene of History, in Literature, Arts, and Struggle for Freedom, (Philadelphia: Ukrainian National Women's League of America, 1955), 12.
5. Bohachevsky-Chomiak, Feminists Despite Themselves, 75.
6. Ibid.
7. Ibid., 105.
8. Natalia Kohuska, "Selected Luminaries of Ukrainian Literature," in Essays from the History of Ukrainian Culture, (Edmonton: Ukrainian Women's Association of Canada, Natalia Kobrynska Foundation, 1984), 166.
9. Ibid., 108.
10. Honore Ewach, "Ol'ha Kobylyanska's Followers," Promin, Vol. 5 (6), June 1964, 17.
11. Ukraine. A Concise Encyclopedia, 1035; Lydia Burachinska, 21.
12. Bohachevsky-Chomiak, 10-11.
13. C.H. Andrysyshen and Watson Kirkconnell, The Ukrainian Poets, 1189-1962, (Toronto: University of Toronto Press, 1963), 254.
14. Ibid.
15. Ibid.; Orysia Prokopiw, An Introduction to Lesya Ukrayinka. (Calgary: The Ukrainian Women's Association of Canada, Olha Basarab Branch, 1971).
16. Prokopiw; Ukraine. A Concise Encyclopedia, 1040.
17. Constantine Bida, Lesya Ukrainka, (Toronto: Women's Council of the Ukrainian Canadian Committee, 1968), 14; Manning, Ukrainian Literatue, 90.
18. Bida, 165.
19. Bohachevsky-Chomiak, 11.
20. Bida, 7.
21. Bohachevsky-Chomiak, 11.
22. Ibid.
23. Prokopiw; Bida, 5.
24. Burachinska etal, 46.
25. Bohachevksy-Chomiak., 163-164.
26. Frances Swyripa, "The Ideas of the Ukrainian Women's Organization of Canada, 1930-1945," in Beyond the Vote. Canadian Women and Politics. Eds. Linda Kealey and Joan Sangster. (Toronto, Buffalo, London: University of Toronto Press, 1989), 239.
27. Bohachevsky-Chomiak, 9-10.
28. Kohuska, 126-127.
29. Clarence A. Manning. Ukrainian Literature. Studies of the Leading Authors, (Jersey City: Ukrainian National Assocition, 1944), 63.
30. Ukraine. A Concise Encyclopedia, 1020.
31. Burachinska et al, Women of Ukraine, 21; Ukraine. A Concise Encyclopedia, 1020.

32. Manning, 53.
33. Ibid., 43.
34. Andrysyshen and Watson, 87.
35. Ibid., 88.
36. Manning, 80.
37. Andrysyshen and Watson, 203.
38. Bida, 29.
39. Kohuska, 138.
40. Andrysyshen and Watson., 204.
41. Kohuska, 139.